Designing Courses for Higher Education

SRHE and Open University Press Imprint
General Editor: Heather Eggins

Current titles include:

Catherine Bargh, Peter Scott and David Smith: *Governing Universities*
Ronald Barnett: *Improving Higher Education: Total Quality Care*
Ronald Barnett: *The Idea of Higher Education*
Ronald Barnett: *The Limits of Competence*
Ronald Barnett: *Higher Education: A Critical Business*
John Bird: *Black Students and Higher Education*
Jean Bocock and David Watson (eds): *Managing the Curriculum*
David Boud *et al.* (eds): *Using Experience for Learning*
Angela Brew (ed.): *Directions in Staff Development*
Anne Brockbank and Ian McGill: *Facilitating Reflective Learning in Higher Education*
Ann Brooks: *Academic Women*
Sally Brown and Angela Glasner (eds): *Assessment Matters in Higher Education*
Robert G. Burgess (ed.): *Beyond the First Degree*
Frank Coffield and Bill Williamson (eds): *Repositioning Higher Education*
John Cowan: *On Becoming an Innovative University Teacher*
Rob Cuthbert (ed.): *Working in Higher Education*
Heather Eggins (ed.): *Women as Leaders and Managers in Higher Education*
Gillian Evans: *Calling Academia to Account*
David Farnham (ed.): *Managing Academic Staff in Changing University Systems*
Sinclair Goodlad: *The Quest for Quality*
Diana Green (ed.): *What is Quality in Higher Education?*
Robin Middlehurst: *Leading Academics*
Sarah Neal: *The Making of Equal Opportunities Policies in Universities*
David Palfreyman and David Warner (eds): *Higher Education and the Law*
Moira Peelo: *Helping Students with Study Problems*
John Pratt: *The Polytechnic Experiment*
Michael Prosser and Keith Trigwell: *Understanding Learning and Teaching*
Tom Schuller (ed.): *The Changing University?*
Peter Scott (ed.): *The Globalization of Higher Education*
Peter Scott: *The Meanings of Mass Higher Education*
Harold Silver and Pamela Silver: *Students*
Anthony Smith and Frank Webster (eds): *The Postmodern University?*
Imogen Taylor: *Developing Learning in Professional Education*
Susan Toohey: *Designing Courses for Higher Education*
Paul R. Trowler: *Academics Responding to Change*
David Warner and Elaine Crosthwaite (eds): *Human Resource Management in Higher and Further Education*
David Warner and Charles Leonard: *The Income Generation Handbook* (Second Edition)
David Warner and David Palfreyman (eds): *Higher Education Management*
Graham Webb: *Understanding Staff Development*
Sue Wheeler and Jan Birtle: *A Handbook for Personal Tutors*

Designing Courses
for Higher Education

Susan Toohey

The Society for Research into Higher Education
& Open University Press

Published by SRHE and
Open University Press
Celtic Court
22 Ballmoor
Buckingham
MK18 1XW

email: enquiries@openup.co.uk
world wide web: http://www.openup.co.uk

and
325 Chestnut Street
Philadelphia, PA 19106, USA

First Published 1999

ISBN   0 335 20049 4 (pb)   0 335 20050 8 (hb)

A catalogue record of this book is available from the British Library

Library of Congress Cataloging-in-Publication Data
Toohey, Susan, 1947–
    Designing Courses for Higher Education / Susan Toohey.
        p.   cm.
    Includes bibliographical references and index.
    ISBN 0-335-20050-8 (hardback). — ISBN 0-335-20049-4 (pbk.)
    1. Education, Higher—Curricula.   2. Curriculum planning.   3. College teaching.
    I. Title.
    LB2361.T56   1999
    378.1'99—dc21   98-36641
                                                                                         CIP

Copy-edited and typeset by The Running Head Limited, London and Cambridge
Printed in Great Britain by St Edmundsbury Press Ltd, Bury St Edmunds, Suffolk

Contents

Acknowledgements   vi

Introduction   1

1 Pressures for Change   4
2 The Course Design Process   21
3 Beliefs, Values and Ideologies in Course Design   44
4 Thinking about Goals and Content   70
5 The Structure of the Course   91
6 Making Learning Opportunities More Flexible   113
7 Deciding on Goals and Objectives for Units of Study   130
8 Choosing Teaching Strategies   152
9 Assessment   167
10 Implementing the New Course   187

References   205
Index   212
The Society for Research into Higher Education   217

Acknowledgements

Thanks are due to many people who contributed to this book. The course designers who were prepared to be interviewed for this book and who spoke frankly about their experiences deserve a particular vote of thanks, as do the academic teachers who contributed examples of their materials. Special thanks are due to Peggy Nightingale and Chris Hughes for reading and commenting on the manuscript; Lindsay Hewson for helping to prepare the diagrams; Anita De Vos and Ina Te Wiata for many discussions of curriculum matters and Anne Maree Austin for transcribing interviews. My colleagues in the Professional Development Centre at the University of New South Wales and the many academics I have worked with in my educational development work have contributed enormously to my continuing education.

Extracts from interviews with academics and students are from my own research and development work unless otherwise indicated.

Most of all I would like to thank Brian Toohey for unfailing support, for reading and commenting on the manuscript and for his efforts to make my prose leaner and more lucid.

Introduction

Teachers in higher education retain a very significant advantage over teachers in other branches of education: their control of the curriculum. In much of primary, secondary, technical and vocational education, course design has been handed over to 'experts', to the impoverishment of the role of classroom teachers. Yet course design is an advantage of which many teachers in universities seem quite unaware. Much of the creativity and power in teaching lies in the design of the curriculum: the choice of texts and ideas which become the focus of study, the planning of experiences for students and the means by which achievement is assessed. These define the boundaries of the experience for students. Of course the way in which the curriculum is brought to life is equally important, but the power of good teacher–student interactions is multiplied many times by good course design.

Many teachers in higher education work in departmental environments that are quite hostile to good teaching and where little thought goes into the design of the curriculum. Their opportunities to contribute to the design of the courses on which they teach may be limited to those units for which they have responsibility. I hope this book will be useful to them. But the limited impact that is possible in one unit of study running over one semester can be greatly magnified when all of the elements which make up the course of study are designed to support each other. An integrated curriculum provides students with the opportunity to explore key concepts and develop essential skills in the contexts provided by different units. For this reason I have emphasized the design of the programme of study as a whole. This may seem an anachronism with the advent of modular courses. But ceding more responsibility to students for structuring their own education requires greater clarity about what each module can offer and how they might be linked together to form a coherent whole.

All aspects of teaching in higher education are under enormous pressure at present. Pressure to teach more students for more hours, to cut costs and increase income have made it increasingly difficult to teach well. At the same time, there are very good examples of course design appearing which apply much of the most recent research into learning in creative ways. I have tried to draw on as many of these examples as possible as a means of offering encouragement to those about to begin the process.

Themes

A number of themes are evident throughout this book. One theme is what I would call (with psychologist Ellen Langer) the importance of 'mindfulness' in course design. This is characterized by willingness to reconceptualize what we are doing, openness to different perspectives and clarity about what we hope to achieve. Rethinking past approaches will be necessary to meet the changing needs of students and contexts. Willingness to explore beliefs and values held by academic colleagues, students and other stakeholders is important if the curriculum is to achieve any coherence. Clear purpose acts as a guiding principle in the many choices to be made.

The need to broaden the higher education curriculum provides another theme. A first requirement is to design courses which foster engagement with the subject matter and reward deep learning. Like many other writers, I believe that the higher education curriculum must aim at more than intellectual development. As researchers like Gardner (1993, 1994), Perkins (1995) and Sternberg (1996) are attempting to show, success in any human endeavour requires more than a well-developed intellect. A certain level of emotional maturity is necessary to enable individuals to work effectively, either alone or with others; so is a capacity for persistence if original ideas are to be pursued to fruition. The future of human society demands that we pay attention to the ethical and moral development of its coming leaders. So throughout the book I encourage course designers to consider all aspects of their students' development and to plan their courses with the growth of the whole person in mind.

Approach and audience

When I started this book I had in mind the academic teachers whom I have taught in workshops, short courses and postgraduate programmes, rather than my colleagues in education. In general those academics have had a very practical focus. They want to learn more about educational design because they are trying to understand the problems that they face in teaching and how these might be addressed. They appreciate the potential significance of the teaching role and have a real desire to delve deeply into the issues without wishing to become educationalists. They already belong to a discipline, and their aim is to communicate more effectively its ways of understanding the world.

Because I want to communicate as directly as possible with practising teachers, I have tried to keep my language simple and the advice I offer straightforward and practical, while not avoiding the complexity of much educational decision making. I have tried wherever possible to illustrate the processes I am talking about with examples that show how other academics have resolved some of the dilemmas. In the often demanding and difficult process of course design I hope that teachers will find in these pages the support of a colleague.

1

Pressures for Change

What kinds of problems arise in designing courses of study in higher education? What are the issues that academics find difficult to resolve? In a typical workshop experienced academics from a wide range of disciplines were asked to identify any difficulties that they had experienced either in planning a programme of study or in teaching on a course designed by others. These are some of the issues that they identified:

My major difficulty has been in designing a unit for our overseas programme. The students in that specific locality have had very different preparation from our local students but the unit must fit within the standard degree framework. (Business law)

We have redesigned our core units but now we need to redesign the elective units so that they support the core units. At the moment there is no fit. (Design)

We have some weak staff members who are not interested in teaching or course design. Our problem is designing the course around them. (Arts)

Our main difficulty in a major course review has been – to what extent should everyone be involved? It seems to be more efficient to let a small group carry most of the work, but what contribution can the others make? And who should have the final decision? (Design)

Ours is the common problem of getting coherence between lectures and tutorials and between units. (Nursing)

The biggest difficulty is the amount of time the process takes and the lack of recognition for this kind of work. (Accounting)

We have no useful evaluation data that will help in reviewing our course. (Computing science)

My problem has been trying to incorporate what I've learned about the research on student learning into my teaching in a very traditional department with very traditional course structures. (Law)

People in our department have very different ideas about what a curriculum should be and different ideas about learning. (Arts)

Some of our subject coordinators are part-time members of staff. To what extent can we ask them to take on the work of course review? (Nursing)

Coordinating delivery of what are supposed to be the same units on different campuses has proved difficult. (Business)

Our course now attracts a much wider range of students. To what extent should we try to cope with different kinds of student backgrounds and different levels of preparation? (Applied science)

Our major concern is lack of coordination between clinical units and the theoretical units. (Medicine)

The problem I had in teaching on a course that I had no part in designing was that there was no design or plan apparent. (Law)

There was a lack of clarity about the goals and objectives and the assessment that I was given. As the lecturer I didn't really understand them and so I was not much help to the students. (Education)

There is always pressure to include more information. We almost never cut anything out. (Engineering)

These are the common problems of course design in universities and colleges of higher education at the present time. Some of them, such as difficulties in integrating theory and practice, are long-standing, but many reflect recent changes in the nature of tertiary education which have had considerable impact on the design of subjects and courses.

During the 1980s participation in tertiary education rose dramatically in most developed countries, and particularly in the UK and British-influenced systems such as Australia and New Zealand. The reasons were largely economic. Increasing automation was making many low-skilled blue- and white-collar jobs redundant. Increasing internationalization of national economies was bringing workers in developed countries into direct competition with much cheaper labour in developing countries. Unemployment was rising steadily in the West as a result of technological change and pressure on manufacturing industries to move operations offshore so as to benefit from cheap sources of labour. It was becoming clear that workers in the developed nations would have to offer considerably more if they were to retain their relatively high wages or even their jobs. One of the solutions seized upon by governments was to create a more highly skilled workforce, capable of sustaining the new knowledge industries which were the best hope for struggling Western economies.

Changes in the student body

This produced a range of results with implications for the higher education curriculum. Firstly, the overall number of students in higher education increased significantly, although in some areas of general education such as the arts and the pure sciences, numbers remained static as anxious students fled to faculties which offered more saleable qualifications. Many more school leavers now seemed to believe that their best chance lay with a university education, and governments pushed the higher education system until it accommodated them. In the desire to get a tertiary qualification, many of these students took the course that they could get into rather than the course they might have wanted. For those who were not particularly academically inclined, the traditional first year pressures of learning how to plan and manage one's own learning were exacerbated. Teachers of entry level subjects struggled to build interest and maintain standards.

The same economic pressures were being felt by those who were lucky enough to have made it into meaningful jobs (as distinct from 'McJobs' – the underpaid and insecure casual jobs in the hospitality and service industries, which often seemed to be the only growth area in the labour market). As large organizations shed thousands of technical and middle management jobs, management gurus proposed that the 'gold-collar' workers of the twenty-first century would be those who 'mentally incorporated themselves' and invested in their own development (Limerick and Cunnington, 1993). Managerial and professional workers keen to maintain their professional skills signed up in steadily increasing numbers for new part-time postgraduate professional degrees. These students brought to their university studies current experience of the professional workplace and the demand that their courses be relevant to it; limited time for study but capacity to complete tasks and meet deadlines; and a willingness to speak out and challenge those institutional practices, particularly assessment practices, which they did not believe to be valid or fair.

At the same time the ethnic mix of the student body began to change significantly. The children of immigrants began to enter universities in significant numbers, as did overseas students whose parents were prepared to pay for the kind of university education not yet available in their own countries. Frequently admitted on the basis of their performance in numerically based subjects, these students often struggled with the language and with an unfamiliar academic culture which expected them to think independently and challenge recognized authorities.

Participation of indigenous students was also an issue for tertiary education institutions in some countries throughout the 1980s. In North America and Australasia, tertiary institutions were sensitive to suggestions that they had failed indigenous people because so few were admitted and even fewer graduated. As a result, a number of special entry schemes were trialled. With indigenous and minority group students came questions about whether the curriculum should place more emphasis on issues relating to indigenous people, and even whether assessment requirements might be adapted to accommodate cultural differences.

Changes in institutions

As the student body changed, the higher education institutions changed along with it. In the UK polytechnics became universities, and in New Zealand they were given degree-granting status – raising the question of what difference there should be between a diploma granted by a polytechnic and a degree from a university, particularly if they are from the same institution. In Australia, Colleges of Advanced Education were amalgamated with older universities to become multi-campus institutions. Academic staff struggled with the problem of rationalizing and amalgamating similar programmes previously offered by different institutions and delivering the new programmes on sites separated by many hours of travel.

While the changes raised the status of some institutions, government demands for accountability increased over the whole sector. Universities had to provide more frequent and far more detailed reporting on student characteristics, student progress and student–staff ratios.

Changes in courses

With higher education's new role as economic saviour direct and indirect pressures came on the curriculum in a number of ways. There was a general concern among governments with the quality of higher education and, in particular, a feeling that degree courses concentrated too much on academic knowledge and too little on the practical skills and development of personal attributes that would enable graduates to be immediately effective in the workplace (Bowden and Masters, 1993; Harvey and Knight, 1996).

In the UK, the movement to make 'enterprise' skills and 'personal transferable' skills a formal part of the curriculum was widespread and received considerable financial support from government. Many universities and polytechnics revised courses to incorporate a greater emphasis on personal abilities such as communication, team work, creativity, problem solving and the ability to manage one's own learning (Elton, 1994). Although less formalized, the same trend can be found in many other English-speaking universities and colleges outside the UK.

Other attempts to ensure quality in higher education had more force behind them; in New Zealand, for instance, legislation required universities and polytechnics to specify the outcomes of all courses and to certify that those outcomes had been met through criterion-referenced (standards-based) assessment (Ministry of Education, 1991). In a climate of reduced funding for higher education, the Australian government offered significant additional funds to those institutions which could convince assessment panels that the education they offered was of the highest quality (Nightingale and O'Neil, 1994).

New technologies in distance education offered other possibilities. Whereas distance education had previously been confined largely to people isolated by geography, it now appeared that packages of learning materials might be used to attract working adults with family commitments and little time to attend college, while at the same time solving the problem of overcrowded lecture theatres and unmet demand from school leavers. Of course, prepackaged distance materials require an investment in course design of a different order to that previously experienced by most academic staff, and the materials produced are open to public scrutiny in a way that traditional university teaching is not.

Attempts to ensure quality in higher education and to encompass a broader range of skills and abilities have largely centred on the design of courses. Over the past decade the pressure has been on tertiary education institutions throughout the developed economies to review, document and defend their curriculum decisions.

Resourcing higher education

Student numbers may have increased, but funding per student has declined. Laboratories and libraries are unable to cope with demand. Staff struggle with questions of resources: What is the minimum number of hours that a student should spend in laboratory work? Is it better for students to have fewer, smaller classes or is it more efficient to maintain mass lectures and cut tutorials? Should students do more independent study? Would they? If we redesigned the course, could we use our existing resources more effectively?

The nature of the academic workforce has changed too. As tenured staff have retired, they have increasingly been replaced by casual staff until higher education has become one of the most highly casualized workplaces. This creates more difficulties in course planning. Casual staff may bring recent professional experience to the classroom. At the same time they are more likely to be inexperienced teachers with a limited repertoire of teaching strategies. They are most in need of the structure which a well-designed course can provide, but least available to assist in the design.

Economic forces represent only one set of pressures on the higher education curriculum. While some academic departments have left it to individuals to find their own ways of coping, many others have responded by redesigning courses and units in attempts to provide the best experiences that they can for students despite increasingly short resources. Such attempts are nothing new. Course design has always been a pragmatic art, aspiring to provide a rich set of experiences for individual students but often settling for what seems achievable given limited time, limited resources and limited human beings.

Research on learning in higher education and implications for course design

A more positive pressure for change has been the emerging body of knowledge on student learning in higher education and the factors which promote effective learning. In the last 15 years, concern to improve student learning has resulted in some radical new curricula in higher education as well as many smaller experiments at the unit level. Much of the inspiration for *problem-based learning, capability-based programmes* and *action learning* has been derived from research into the nature of learning in higher education.

What makes for success in higher education? What enables students not only to pass their exams but also to engage in the powerful learning that produces lasting knowledge and understanding? What encourages students to tackle real problems and to discover knowledge for themselves? Since the fifties, researchers in higher education have attempted to identify the characteristics of students, the institutional supports, the qualities of lecturers and the factors in the learning environment which produce success in learning.

Approaches to learning

Marton and Säljö in Sweden were the first to investigate students' approach to learning. They asked students to read academic articles, and then to describe what they had learned and how they had gone about learning it. They identified two different approaches with very different outcomes, which came to be called the *deep* approach and the *surface* approach (Marton and Säljö, 1976).

Independently, researchers in the UK and in Australia were also investigating the ways students went about learning – this time using factor analysis of students' responses to questionnaires on their study intentions and behaviour. This research produced remarkably similar results to those of the Swedish researchers. Again, the deep and surface approaches stood out as consistent and fundamentally different approaches to studying (Biggs, 1979; Entwhistle and Ramsden, 1983).

When students adopt a deep approach to learning their motive is to gain understanding; they adopt strategies such as reading widely and discussing the concept or topic with others; they seek to make sense of new knowledge in terms of what they already know about this topic and related topics. Students adopting a deep approach are not always interested in achieving high marks. The need for learning to be recognized in the form of marks or grades turns out to be an independent factor, called an 'achieving approach'. The desire for achievement may be combined with either a deep or surface approach to study. Students who take a deep/achieving approach will study all of the topics on which they may be examined, try to predict questions and plan their study time carefully; those who are not concerned with achievement will simply follow their interests and let the exams fall out as they may.

Students adopting a surface approach are primarily interested in meeting the demands which the system places upon them. Their usual strategy is to reproduce enough of the information they have been given to satisfy the assessment requirements of the unit. They often resort to rote learning and are satisfied if they can retrieve what they have memorized, even if they don't fully understand it. Many students who adopt a surface approach are only concerned to pass, but some aim for higher grades. They believe that higher grades will be obtained by reproducing more information, and they may also use study skills to plan and manage their study time.

It is not difficult to distinguish between deep and surface approaches. While a few students are strongly attached to one approach, most select the approach they deem appropriate in the circumstances. Listen to a selection of students talking about the way they study:

> I must admit that I do sometimes study more successfully than at other times. I am more successful in my studies if the assignment is challenging and I have to apply my whole mind to it. If, on the other hand, it is 'busy work' then I find myself thinking about other things and while I might get a good grade I have retained nothing. (Theology student)

> Understanding all the concepts behind it, that's what I think it [good learning] is. It's not rote learning, it's understanding the full concepts behind things, why things happen, how they are happening, and OK, be able to apply what you know to any kind of question or situation. That's what I think is really good learning . . . But what I did for one subject, I just memorized a whole set of reactions and then when I came to the exam I think 'Ooh, I've seen that reaction before and I can do that!' But if I saw something even slightly different, I mean, I wouldn't know what it *was* even . . . when I don't understand concepts behind things, when I'm just relying on what I see in notes and what I've memorized, then I think that's learning badly. (Industrial chemistry student)

> I've done a lot better the last two years, since I've stopped reading cases, huge waste of time, doesn't work . . . I didn't use them in the exam. (Law student)

> When I am revising [for an exam] I aim to memorize the things I have learnt. In revising it's more memory work. Whereas in preparing for a class meeting it's getting an understanding, trying to understand it. Not really memorizing what word means what. Understanding basically what the whole concept is. (Human biology student)

> I get satisfaction out of understanding something . . . I prefer to understand but if knowing gets me through it, then – I've gone into a lot of exams knowing things but not really understanding them. (Law student)

The most important thing to remember about the two approaches to learning is that most people are capable of both. The approach chosen on any particular occasion will be the result of individual characteristics and the pressures or demands of the learning context. The brightest student may decide on occasions to do just what needs to be done in order to pass and no more; the student whose work is often scrappy, disconnected, showing minimal understanding, may at weekends be displaying a deep approach to motorcycle maintenance or musical composition for the guitar.

The outcomes of different approaches

The work on approaches to learning has now been tested and reproduced in hundreds of studies carried out in Europe and Australasia. Students have been interviewed in depth, surveyed using the 'Approaches to Study' Inventory (ASI) (Entwhistle, 1981) and the Study Behaviour and Study Process Questionnaires (SBQ and SPQ) (Biggs, 1987), and samples of their work and their examination results have been analysed. The results show very clearly that a deep approach is always associated with higher-quality learning outcomes. Students who take a deep approach retain knowledge longer, have better understanding, produce logical and coherent work, and can make more connections between different topics.

John Biggs, one of the original researchers on approaches to learning, went on to develop a system for classifying student work according to its quality. It is called the SOLO taxonomy – SOLO standing for 'structure of the observed learning outcome' (Biggs and Collis, 1982).

Using the SOLO taxonomy, student work can be classified into one of five categories:

- *Prestructural*: no knowledge is apparent.
- *Unistructural*: the student shows some understanding of one aspect of the topic.
- *Multistructural*: the student has grasped a number of ideas about the topic but does not relate them to each other or to the central question; the information is presented as a list or description.
- *Relational*: all of the significant aspects of the topic are related to each other and brought together to form a coherent point of view; the work stands as a whole.
- *Extended abstract*: as with the relational category, all of the aspects have been brought together. But here the student goes further and is able to reason about applications beyond the scope of the immediate question, theorize about related issues or reflect on his or her own actions and understanding.

For many teachers in higher education the SOLO taxonomy will fit quite easily with their conceptions of grade standards. Biggs himself has suggested that it might form the basis of a grading scheme, with prestructural work equivalent to a fail, unistructural a 'D', multistructural a 'C', relational a 'B' and extended abstract an 'A' (Biggs, 1992, 1996).

The SOLO taxonomy has frequently been used to classify students' work and compare the results with the approach that they took to their study. In one such study (Van Rossum and Schenk, 1984) 69 students were interviewed about their approach to learning. Thirty-five were identified as taking a pre-dominantly surface approach and 34 as taking a deep approach. They were then given a chapter to read and later asked to write an account of it. The accounts which the students wrote were analysed using the SOLO taxonomy. Of the 35 students who took a surface approach, none produced an account that was at a higher level than the multistructural (the third level of the SOLO taxonomy). Of the 34 who took a deep approach, six produced an account at the multistructural level, 25 wrote papers that were considered relational (the fourth level of SOLO) and three reached the extended abstract level. So while students who took a surface approach could only manage to list and describe, almost all of the students who took a deep approach could synthesize the material they had read and produce logical arguments and conclusions.

Many studies of this nature have been done, and the results are always simi-lar (see, for example, Watkins, 1983; Prosser and Trigwell, 1991; Trigwell and Prosser, 1991). Some studies have shown that a surface approach can produce a slight improvement in the ability to recall specific items of information in the short term, but for long-term retention and understanding the deep approach has always proved superior. (This comes as no surprise to those of us who have crammed for the 24 hours before a final exam, only to feel all of that rapidly acquired knowledge slip away from us as we left the exam hall).

Is this a problem that will go away?

It is tempting to consider the surface approach as a sign of immaturity. We accept that students may come to university with an idea from their school experiences that knowledge is about acquiring information and reproducing it, but we hope that as they come to understand what is required of them at uni-versity, they will give up the surface approach and take on a deeper approach to learning.

Some of the most discouraging research for university teachers in recent times has been John Biggs's very extensive studies of the approaches to learn-ing adopted by university and college students over the years of their tertiary education (Biggs, 1982, 1987). Biggs surveyed more than 2000 students from faculties of Arts, Education and Science in Australian universities and what were then called Colleges of Advanced Education (similar to polytechnics in other tertiary education systems).

The results showed that far from students changing to a deeper approach as they gained maturity and progressed in their studies, they were more likely to take a surface approach the longer they had been at university. The same find-ing applied to students at the Colleges of Advanced Education. Although this tendency was slightly more pronounced among science students than students in the arts and education, it applied in all disciplines. The only exception was the relatively small group of students who were planning to go on and do an additional honours year. They clung to a deep approach. In a similar study in the UK a surface approach was found to be common, and even more prevalent in universities than polytechnics (Ramsden, 1983).

Clearly, the majority of students during their time at university or college are not developing the kind of involvement with their discipline or profession and the commitment to learning that most teachers would hope for. Indeed, it seems that it is the university or college experience itself which pushes students towards a more superficial and instrumental approach to their studies.

Which aspects of teaching or course design encourage a surface approach?

Graham Gibbs (1992) and John Biggs (1995) both cite factors which have been shown to push students towards a surface approach. These include:

- time stress usually brought about by a heavy workload; high class contact hours; an excessive amount of course material; an emphasis on coverage;
- an assessment system which tests and rewards only low level outcomes, rewards students for recalling isolated scraps of information and causes undue anxiety;
- lack of choice over subjects, choice of topics to pursue in depth and method of study;
- a classroom and departmental climate which promotes negativity and cynicism.

Let's look at these factors more closely to see how they influence the approach that students take.

Heavy workload / high contact hours / excessive material / emphasis on coverage

The explanation for these first factors is obvious enough: a deep approach to learning requires a certain amount of time to think about and explore each topic. The more that the day is crammed with lectures and compulsory activities the less time is available for processing the information provided in the classes and the course material. These findings are of course likely to relate to typical university classes, which are heavily based on information giving. In theory at least it would seem possible for a deep approach to be compatible with quite high contact hours. But this would require students to spend much of that class time in discussion and activities that required them to 'process' new knowledge in a way that hours of note-taking in lectures does not.

Many teachers, particularly those responsible for introductory units, feel a responsibility to 'cover the territory'. Regretfully they will admit that their students never get the chance to look at any topic in depth – there is always too much to be covered. They know that students have no real understanding of what they have supposedly 'learned'. However, they hope that in future, when students are required to use their knowledge in professional practice or in further study, they will remember that it was 'touched on' in their introductory units and will know where to start looking for information when they have to learn about the topic – this time for real.

While it is possible that students will take a deep approach to learning when they actually need to know about the topic, it is unlikely that the introductory survey course will contribute much to the process. Students on a wide-ranging introductory course have had no experience of learning how to learn for themselves in depth. Instead they have been taken on a quick tour of the high points of the landscape which may leave them struggling when it comes to negotiating their own way through the swamp.

Demands on students may be exacerbated by poor coordination of assessment tasks and deadlines among different subjects, and by the fact that many students take on part-time employment in order to support themselves.

The assessment system

Most teachers in higher education espouse goals of critical thinking, logical argument involving selection and use of relevant evidence, systematic problem solving and self-directed learning. But far too frequently the assessment tasks do not require evidence of any of these, but instead allow students to pass by replaying information from lectures and textbooks. In such a situation, the assessment system will be a far more powerful influence on the approach students take than the expressed goals. Students quickly learn that whatever the lecturer says, a surface approach will suffice in this unit. Those who continue to take a deep approach are not necessarily advantaged under this kind of assessment system. One former student, now a lecturer in philosophy, described his experience of studying psychology:

> As a student I majored in philosophy, but I began to realize that in many respects psychology and philosophy were talking about the same ideas but from different perspectives. So I thought it would be useful to study some psychology and enrolled in the first-year course. I read widely and I organized all the notes from my reading together with my philosophy notes and arranged them around concepts – so that on any concept I could see and compare the view from philosophy and the view from psychology. It was only when I came to the final exam in psychology that I realized what a mistake I had made. It was all about facts, definitions – questions that I was not well prepared for at all. I passed but I did not do well . . .

Assessment (particularly in the form of examinations) which emphasizes recall of a wide range of very specific information and problem solving by formula is also most likely to induce a high level of anxiety. While a small measure of anxiety can be useful in helping students focus their study (Heywood, 1989), significant stress will make learning more difficult and cause students to concentrate on meeting the minimum assessment requirements. Students will try to memorize as much information as possible in the time available, to the detriment of any concern for what the information means, how it relates to knowledge already acquired and how it might be applied in new contexts.

Lack of choice over subjects, topics to pursue in depth and methods of study

> If you choose dentistry it will be the last choice you make for a very long time. You cannot choose electives, lectures, tutorials or make timetable changes.
>
> (Quote from Student Association alternative handbook)

Students who make their own choice of units are more likely to take a deep approach to learning because they are choosing to pursue an area in which they already have some interest. Within prescribed units a similar level of motivation can often be achieved by allowing students the choice of topic for a major assignment. Choice helps to promote ownership and responsibility. It is unlikely that students will take responsibility for their own learning when all the decisions about what topics or skills are most relevant, and what evidence of learning might be presented, have already been made by someone else. Where the unit is prescribed, where there is little or no choice in assessable work and all of the assessment requires a similar response, students are more likely to opt for a surface approach in order to meet requirements that they feel little commitment to.

Classroom and departmental climate

Some teachers and some academic departments create a climate of negativity and cynicism among students. This can happen where students are regarded as inherently untrustworthy, needing to be controlled and monitored and incapable of any input into decisions about their own learning. The department may put a heavy emphasis on student compliance with rules and deadlines but tolerate academic staff who miss classes or fail to return work. Examinations may be used to assess trivial or esoteric knowledge in order to 'sort students out', and assessment requirements may be changed for administrative or staff convenience. Students who ask questions or answer incorrectly in class risk sarcasm and humiliation. Students treated in this fashion come to feel that the educational contract has been broken and respond with cynicism themselves. If teachers do not treat the process seriously why should students? Better to take a surface approach and beat the system if you can.

To a large extent these factors which push students towards a surface approach are related to the design of the course. As such, they may be beyond the power of an individual academic, responsible for one unit of the programme, to modify significantly. The structure of the programme, and its assessment requirements, professional accreditation requirements, expectations of colleagues and departmental norms limit the degree of change which an individual can bring about. These are issues which are best tackled cooperatively. Together they make up a system which, if it is be made to work more effectively, must be considered as a whole.

What kinds of teaching might encourage a deep approach?

Surprisingly, perhaps, many of the factors that have conventionally been considered indicators of good teaching have very little impact on the approach that students take to their learning. What we are talking about here are the kinds of statements which frequently appear on instruments for student evaluation:

The teacher:

- presents information clearly;
- arrives at class on time;
- is well prepared;
- is friendly and helpful to students;
- uses appropriate audio-visual aids.

Students are asked to rate such statements on a scale from one to five, 'strongly agree' to 'strongly disagree'. While such information may show the teacher as more or less hard working, conscientious and organized, it will say very little about what kind of learning went on in the class and whether it was valuable or not. Most students, whether they are taking a deep or surface approach to learning in a particular unit, will prefer a teacher who is well organized, well prepared and presents clearly. Students taking a surface approach may value such attributes even more than students taking a deep approach since it may make it easier for them to distinguish which information is likely to be on the exam and which information they can safely ignore.

Because such items attempt to measure the behaviour of the teacher, they are largely irrelevant when it comes to drawing any conclusions about the learning that took place. As Shuell says:

> If students are to learn desired outcomes in a reasonably effective manner, then the teacher's fundamental task is to get them to engage in learning activities that are likely to result in their achieving those outcomes . . . It is helpful to remember that what the student does is actually more important in determining what is learned than what the teacher does.
>
> (quoted in Biggs, 1995)

What we need to consider in judging the effectiveness of the teaching is what the *students* were asked to do in that unit. What they may be asked to do will range over the kinds of formal assessment tasks they were given, the exercises they were set in tutorials and laboratories, and the kinds of questions they were asked to answer.

Factors which encourage a deep approach

Biggs (1989) has pulled together from the results of many research studies a list of the four principal factors that have been shown to encourage a deep approach to learning in students. They are:

- an appropriate motivational context;
- a high degree of learner activity;
- interaction with others, both peers and teachers;
- a well-structured knowledge base.

Motivational context

Larson (1993) pointed out that professors are likely to assume that enrolment in a course is tantamount to being motivated, while students feel that it is part of the professor's job to motivate them to learn. We tend to think that motivating teaching results from the personality of the teacher, and faced with student apathy many academics feel incapable of generating the sort of excitement that they associate with 'motivational speakers'. But many of the factors which arouse motivation are aspects of the course or unit design and need to be built in at the planning stage. The unit can be designed around real-life problems or issues which help to establish its relevance. Students can help to identify the projects that they wish to work on and the areas of knowledge that they wish to specialize in, thus creating some ownership of the material. Learning activities and assessment tasks can be structured and sequenced so that students are clear about requirements and get sufficient informal feedback on progress to give them a good chance of being successful in formal assessment tasks.

The atmosphere within the classroom or lecture hall obviously has an effect on motivation. An alienating climate where students feel that no one knows or cares who they are and whether they attend or not will undermine motivation and willingness to persevere with difficult material. Time spent in activities which help to establish cooperative and mutually supportive working relationships among students will help to establish other routes to understanding than reliance on the teacher alone.

Learner activity

As mentioned above, it is what the learner does in studying a subject that matters most. Students need to be involved with their topic from the beginning, generating questions, identifying prior knowledge and areas of ignorance, attempting to apply the newly acquired knowledge in answering questions and solving problems. It is in the act of engaging with the material that learning begins.

Interaction with others

Learning activities which require interaction with others may be introduced into a course because they help to develop the skills of team work, but there is another and perhaps even more important reason for including collaborative work. Working with others, whether in a tutorial discussion or group project, requires students to test their understanding of the topic by putting ideas in their own words and offering these for scrutiny by others. In the to and fro of discussion, understanding is challenged, clarified, worked on and strengthened in ways which are far more difficult for the solitary student to achieve.

A well-structured knowledge base

The idea of a well-structured knowledge base does not refer to the knowledge as it is structured in the mind of the lecturer: unfortunately it is not possible to transfer those structures intact to the minds of the students. So, although it is useful if the lecturer can present information in a clear and well-structured way, it is equally important that the student is required to integrate new information with his or her existing knowledge structures. How, for instance, do students integrate the new 'academic' knowledge with what has been learned through day-to-day experience? Some studies have shown that many seemingly successful students are unable to do this. They continue to hold significant misunderstandings about fundamental concepts in their discipline because they have never attempted to reconcile what they have learned at college or university with the beliefs that arise from everyday experiences (Dahlgren, 1984). A surprisingly large number of science students in the United States have been shown to believe in a fundamentalist creation theory to explain the beginning of the universe at the same time as they are successfully studying biology and physics. This is possible because these students have been able to quarantine different areas of knowledge and different kinds of knowledge, and have never been asked how they might reconcile the two in one personal belief system.

Deep learning and course design

To create those conditions which foster deep learning – the right motivational context, the appropriate activities for learning, the opportunities to interact with others and to build one's own well-structured knowledge base – is more than anything else a challenge for the teacher as course designer. It is most unlikely that such conditions will occur spontaneously. Instead, they require careful thought, preparation, creativity and collaboration with students and other faculty members.

The elements which enable deep learning must be built into the design of the course. If they are not, individual teachers, however creative they may be, will always be struggling to overcome the structural limitations of the course. If, for example, the content to be covered is too broad, the assessment requirements too narrow and prescriptive, and the teaching methods too confined by timetabling, class numbers and accommodation restrictions, it will be very difficult for the individual teacher to achieve an environment in which students really engage with the subject.

Course design and economic pressures

In the early part of this chapter we discussed some of the political, economic and social factors which have had a significant impact on higher education in the past decade. These factors – increasing numbers of students with differing backgrounds and expectations; more complex institutions expected to offer a broader range of courses through more flexible delivery systems; and reduced public funding for higher education – are currently pushing the system to its limits. Many people within higher education itself, and in government and professional bodies, propose new models of course design as the only realistic way to handle these pressures and maintain current standards.

Sometimes the course design solutions proposed are of the most sophisticated kind. New technologies promise that students will be able to work on problems and exercises, using the highest-quality information resources available through the Internet and CD-ROM. They will be able to construct personal databases as they learn and take those databases with them into professional life. The need for face-to-face teaching, and investment in infrastructure such as classrooms, libraries and laboratories, will be dramatically reduced once a very substantial initial investment has been made in designing and setting up the new computerized learning systems.

On the other hand, sometimes course design solutions of a far more brutal and less considered kind are suggested and implemented. To address resource problems, student numbers in mass lectures are doubled, tutorials are abolished and all small-group work is abandoned. Assessment is restricted to 'objective' tests which can be computer marked. Students receive no feedback on their assessment other than a final mark. To save the expense of having to develop a larger bank of exam questions, completed exams are not returned to the student. Costs are held in check, but at the expense of increasing alienation of faculty and students from each other and from the discipline itself.

Both of these responses represent course design solutions to the changing nature of contemporary higher education, although they are radically different in the resources they require, and the demands they make of teachers and students.

At the present time more attention is probably being given to course design in higher education than at any time since the beginning of this century. Much of it is being done for reasons of cost and expediency. At the same time, as a result of the research that has been done in the last 30 years in higher education, we know more than ever before about the conditions that are likely to promote effective learning at the tertiary education level. Clearly, there is an opportunity to bring together the need to rethink higher education provision with what we know about encouraging effective learning, so as to produce course designs which offer greater possibilities than some of our present solutions. It will not necessarily be easy or automatic. What the research tells us about the conditions that promote effective learning does not easily fit with the need to reduce resources and make provision more 'efficient'. In education, efficiency sometimes comes at the expense of effectiveness. It is, however, a challenge worth responding to. If we fail, we run the risk that when redesigning higher education to meet market pressures we will lose those qualities that have characterized its graduates: the ability to think critically, to analyse, to solve complex problems and to create new knowledge. Instead, students will be force-fed ever-increasing quantities of information, without acquiring any experience in how to evaluate it, when and how to apply it, and when to discard it.

2

The Course Design Process

Where does the design of a new course begin? What are the factors that make it desirable to change an existing course? What needs to be done in order to produce a new course and who is best suited to carry out the work? In this chapter we look at some of the answers to these questions.

Most models of course design suggest that a comprehensive needs analysis should be the first step in the process. Various market research techniques are suggested which will establish the extent of demand within the community and the characteristics of the potential student body. As a variation on this theme, evaluation data from existing courses should identify aspects of the course which need to change. Once the need is established, and the decision to go ahead with the course design or redesign is approved, the goals and objectives can be determined, the structure of the course decided, the teaching methods and materials planned and assessment methods set down.

A typical model of the course design process (see, for example, Diamond, 1989: 7) looks something like Figure 2.1.

In practice the need for new courses is rarely determined on this logical basis, and development does not follow a linear pattern. New courses come into being for a whole range of reasons related to departmental survival, institutional prestige, desire to experiment with new kinds of teaching, unmet demand from prospective students, or the need to create demand for higher education where none previously existed. Sometimes research into community need and student demand is carried out, but it is most likely to be after someone

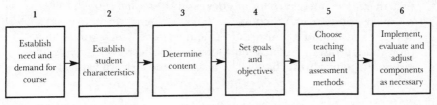

Figure 2.1 A typical model of the course design process

has decided that the new or revised course is a good idea and should go ahead. Here are six scenarios, based on real cases, that suggest how new courses come to be started or existing courses radically changed.

An elite science degree

In recent years the demand for science degrees has fallen considerably. Entry standards have had to be lowered in all universities in the region in order to fill the number of existing student places. As a consequence, lecturers in science departments find themselves teaching students with a much wider range of abilities than previously. Although there is still a handful of very bright students whose first choice is science, a considerable number of students enrol in science because it is the only degree which will accept them. These students barely cope. A large research university in the region decides to deal with the problem of student ability by creating an elite science course which will enrol only the most highly qualified students. A basic science course will continue to be offered for those students who only want to do one or two units or who must take some science as part of another degree. But the plan is to attract as many as possible of the best students, who might otherwise have been thinly distributed between half a dozen universities, by offering a prestige course, with high entry requirements which will be heavily promoted in high schools. The course will need to be specially designed so that it is both challenging and satisfying for these very bright students.

A course-work master's degree by distance education

A well-regarded regional university offers an undergraduate degree in communications with a specialization in journalism. Students are mainly school leavers. Staff on the programme would very much like to offer postgraduate course work to those already qualified and working as journalists. This would not only provide a wider range of teaching and students but would also enable stronger academic/professional networks to be established. However, as the university is located in a regional city which supports only one newspaper and one television station, there does not seem to be any possibility of getting enough students to make postgraduate courses viable. When the university is approached to join a consortium of universities which will produce postgraduate distance education courses to be offered via national television, the journalism school is the first to come forward with a course proposal.

Innovative course design as a means of attracting business students

In the past five years, four out of five universities and colleges in a single region have introduced an undergraduate degree in business studies. It seems as though four courses should be enough to satisfy student demand, but the fifth institution, the region's largest polytechnic, is still to enter the field. Although other institutions have managed to get programmes up and running sooner by offering new combinations of existing units, the polytechnic believes that the innovative nature of its new business degree will prove a real attraction to students. A team of people seconded from the accounting, computing, management and marketing departments has been working full time for the past year on the design of the new business degree. It is 'capability based', with a strong focus on problem solving, team work and communication as well as technical competence. Class sizes will be small. The programme will feature a six-month industry placement for each student, clearly integrated with the rest of the programme. Strong links have already been established with major organizations in the area which will provide guest teachers, student placements and cooperative research projects.

Continuing education workshops become an accredited course

The continuing education department of a city university has for some time offered a number of short courses and workshops on different aspects of training and development. Some of these short courses are taught by casual staff and others by staff from the Faculty of Education. The short courses are popular and participants often inquire about the possibility of follow up workshops. Staff from the Education Faculty who teach on the continuing education programme propose that the courses be brought together and accredited as a diploma course in training and development. They believe that this would be advantageous for many students, who would receive more recognition for their participation, while the additional time needed to complete the diploma would allow more application of theory and analysis of practice. The popular workshop-based teaching format would remain, but project work would be added for assessment. The programme would be offered only on a part-time basis, as students are expected to be already employed in the field.

A new postgraduate degree designed for both local and overseas delivery

The Bachelor of Health Management degree has been offered for some years. It attracts nurses, social workers and other professionals who are moving into hospital administration. But enrolments have been steadily falling. Research by the Faculty reveals that the proportion of managers in the health sector who hold tertiary qualifications has gone from 20 per cent to 70 per cent in a decade. This means that an additional bachelor's degree is no longer particularly attractive to the target group. Enrolments in the master's programme remain steady and the course attracts quite a number of overseas students. Still there seems little likelihood that numbers will increase and it appears that the department is facing a slow decline. After an overseas study leave, the head of department returns with a radical proposal. The bachelor's degree should be dropped and the master's degree should be restructured. The new more flexible master's programme should be offered in the country from which many of their foreign students come. The department has built up a good reputation and contacts in the health system and local university there; and there is unmet demand from students who cannot afford to study abroad. Ultimately the number of foreign postgraduate students could replace the undergraduate students. Discussion with overseas providers of health services suggests that they are not interested in distance education, but in face-to-face teaching which can take account of local conditions. Staffing such a programme would mean employing some locals, but a considerable amount of teaching would need to be done by existing staff, who would spend some weeks each semester at the overseas campus.

A new approach to teaching agricultural science

The Agricultural Science degree at this college has been established for some time. It is a fairly conventional curriculum of science, applied science, technology and management subjects, taught by discipline-based departments through lectures and practical classes. There has been a level of dissatisfaction with the programme for some time: many staff feel that it is not particularly relevant, and students are difficult to motivate. Attempts to make changes by negotiations among the different disciplines have led only to failure and frustration. The situation is turned around when a new college principal is appointed. A charismatic leader, he is able to articulate a different educational philosophy based on experiential learning and a vision of the new breed of agriculturist which the college might produce. His energy and enthusiasm persuade key staff members to begin a radical transformation of the course structure and the teaching and learning methods used.

As these examples show, courses appear or change for all sorts of reasons. What is interesting is that at the point when the decision is made to act, one component of the course is usually fixed. Logical systems, as represented in the instructional design flow chart, have their own attraction, but course design rarely follows that pattern. It is usually a far more holistic process and, as we can see in the examples above, it tends to pivot on one aspect which is decided at the beginning of the process. In the case of the science course it is the nature of the students who are to be attracted: if they don't enrol the course is a failure. In other cases it is a decision about the delivery mechanism. From the beginning the journalism degree was going to be a distance education programme delivered through television and print materials, with no face-to-face component. In the health sector management course, the decision was almost the opposite: a strong face-to-face component was to be retained and the course taught on different campuses in different countries.

Sometimes a course is completely revised because enough individuals who share a particular philosophy of education want to reshape it to fit with their beliefs and values. On other occasions, the stimulus is a successful new method of teaching, as in the postgraduate programme based on the workshop model; or a commitment to try new and different methods of teaching, as in the business degree.

To say that course design can begin with any dimension of the course is not to say that in these cases the process was illogical or sloppy or badly thought out. It is simply to recognize that new courses come about in all sorts of ways – as a matter of departmental survival, because a group of teachers want to express their creativity, or because they want to create a course that will shape students' intellectual and personal development in certain directions. In fact these may be more powerful stimulants to educational change than simply responding to unmet student or community demand by creating another conventional degree programme. Indeed many of the programmes in the examples cited above went on to develop into innovative courses, attractive to both students and staff and often held up as models of creative educational planning.

But once a decision has been made to have a new course, and maybe one or two of the variables have been fixed, what is the next step? What sort of process should be followed and who should be involved? Is this a process that can be handled within the faculty or should other assistance be sought? Should all the staff be invited to participate or is it more efficient to hand over development to a small team? What questions are best resolved as a group and what can be left to individual teachers to decide? In what order should the various issues be tackled?

The central questions in course design

The central question which has to be answered through the course design process might be expressed as *What is most important for these students to know and what might be the best ways for them to learn it?*

But in attempting to answer this seemingly simple question, a series of other questions arises:

- What characterizes knowledge in our discipline or profession?
- How does learning occur and how is it best facilitated? What should be the role of teachers and what should be expected of students?
- What goals and objectives are worthwhile – and how are they best expressed?
- What content must be included and what might be left for students to learn in other ways? And how will the content be organized?
- What purposes do we need assessment to serve and what forms should it take?
- What resources and infrastructure would we need?
- Who else has a legitimate interest in this curriculum? What is the relationship between the faculty and professional associations, funding bodies, the university itself?

Those involved in designing a course will need to return to these questions at many stages of the process. They need to be addressed when considering the shape of the whole programme of study and again at the level of individual units. All of the questions are interlinked and an answer to any one will affect the answers to others. Because the questions that have to be resolved are so interrelated, the course design process, at least in its initial stages, does not usually consist of a series of sequential steps, but of a group of parallel processes.

First stage in the course design process: determining the framework

The processes which in the initial stage of a course design or redesign tend to happen in parallel are set out below, together with many of the questions that will need to be considered at each point.

Collecting and analysing information on what should be taught

What are the fundamental ideas, knowledge, skills, attitudes which must be developed through this programme of study? What is desirable but not essential? Are there programmes of a similar nature to ours? What do they teach? Will professional bodies or accreditation agencies want to put requirements on what is taught? What can we find out and what can we assume about students' prior knowledge or relevant experience?

Sorting out beliefs and values about education and agreeing on broad goals for the programme

If other colleges or universities arrange their programme differently from the way we would like to arrange ours, what does that show about our beliefs about education and the kinds of learning we value? Does our own institution have a particular character which will influence our approach? What qualities do we think should characterize the graduates of this programme? Are there particular kinds of abilities – intellectual or professional – that we would like to develop in students? What are the goals of this programme and its rationale?

Thinking about how the programme might be structured

What do our educational beliefs and values suggest about the kinds of teaching and learning in this course? Should knowledge be organized into discipline-based subjects? What should students encounter first, theory or practice? Do students need to learn professional roles and tasks, mastering the knowledge and skills related to each? Should students develop knowledge and skills through working on real-life problems and challenges? How much choice can students have in what they learn? How will students learn in this course – from working with others, from working on individual projects, from lectures or from resource materials? What elements of this programme will require students to be physically present on campus? Could students start the programme at any time or only at fixed times of the year? Can they work at their own pace?

Identifying entry requirements for students and the kinds of support they might need

What prior knowledge and skills are we assuming on the part of students? Should these be formalized as prerequisites? Are students expected to have relevant work experience? How will the expected characteristics of our students (full-time, part-time, employed in the profession or not, resident locally or not) affect the structure and timing of the course? Will it be desirable to provide language assistance to overseas and foreign-born students, assistance with study skills, academic writing or maths requirements for students who have been poorly prepared or out of formal education for a long period? To what extent can different assessment and attendance options cater for needs of different kinds of students?

Thinking about assessment and identifying any constraints

What kinds of assessment are appropriate for the kinds of learning in this course? What kind of grading system would we prefer? Does our institution have rules about assessment? How flexible are they? Does the relevant professional body or accrediting agency put any requirements on assessment?

As information is collected and analysed, as different possibilities for goals and structure are explored and any external constraints (such as requirements for professional certification) are identified, the programme begins to take shape. Each of these areas will need to be revisited on more than one occasion until the programme is defined more precisely and agreement is reached on the key variables. Diagrammatically the process might look like Figure 2.2.

Once these dimensions of the course have been resolved, more detailed development work can commence on individual units, or on groups of units. Similar questions will now have to be answered in relation to each unit or group of units. What should be taught in this particular unit? What should students be expected to achieve? How might the unit be structured? Are there prerequisite requirements for students? How will the unit be assessed? These decisions in relation to individual units will be strongly influenced by decisions made in determining the course framework, but they will not necessarily be the same. The nature of the knowledge or skills taught in a particular unit or module may dictate a certain sort of structure which is different from the larger part of the programme; if the unit is taught in the field or in the workplace, this will affect the nature of the objectives and the assessment and so forth. The second stage of the process looks like Figure 2.3.

Who should be involved in developing the framework?

The development of a new course is going to involve many people, including academic and administrative staff and other specialist staff. Cross-disciplinary courses will involve staff from more than one department. At times they will need to work together and at other times they will work individually. There will be many deadlines to meet – for course approval, for advertising, for production of materials and resource lists, for enrolment of students and employment of additional staff.

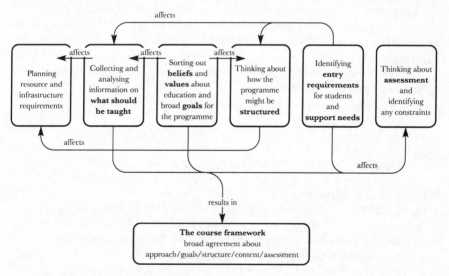

Figure 2.2   Determining the course framework

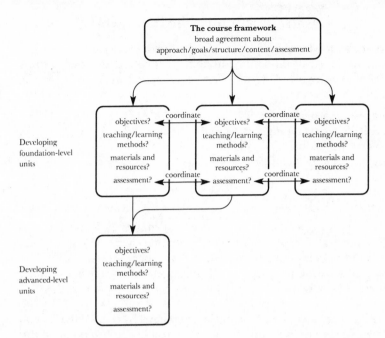

Figure 2.3   The course design process – second stage

There are many models for how a project like this might be run – probably almost as many models as academic departments. At one extreme is the model where everyone is involved – the course design team includes all of the teaching staff, plus representatives of professional groups, the student body and other interested parties. Coordination of activities may be attempted at meetings or may fall to the head of department or the administrative staff. While this model is intended to engender ownership and commitment to the new course it sometimes has the opposite effect. Over-large meetings can become difficult to manage and result in frustration and disillusionment with the project.

At the other end of the spectrum the course design team may be kept lean and efficient by limiting it to representatives of interested groups or to those interested enough to do the work. Individuals may represent the disciplines or sub-disciplines involved in a course, the different levels of the course, or even the different philosophical positions within the school or department. Representatives of interested parties outside the department itself may be included on the course team or called upon for advice at appropriate times. While this model benefits from reducing the course team to a manageable size, it also generates its own problems. The chief problem is likely to be that those who were not directly involved in the design process will feel little commitment to the programme which results. They may operate on the basis that whatever is on paper is only there in order to get the course approved and that they will continue to teach as they like in their own domains.

Roles and functions in determining the framework

When thinking about who should be involved in a course design project it is useful to distinguish the roles and functions that are involved and then to think about who needs to be involved in each. The questions that will then need to be answered are:

- Who manages the project?
- Who is involved in developing ideas and design options?
- Who makes the decisions?
- Whose advice would be helpful?

Who manages the project?

Obviously a complex project like this will need coordination. While individuals may ultimately take responsibility for developing single units, someone needs to decide at which points they need to work together. And while the whole faculty group will definitely want to come together to make many of the decisions, they are usually too large and unwieldy a group to manage the project efficiently.

So it makes sense to have the whole project managed by a small team. The job of these people is to design and manage the project – not to do all of the development work themselves. They need to determine the time frame for the project, the decision points, the schedule of meetings and the deadlines for completed tasks. They also decide what information and options need to be collected and presented to the large group.

The selection of people for the management team is important because they need to have both good organizational skills and good interpersonal skills. Their work will involve planning plus considerable liaison and communication with colleagues. In his work on change in vocational education Scott (1999) suggests that key selection criteria for membership of a team like this are that those selected, first, see the innovation as being desirable, and secondly, have the skills to make it work.

In particular the skills which he believes are necessary are the ability to work well with others and to be able to think creatively, reflectively and contingently. This kind of thinking involves:

- being able to analyse situations and contexts to determine which features are distinctive and need to be addressed;
- being able to create or adapt solutions to fit specific situations and contexts; and
- being flexible enough to resolve problems as they arise.

Who is involved in developing ideas and design options?

The project management team is likely to be heavily involved in developing ideas and options for the new course, but will almost certainly want to include more people at this point. If the number of people who will be teaching on the new programme is reasonably small it may be possible to involve them all in this stage. Otherwise a smaller group will need to develop options for everyone to consider. This may be the time to bring in specialists in educational design to work with the project team.

Whose advice would be helpful?

There is a range of people whose input and advice can be extremely useful on a curriculum design project but who do not need to be part of the project team or involved in the making of decisions about the course. These include educational specialists, leaders at the cutting edge of the discipline, representatives of professional associations, students and graduates. Sometimes it is worth bringing in individuals for working sessions with the project team or with the whole staff. Sometimes it is sufficient for one of the team members to canvas opinions and bring back the results. Sometimes the information needed may be already available through research conducted by professional bodies, surveys of students and graduates and so forth. Where the course has to satisfy external requirements as some professional courses do, it may be advisable to bring some of the key people into close contact with the programme from its earliest stages. One way to do this is to create an advisory group for the project. This group can review and comment on the course proposals at various stages. While it is important to get their advice about any factors which they may consider problematic, meetings with the advisory panel can also provide an opportunity to influence and educate key members of the discipline.

Who makes the decisions?

During the first stage of the design process it is desirable to involve all of the staff who will be teaching on the programme in detailed analysis of the options and decisions about the final shape of the programme. It is also worth including staff who will administer the programme and who may be responsible for advising students and scheduling.

This stage of the process is likely to uncover philosophical disagreements, differences in beliefs about teaching and about the importance of different areas of content. It is tempting to think that conflict might be avoided by limiting the process to a few key people of like mind. But although this may be an efficient way to draw up a course design on paper and produce the associated documentation for institutional and accreditation requirements, in the long run it is self-defeating.

The implementation of a new course or a major revision of an existing course usually requires individuals to make significant changes. These may be changes in the way they teach, or in the content that they teach, in the focus of their teaching – the kinds of abilities they try to develop in students – or in the amount of structure or degree of autonomy they offer. These sorts of changes are not easy, even when one is committed to the need for change. Mastering new knowledge and skills is difficult but even more difficult is the kind of change in professional identity which is sometimes required. Bocock quotes a letter to *The Guardian* (in the UK) by an academic which typifies this kind of conflict:

> I am not a teacher. I am not employed as a teacher and I do not wish to be a teacher, I am employed as a lecturer and in my naivety I thought my job was to know my 'field', contribute to it by research and to lecture in my specialism.
>
> (Bocock, 1994: 120)

The change in the nature of the job which is reflected here can be devastating to the unprepared. At best, teaching tends to be an isolated activity, and the discomfort involved in change can be difficult to sustain unless one is truly convinced that the effort is worth it. Developing the course framework therefore needs to be a learning process for many if not all of the teaching staff. It may involve challenging long-held but unexamined educational beliefs and considering the evidence for and against different approaches.

The planning process for a new course or a major review of an existing course cannot be an inward-looking exercise. It should provide an opportunity for the faculty to systematically seek information and opinions from the community, the profession or discipline, students and graduates about the success of past courses, the directions in which the profession or discipline is likely to move, the needs of future graduates and the characteristics of current or potential students. Even if, at the end of the review/design process, individual staff members will continue to teach familiar content, the process of coming to grips with this kind of information can help to stimulate and refocus their teaching.

The process of agreeing on and clarifying the goals of a programme of study and the content and strategies through which these will be achieved will also be instructive. Course design is always a matter of compromise – there is never enough time, resources, people or money to do all that we would like to do, or even to do what we think is necessary. The question of what should be given priority will of necessity involve argument, negotiation and examination of long-cherished beliefs about what is important. The process of coming to an agreement on the goals, and the most promising ways to achieve them given the resource restraints, can be invaluable in generating understanding of and commitment to the programme. Just as deep learning and the creation of understanding in students usually require opportunities to 'process' new ideas – to examine them, challenge them, attempt to integrate them with what is already known or believed – so deep learning about educational design requires the same kind of process. Like deep learning in students, it too requires time.

Using specialists

While a small group may drive the process of developing the course framework, deciding what meetings to have and when and what information is to be collected and presented, general participation is needed in all decision making. Where significant change is considered, leaders should be prepared to bring in specialists to talk to the whole group and answer questions about the nature of the proposed changes, the reasons for them and the impact that they might have on individual teaching. Such specialists might include leading-edge exponents of the discipline, or specialists in different models of course design such as problem-based learning, or in new delivery systems such as Internet-based teaching.

Where the changes involved are significant or likely to be contentious it can be very helpful to use an educational designer as a consultant. Such a person will design the process, planning meetings, setting agendas, suggesting the information to be collected and the people who should be involved. The educational designer can also be used to chair meetings and facilitate working groups. Having as chairperson an outsider who is a skilled facilitator can prevent disagreements becoming acrimonious and destructive and keep discussion moving.

Educational designers can also play a valuable role in helping the subject specialists who make up the academic staff to analyse the kinds of knowledge, skills and dispositions that together determine effective performance in their speciality. Experts often lose touch with many aspects of their own performance because it has become automatic. As an outsider, an educational designer can help subject experts examine the full range of knowledge and skills that go into performing a particular task or role, the goals that have not been fully articulated and the assumptions that are being made about students' entry-level knowledge and skill.

In summary then, what we ought to expect from the first stage of the course design process is:

- an opportunity to align the course more effectively with the needs of students, the community and the directions being taken by the discipline or profession;
- an opportunity for the staff to clarify the goals and purpose of their teaching, to explore areas of philosophical difference and how these might be handled in teaching;
- a set of principles which will act as a guide to individual faculty members or teaching teams in the selection of content, the choice of teaching and learning strategies and the assessment of students;
- documentation of the goals of the course, the principles on which it is founded and the methods which it employs, which provides the basis for approval by the institution and which is open to critical scrutiny.

The second stage

In comparison with the first stage, the second stage of the design process is more straightforward. Now the work of developing single units, or groups of related units, can be handed over to the individuals or teaching teams who will take responsibility for them. Units may be developed individually, or small teams may be set up to plan all of the teaching at each level of the course or to prepare sequences of units. The development of groups of units in concert may help to reduce overlap and improve the coherence and sequencing of related units.

Membership of design teams for units or groups of units

While the development of some units will be the responsibility of an individual, others will involve a number of teaching staff. It is also worth thinking about whether other staff who work with students ought to be included as well. Teaching assistants and laboratory staff may have much relevant experience of the student body to contribute, including knowledge of which concepts and skills students find most difficult to acquire. Their future work with students is also likely to benefit from the deeper understanding of the course aims which involvement in the design process is likely to give. Educational designers and specialists in the design and production of materials may also contribute to the design team for a particular unit or group of units, particularly if the course is to be offered in distance mode.

The work of the unit teams

Unit teams are charged with working from the principles, the approach and the goals which were accepted as the course framework and coming up with detailed specifications for their unit or group of units. These specifications will include:

- the relationship of this unit to others in the course, such as level of the unit, specified prerequisites and the student knowledge and skills that are assumed;
- aims and objectives;
- an outline of the main topics, concepts, methodologies, etc. that will be included;
- a description of the teaching and learning methods that will be used (such as lectures, laboratory exercises, project work) and the media (such as textbooks, audio and video tapes, Internet discussion groups, telephone conferences);
- the expected study time for students (how many weeks and how many hours per week will need to be spent in learning activities and private study);
- the assessment requirements.

Ultimately these specifications form the basis of a student guide and the advertising for the programme.

The biggest difficulties for unit teams and individual developers of units are likely to occur in preparing work to meet the project deadlines. Draft materials are usually circulated to other teams for comments and this can be very important where units are supposed to be related or where there may be unintentional overlap. But the time required to read and comment on drafts may be considerable and should be built into the project. Academics who have previously had sole responsibility for designing their own teaching may initially feel uncomfortable when all of their work is open to the scrutiny of colleagues. But virtually all tertiary education teachers who have worked with one or more colleagues in developing a unit quickly appreciate that the wealth of suggestions generated about alternative approaches, different learning activities and materials outweighs the discomfort.

A case study of the design process for an environmental engineering programme

To illustrate some of the processes I have been talking about in this chapter I decided to talk to an academic who has recently been involved in a major review and redesign of a fairly traditional environmental engineering degree. As director of the environmental engineering programme, Garry Mostyn led the review team. The review was initiated to address problems of lack of integration between the many separate units, work overload for students associated with a very high number of contact hours, a desire to give more attention to the development of generic skills such as communication and team work, and a better understanding of economic and social issues and their impact on engineering projects. The review resulted in a significant redesign of the course, with a substantial reduction in the time given to discipline-based units and the introduction of a 'practice' strand in each year of the course. The practice strand aims to get students to integrate the knowledge that they acquire in other parts of the programme through cooperative work on major projects. The projects also provide opportunities for the development of generic skills which are taught and assessed as part of the programme (Mostyn and Luketina, 1995).

Composition of the team

I asked Garry Mostyn to describe the make-up of the team which reviewed and redesigned the course and to comment on any particular factors which helped or hindered the group's functioning. Two points he highlighted were the value of having staff members with expertise in education and the important role played by student members of the review team:

> The review team was set up by trying to make sure that most of the interested parties had a seat at the table. The School of Civil and Environmental Engineering runs about 60 per cent of this course, so it was natural

that we had a fairly large representation. A number of our staff who were on the review committee were in the process of doing the master's programme in higher education and they were able to contribute in a very large measure to the review process and to the design of a new degree. Each of the departments in the school which represent water engineering, geotechnical engineering and transport engineering was involved. Then we also had staff involved from the School of Chemical Engineering and Industrial Chemistry, who are fairly large stakeholders in the course. We had the Director of the [Research] Institute of Environmental Studies involved. We also had two student representatives and they were extremely important in giving valuable feedback. We were lucky to have two very vocal student representatives who contributed in a very major way to the success of the programme.

The two students were in their final year. They were students who had entered the very first year of the environmental engineering programme so they had been guinea pigs in the existing course. They had a good understanding of the objectives of the existing course and they were able to provide very good feedback as to whether they were being achieved or not. When people would make assertions about 'Well, we had people work in teams in this unit', the students would say, 'No, we didn't do that.' They were able to say the stuff that you often only hear anecdotally, about how the students had just studied the night before and they had no recollection about what they did in a unit. The students would say, 'Yes, we did this unit but Lord knows what we got out of it. Yes, we passed and I got 87 marks but the fact is I don't actually remember much.' So having the students there was a very good brake on our own assertions about how successful we had been in the past.

One of the things that we had considered was to have industry representatives on the review team. The initial course had been formulated in consultation with industry. But we wanted to get the review process going fairly quickly and therefore thought that it was necessary to confine the group to people who were local to the campus. We have a visiting committee and feedback from industry had actually triggered the course review, so we felt that in fact we had already had fair feedback from industry about what they wanted in terms of outcomes.

Because we had two course reviews going through at the one time – one for civil engineering and the other for environmental engineering – the head of school was a guest on our committee, rather than a full member. He chaired the civil engineering review and because I was the director of environmental engineering I chaired the environmental review and was also a member of the civil engineering review committee. There was deliberately a degree of overlap between the two committees. Whether it's important to have the involvement of the head depends on the particular head, I expect. It would not be good to have the head of school if the head of school was not supportive of the process, because it would not enable the individuals to achieve the goals that they were set. In fact the school now has an undergraduate studies committee to do this sort of curriculum review, and the head of school is not on that committee. It is charged with carrying out the review process, and the committee's view is that once it has done this work it does not expect it to be changed in any serious way. We expect to have the head's support for whatever we do.

So there were up to ten on the course review team altogether, but in a typical meeting we'd have seven or eight. It was a manageable number, but there were a number of very tough issues to be resolved and in a way the larger committee made resolving some of those more difficult. But at the end I think the final product benefited. In a way a smaller group would have worked more harmoniously and faster but maybe the final product wouldn't have benefited as much.

Getting agreement from all staff

The new course design proposed by the review team was quite radical. It involved a reduction of about 25 per cent in the time given to discipline-based units to accommodate the problem-based 'practice strand'. This meant that the new design had significant implications for everyone who taught on the programme, not just those who were teaching the new units. I asked Mostyn if there was much resistance to the proposal and how conflict was managed. He emphasized the difficult balance which needs to be found between listening to people's concerns and trying to address them, while holding on to the essential features of the proposed change:

> We have a very big School of around 40 academic staff and you could divide the staff into three groups. The first group were very much on side with this approach. There was another group of probably about a third of the staff who really thought the way we've been teaching in the past was acceptable. They thought that what we were doing now was softening our course at the expense of technical rigour. It's been a long battle – or not a battle perhaps, but a long process of trying to get that particular group of staff on side. The remaining third of the staff were really bench sitters and were quite happy to go one way or the other. But universities are fairly conservative and therefore it was difficult to get staff to just suddenly throw out all their teaching plans from the past, and all their assignments, and try and redevelop their teaching with the focus on the practice strand.
>
> We had a number of staff meetings which all the staff were invited to. We discussed the proposal before it was finalized and then after it had gone through the academic board of the university and again after that. We had about four or five plenary staff meetings where we tried to convince the staff, saying 'This is what we are proposing to do, what feelings do you have about it?' and then trying to address those feelings. There is no way everybody left thinking that all their concerns had been answered

but the way forward was evident. Our attitude was, 'This is what we're going to do; we think it makes a lot of sense; if you've got concerns let us know what they are and we will see if we can address them.'

Designing and implementing the new units

The design of the units in the practice strand was undertaken by small teams, but the original design underwent constant monitoring and evaluation in its first year. Once again student input has been valuable in fine-tuning the design. Mostyn described the mechanisms that have been used to support the implementation of the new curriculum as follows:

> The development of the practice units involved small groups of about four or five staff developing each unit, sitting together having multiple meetings, putting together the required courseware [course materials] for those units. We have appointed year managers, so there are two staff who look after each year of our new course and their job is to make sure that the units within that year are meeting their objectives. We talk to each of the unit coordinators at intervals, but to some extent this monitoring is done retrospectively letting a unit run for a year and then looking at what happened in that year. We also have student focus groups which meet twice a year. They're not set groups of students, but twice a year we go and get students from each year of the course and sit down separately with them and work through the strengths and weaknesses of what we're doing. They give very valuable feedback.
>
> It's always difficult to make sure that you've got a reasonable cross-section of students, because the more communicative students are the ones more likely to volunteer and they tend to be the better students, so my practice is to try and press-gang a broader cross-section. Of course, when you get them into the room the good communicators tend to dominate again. It's always a bit difficult, but it's important to give some weight to the few words you might get out of the poorer students. Very often you have to address much more focused questions to the poorer communicators to get some feedback from them. The school and the faculty also have standard surveys that are issued for every single unit across the school, and they give valuable feedback in terms of whether the workload is too big, whether the assignments appear to be useful and the quality of lecturing.
>
> In allocating staff to the new course there were a number of issues. The school has made a policy that these practice units are the first units allocated when we come to staff allocation, and for that reason we have been able to allocate staff who were on side, were keen to see this succeed, and have a reputation as the good teachers within the school. For that reason I think we have actually got the staff teaching these units who will be able to carry the project through to fruition. Quite a few of the lead teachers in

the practice units have done postgraduate study in higher education. We see the practice strand as so fundamental to where we're going that we've got to devote the school's most appropriate resources to it.

In the early days of a new programme, constant vigilance is required to ensure that less committed staff do not give up on the difficult work of implementation and slip back to familiar ways of doing things. Continuous discussion, feedback and evaluation of the new programme are essential to maintain the new educational strategy. Garry Mostyn described how his team carried out this monitoring process:

The programme is now in its second year, and it's going very well. I've had formal feedback on our first year (i.e. last year) and informal feedback on our second year, which is two-thirds of the way through at the moment. The students ranked the practice units very highly. The focus groups report very favourably on them. The workload is still high and in fact some of the units don't appear to have trimmed the work to suit the new hours. If you talk to somebody before they offer a unit you very often get assurances that yes, they've tailored it for the time available. It is really the student feedback afterwards that gives you a different picture. What we've done is to go back and, particularly in some of the servicing areas, talk to the people who are offering the unit and say, 'We understand that you're just doing far too much in the time, you've got to do less.' That will be a bit of a battle for a while yet. It is a concern to us because we believe that in some of the servicing areas, because they are trying to teach too much, they're not achieving the aims we set for them. In other words the students aren't learning the lot that they're being asked to learn and they're not learning the little that we'd like them to learn. So that's been a concern and it will take some time to work itself out.

Managing curriculum change

Research in adult and school education shows that much innovation is done badly; that people asked to implement a particular change often have quite contradictory ideas of what they are to do and therefore work at cross purposes; and that the people involved are also often unclear about the extent and type of change envisaged (Fullan and Stiegelbauer, 1991).

The first stage of planning a curriculum project, when it seems likely that significant change might be involved, is also the time to think about how such change might best be managed. Reformers, as Bernard Shaw pointed out, have the idea that change can be achieved by brute sanity. Academics in particular can be seduced by the idea that rationality ought to carry the day. Force of argument about the logic of the plan for action, backed by status and authority, may get change on to the agenda, but the investment that many participants will have in maintaining the status quo is often overlooked. Because of the nature of teaching there are many opportunities for the uncommitted to subvert the intentions of reformers when it comes to putting change into practice, as can be seen in the Environmental Engineering example, when staff from other departments who provide some units prove much less committed to the idea of reducing content.

Michael Fullan (Fullan and Stiegelbauer, 1991; Fullan, 1994) is one of the foremost researchers on educational change and specifically curriculum change. Much of his work has been devoted to identifying the factors which distinguished those projects which were successful from the many educational innovations which failed to take hold. Many of these factors relate to the implementation phase, and we will look at the implementation of a new course later in this book; but some success factors are established at the stage when the idea of change is introduced.

Success factors in curriculum change

Among the success factors that are important in the planning stages of a curriculum project are its leadership; agreement about the desirability of change; the availability of staff development; clarity about the nature and extent of the proposed changes; and institutional and community support.

Leadership

The quality of the leadership of the course design project, and particularly the extent of support for the project from the head of department, turn out to be particularly important factors. The head has three important roles in a course design project. One is to understand and articulate the goals of the project and to understand and acknowledge the difficulties that staff may experience in designing and implementing a new course. The second is to ensure that adequate resources and assistance are available to the staff involved, and the third is to make it clear to all members of the department that curriculum change is a priority and that planned changes must be carried through. The head does not need to be the person in charge of the project – that role may be delegated to another member of staff. But unless the head both supports the project with resources and applies some pressure for change it is very difficult for a course design project to succeed. In a case study of major curriculum change in a management school, Cowen identified the need for multifaceted leadership (Boyatzis *et al.*, 1995).

Intellectual leadership provides the ideas for the project. These ideas, typically to do with the curriculum approach or key values, provide the shape and rationale for the new design. Should we consider a problem-based curriculum or a competency-based curriculum? What other options might there be? What are the reasons which would lead us to choose a particular approach for our situation? Intellectual leadership provides the answers to questions like these.

Inspirational leadership is needed to convince the staff that the project will be worth the time and effort required. In any human endeavour, the people involved need to feel that their work has purpose and value. Inspirational leadership reminds the faculty of the significance of the educational role and the importance of getting it right. As the leader of a course design team in obstetrics and gynaecology once explained, 'We used to just deliver babies and save lives, but now we are involved in something much more important: educating the doctors of the future!'

Process leadership is needed to plan and implement effective processes which will enable different opinions to be heard, different talents to be used effectively, deadlines to be met. Process leaders take responsibility, not only for designing the process but also for moving everyone on through the different stages. They are the ones to decide when discussion has gone on for long enough and commitment needs to be made to a particular course of action.

Political leadership is another necessity given the nature of academic departments. Political leaders are those who will take the time and effort, often in one-to-one conversations, to convince others of the desirability of a particular path. It may be important to gain the support of leaders of factions or sub-groups in order to achieve consensus. In order to persuade others, political leaders must be seen as people of principle who have the interests of students and staff at heart. They need to be people who are capable of listening to an opponent's point of view, as well as putting forward their own.

It will be evident that all of these different aspects of leadership ability are unlikely to be found in the same person. For this reason, it is important that a course design project be led by a team of individuals who between them are able to make the project work.

Establishing the need for change

Another crucial factor in all curriculum change projects is the importance of establishing the desirability and need for change. This will mean identifying problems or gaps in current provision and analysing any relevant data which is available or can be collected. One of the reasons for the success of the major redesign of the Health Sector Management degree described earlier was that there was a very clear need for change. Without a new programme that would attract many more students, academic jobs were at risk. Perhaps not surprisingly, some of the courses that are most likely to go for very long periods of time without any significant review or change are high-demand courses like law and medicine at the oldest and most prestigious universities. The combined status of the institution and the degree means that there is never any shortage of students. Although students and staff may grumble there is little real impetus for change.

Providing support for staff

Probably the most crucial success factor throughout all the stages of curriculum projects is the quality and availability of staff development and support. In the early stages of the project (that is in the planning and design phases) effective support to staff is most likely to take the form of discussion sessions with experts who may be educational specialists, colleagues teaching on similar programmes at other institutions or expert practitioners and subject specialists, who can help to open up the range of options that can be considered.

Once initial decisions have been made about the content, goals and structure of the new course and the characteristics of the students for whom it is designed, the next success factor lies in *clarifying the nature and complexity of the change for the people involved.*

Clarifying the nature of the change

Scott (1999) has identified the range of course components which might represent significant areas of change in a new or revised course. They include:

- the kinds of aims or objectives that the course hopes to achieve;
- the teaching and learning methods that will be used;
- the kinds of materials and learning resources which will need to be used or produced;
- the location where teaching and learning take place (home, workplace, lecture hall or classroom);
- the kinds of assessment that are to be used;
- the kinds of people who will staff the programme and their roles;
- the way in which students will be selected; and
- the expected backgrounds, ability and experience of the target student group.

The course design team needs to identify exactly which of these components will be affected and to what extent. The more components that will change, the more complex the change will be and the more support will be needed for staff. Some changes such as those concerning the structure of a course, or the kinds of materials used, may involve very little real change for those teaching on the programme. Other changes which require academics to change their beliefs about teaching and learning are much more difficult to achieve and will require much more support throughout the process of change.

Fullan's research has shown that while simple changes may be easy to carry out and therefore more likely to be 'successful', they may not make much of a difference. In particular, they are likely to make no difference to the quality of the teaching and learning which takes place. Complex changes, which demand more personal effort and organizational support, are more risky but are more likely to lead to significant results (Fullan and Stiegelbauer, 1991).

Seeking wider support

As well as doing everything possible to build understanding and support for the project within the faculty, it is important to identify those outside the faculty whose support will be needed. These might include groups beyond your organization which will have power or influence over your programme, such as professional groups, politicians, bureaucrats or major employers. Influential outsiders have the power to sway community acceptance and support and may even be able to withhold accreditation or funding. It is important to identify these people and to seek their advice and support in the early stages, in the hope that they will become allies rather than opponents.

It is equally important to identify and involve those within your organization – senior managers and policy makers, administrative staff and providers of support services – who can affect the success of your programme. Sometimes curriculum developers have naively assumed that while they may have to deal with opposition elsewhere, they can expect support for innovation from within their own institution. In one recent case a head of department spent two years negotiating a new degree programme which was to be offered on a new international campus. The project required extensive negotiations with representatives of the foreign government who would sponsor many of the students involved, and who wanted a significant voice in the content. It also involved an extensive collaborative design effort with his own staff, who were concerned about the adaptations they might need to make for foreign students and the working conditions that they might expect overseas. Everyone was consulted, it seemed, except the members of the academic council at the home university which had final approval of degree courses. After years of negotiation, when the final proposal – a joint effort of the department and the foreign government – was put forward, the academic council refused approval because it required unprecedented flexibility in the university's usual degree requirements. A year later that project is still on hold. Managing the political relationships can be as important to the success of a course design project as the design itself.

3

Beliefs, Values and Ideologies in Course Design

What is most important for these students to know and how might they best learn it? It may appear that the answer to this question is relatively straightforward. In many cases, particularly where a course has not undergone review or significant change for a long time, it often seems that the question of what should be taught is self-evident. 'All first-year chemistry courses are the same, wherever you go', a chemistry lecturer tells me.

But other approaches might be conceivable, even in chemistry. What prevents us from imagining other possibilities is our strongly held beliefs about what should be taught and the best ways to teach it. Elliot Eisner, one of the most influential writers about curriculum development in schools, calls these beliefs 'curriculum ideologies'. He defines them as 'the value premises from which decisions about practical educational matters are made' and 'beliefs about what schools should teach, for what ends, and for what reasons' (Eisner, 1994: 47).

Such beliefs are no less important in structuring the higher education curriculum. They have developed out of our own previous experience of education, particularly our understanding of our discipline, and our personal, cultural or political values. For some university teachers they are consciously held, and can be clearly articulated – the result of a process of examining and refining their own values and working out how these might be applied in their classrooms. But for many others, beliefs about curriculum are tacit and unexamined. The conceptions on which beliefs are based may be so long-standing, and so commonly held in the discipline, that they are accepted without question. Those who hold them may never realize how their own beliefs have been shaped. Alternative views are literally 'unthinkable'.

These tacit beliefs about education are not purely an individual matter. They surface in the language that is used to describe educational goals, in the choice of what is to be taught, in the design of teaching spaces, in the allocation of time within the course, in decisions about assessment.

If we examine the values in the language that has been recently used about the goals and purposes of higher education a clear trend is evident. Overwhelmingly, over the past decade, higher education has been described in terms of its role in economic competition. It must 'produce new graduates who will lead . . . industry to victory in the worldwide technological competition' (Spring, quoted in Hart, 1992: 69). Education is promoted by university leaders as a product whose sale may improve the balance of payments, and governments are encouraged to continue funding on that basis. In this context what do we understand about the current status of the long-running argument about the importance of vocational preparation versus liberal and general education? The concept of tertiary education as preparation for employment has become so dominant that the idea that graduates might question the ways in which work is organized and distributed in society seems unpatriotic. We see the effect of these beliefs in the higher education curriculum, as degree programmes in humanities and fine arts are redesigned in order to offer students preparation for a career in government service or arts administration.

Curriculum ideologies also surface in the choices that are made about what content should be taught. There are some subjects that are axiomatic – they will always be included. Thus a medical degree which does not include the study of anatomy is unheard-of. Then there are those subjects which are problematic. Should medical students be formally taught about interpersonal communication? The decision could go either way. But, as Eisner points out, while the subjects which are included 'by right' enjoy a certain security, they are generally the focus of much more attention than those which are considered problematic. Student performance in these core subjects will be carefully scrutinized and rigorously assessed. On the other hand, teachers of subjects which enjoy only fluctuating support are generally given far more freedom over how units are designed and what content is included.

What distinguishes these decisions about choice of content is that they are not made strictly on the basis of relevance to the programme of study and potential usefulness to the student or practitioner, but on the faculty's beliefs about what is 'appropriate' and its level of comfort with the decision. Should lawyers study ethics or is law a 'value-free' zone? Must a degree in English literature include the study of Shakespeare? Should computer scientists have to explore the social impact of computerization? Questions like these arise in all disciplines. Sometimes they are the subject of vigorous argument. Sometimes the level of discomfort at having long-held beliefs questioned is so high that any debate about them is immediately squashed.

Beliefs about knowledge and the nature of learning are also revealed in the ways in which teaching spaces are designed. I once worked in a new purpose-built building which was shared by the Faculty of Commerce and Economics and the Faculty of Adult Education. In the part of the building occupied by Commerce and Economics were lecture rooms of all sizes, accommodating between 50 and several hundred students. Floors were raked and seating was fixed. In the other end of the building, occupied by Adult Education, there were no lecture theatres. Most rooms held a maximum of about 30 students, the floors were flat with no dais or podium, and the furniture consisted of tables and chairs which were moved around at will. What views about knowledge and understanding do these differences reveal? In this particular Faculty of Commerce and Economics, knowledge appears to be handed down from authority figures to well-disciplined recipients. Given the numbers involved and the room arrangement, it seems that there is no intention that individuals should challenge or discuss the prevailing wisdom. In the Faculty of Adult Education there seems at least the possibility that students will be involved in working together, discussing, questioning and generating understanding.

Mass teaching arrangements are often explained on the grounds that resources are limited and this is the best that can be provided. However, in the situation described above we see the choices made by two faculties of the same university which were both asked to specify their preferred teaching arrangements at the same point in time. I suspect that frequently these choices about infrastructure which appear to be made on the basis of resources are instead made on the basis of beliefs about teaching and learning.

Allocation of time within a course is another indicator of where values lie. This applies not only to the amount of time given to different topics, but also to the time available for acquiring different kinds of knowledge and skills. Psycho-motor skills – those which involve using knowledge and finely discriminated physical movements in combination – are usually time-consuming to learn. They involve much practice, ideally accompanied by expert feedback so that the novice can try to bring his or her performance closer and closer to the ideal. Teachers in the performing arts are very familiar with this style of teaching, and the singing lesson might serve as an example. There are many occasions when students must acquire psycho-motor skills as part of their university course, yet often not enough time and assistance are allocated for the students to become even marginally competent.

Why is this? Is it because of costs and resources or is it because this kind of knowledge is not valued in the traditional university? If universities are primarily concerned with abstract and theoretical knowledge, then perhaps a course which spends considerable time developing students' psycho-motor skills belongs in some other (less prestigious) institution.

The education of nurses has moved into universities and colleges comparatively recently after a long history of hospital training. The following comment by a lecturer in nursing suggests that there is now much less emphasis on developing psycho-motor skills:

> In third-year medical–surgical nursing we were demonstrating a new skill each week. The assumption was that students would then go away and practise it. But the majority weren't practising the skills regularly and there were bottlenecks in the labs at the end of each semester as students rushed to try and learn the skills. One of the benefits of introducing video-taped self-assessment of nursing skills early in the semester is that students realize for the first time how much practice it really takes to master a skill to the required standard.
>
> (Lecturer in nursing)

What does assessment tell us about what is valued? Undergraduate education in the United States is often evaluated through multiple-choice tests which can be machine marked. What types of knowledge and skills do these kinds of tests assess? By and large, factual knowledge and the ability to reason along well-practised lines. There is little possibility in the multiple-choice test of showing that one is able to bring together knowledge from different subjects, that one can build an argument which is supported by evidence or indeed display any creativity at all. But this kind of assessment is seen to be fair, objective and reliable. Tests can be scheduled two or three times a semester and thus provide students with regular feedback on progress. The test will stand up to challenge and different markers will rarely disagree over the results.

In Europe, on the other hand, it is common for even undergraduate education to be assessed by an extensive oral examination which ranges over the content of many separate units and is conducted by a panel of assessors. Students are expected to show how they can integrate what they have learned, and assessors can delve into any aspect in depth. An oral examination of this type is not particularly reliable: different examiners are quite likely to disagree about interpretations. The fact that it is often the student who must schedule her own examination when she feels ready may mean that many students take longer over their degree than they need. Both systems have different strengths and weaknesses, but the fact that there are such different systems at the same level of education indicates very different values at work.

If we examine universities and colleges of higher education – as Eisner has done for the primary school system – to see what values and beliefs are transmitted through day-to-day operations, a number of patterns emerge.

- There is a tendency to isolate knowledge and different ways of knowing. Many disciplines present different ways of understanding human experience or the natural world, but in general, students are not encouraged to bring different perspectives together. The emphasis is on mastering each individual approach, as exemplified in a discipline or a particular methodology, rather than on integration.
- Theoretical and abstract knowledge is valued over practical skills, creativity, self-understanding and interpersonal skills. Of course original work is welcomed. In professional courses the importance of interpersonal skills in dealing with clients may be recognized. But there are few attempts to consciously develop these abilities in students. Where these kinds of skills and abilities do form part of the curriculum they are usually not valued in the assessment system in the same way as theoretical knowledge.
- There is an emphasis on individual rather than cooperative achievement, and a need to compete for limited rewards. Occasional group work projects are assigned, but most emphasis in assessment is on sorting out students on the basis of individual achievement. Students are often highly conscious that only 5 per cent can get the highest grade, and sometimes resort to practices like stealing library materials in order to weight the odds more heavily in their favour.

- Verbal and mathematical modes of expression are most valued. This is particularly exemplified in the current debate over whether candidates for postgraduate degrees in art and design should be required to produce a written explication of their intent and their creative process as well as a major work of art or series of works. So far, those in favour of additional writing are winning out.
- Students are taught respect for authority. Early in their academic careers they learn that previous academic work on their topic must be sought out and cited, that teachers are the ones to decide what questions to ask and to judge the quality of any work that is produced. There is little space for students to develop their ability to evaluate themselves and great reluctance on their part to do so – on the rare occasions that they might be asked to. This is despite the fact that one of the criteria used to distinguish professional practice from other areas of work is the supposed ability to evaluate oneself and regulate one's own performance.

The fact that we can identify these recognizable patterns in higher education is not to say that they are wrong. But they are the result of choices that have been made, sometimes consciously, sometimes without much consideration of what the alternatives might be. Those choices have been made according to the predominant values in the academic community. Values will inevitably vary between disciplines, and will be challenged as the composition of the university community changes and values in the wider community change. With this in mind let's consider a range of different approaches to curriculum in higher education, including both those which reflect traditional values in universities and those which reflect more recent beliefs about how the student's path to understanding might be constructed.

Writers on curriculum in schools (Kemmis *et al.*, 1983; Eisner, 1994; Posner, 1995) have identified a range of different philosophical approaches to curriculum, of which some can also be found in higher education and others cannot. The five approaches which I believe can be identified in university and college courses might be categorized as:

- traditional or discipline-based;
- performance- or systems-based;
- cognitive;
- personal relevance/experiential;
- socially critical.

Let us again consider the fundamental questions of course design which were identified earlier:

- What characterizes knowledge in our discipline or profession?
- How does learning occur and how is it best facilitated? What should be the role of teachers and what should be expected of students?
- What goals and objectives are worthwhile and how are they best expressed?
- What content is essential and what is desirable? And how should it be organized?

- What purposes do we need assessment to serve and what form should it take?
- What resources and infrastructure are needed?

Each of these questions would be answered differently according to which of the five different philosophical positions was adopted. Each different perspective represents a coherent set of assumptions about these key factors in education.

In order to contrast the different perspectives and bring to light the assumptions that underlie each approach I have treated them here as though they are always discrete. In fact, given that university courses are often not developed as a coherent whole but as a pastiche of individual units, there are many examples of courses which reflect a range of different approaches. There are also many examples of courses which espouse fashionable values, such as a commitment to developing lifelong learning or critical thinking, or adopt features of a particular approach, such as the specification of objectives, but fail to follow through by making these part of what is taught or assessed. The most accurate picture of the educational values and beliefs inherent in a course is usually to be found not in the statement of goals but in the way time is allocated to different topics and learning activities and in the nature of the assessment.

Traditional or discipline-based approach

The design of most university and college courses has traditionally followed the structure of knowledge in the discipline. Programmes of study are divided into units and topics based around important concepts, and each topic will be structured in some rational manner. For example, an English literature course might be divided according to the major forms (poetry, prose and drama) and then according to the historical development of each form – Elizabethan drama, Jacobean drama and so forth. Within an economics course the subject divisions are made on the basis of the scale of operations: microeconomics (the economic behaviour of the individual and the firm); macroeconomics (economics at a national level); and international economics. In Euclidean geometry the theorems are arranged from the most simple to the most complex. In geology, students may follow a sequence based on the cause-and-effect relationships which result in the formation of certain kinds of geological features.

The important point to notice here is that whatever logical basis is used to structure the course – chronological, causal, scale of operations, form of expression – it exists within the subject matter itself and the way in which the discipline is usually structured. It is not related to student interests, the way people learn or the ways in which problems present themselves in everyday life.

The view of knowledge

In this perspective on the curriculum, knowledge is conceived as existing independently. It forms a body of theory which has been developed, refined and tested over time. It exists in books and published records, waiting to be accessed by students. Most emphasis is placed on the technical, rational and managerial aspects of knowledge which help to give greater control over the world, rather than on personal or expressive knowledge. There is a strong leaning toward abstract and theoretical knowledge, to the point where even highly relevant skills such as report writing or library research may not be considered appropriate to be taught within the course.

The process of learning, the roles of teachers and students

If knowledge consists largely of information, facts and concepts, the role of the teacher is to sift through it, select what is most important for students to know and transmit that to them. Teachers may also provide exercises for students, designed to confirm what is known or to give practice in the mode of inquiry of the particular discipline. Students are conceived as more or less motivated and prepared to learn, more or less diligent in carrying out their assigned tasks and memorizing important information.

The learning goals and how they are expressed

Students in these kinds of courses are expected to acquire a broad knowledge of the field, the key concepts, and the methods of inquiry used within the discipline. Goals are often expressed as lists of important topics with which the student will become familiar.

How content is chosen and organized

Content is frequently chosen for breadth so that students obtain a representative picture of the field. Coverage is considered important, and the opportunity for deep investigation into any one area will often be sacrificed in its name. Content is logically structured and sequenced according to the nature of the discipline.

What purpose does assessment serve and what methods are used?

Assessment is used to confirm the extent of knowledge and to rank students for further study, honours, awards and so forth. The predominant methods are paper-and-pencil tests, ranging from multiple-choice and short answers to long essays. Student efforts are usually marked on a finely discriminating scale (e.g. 1–100) and the results are norm referenced (students are ranked against their peers).

What kinds of resources and infrastructure are needed?

With this approach, education can be economically delivered to large classes. It is an efficient use of the subject expert's time because one person can lecture to large numbers. Much of the tutorial work, laboratory classes and marking can often be assigned to teaching assistants because exercises are specified in advance and outcomes clearly defined. Textbooks and printed lecture notes distil important knowledge and reduce demand on libraries and primary sources.

Examples of traditional, discipline-based courses abound in universities and colleges of higher education. Here is just one extract from a university handbook which suggests a traditional, discipline-based approach to the course design:

> *Japanese linguistics and Japanese literature*
> The Japan Centre offers units in Japanese linguistics and in Japanese literature. Linguistics units cover descriptive and applied Japanese linguistics as well as translation; they may be combined to form a major in Japanese linguistics . . . Literature units offered by the Centre deal with a variety of Japanese literary genres, both traditional and modern, including drama.
> (Australian National University: undergraduate handbook, 1997)

Performance or systems-based approach

A very different approach is that taken by educators who see the course design problem not as one of values or philosophy, but as technical, a question of what means to use to achieve certain desirable ends and of how to measure results so that improvement can be soundly based. By introducing a 'systems approach' to course design, educational technologists promised to bring the methods of applied science to education. The systems approach developed out of the work of Ralph Tyler, who stressed that education should be a purposeful activity, that schools needed to define their goals, teach toward them and then evaluate students' progress to see whether the goals are being achieved (Tyler, 1949).

Tyler's four questions for curriculum developers

1. What educational purposes should the school seek to attain?
2. What educational experiences can be provided that are likely to attain these purposes?
3. How can these experiences be effectively organized?
4. How can we determine whether these purposes are being attained?

Tyler's work was refined and elaborated (see, for example, Taba, 1962; Wheeler, 1967; Kemp, 1977; Nicholls and Nicholls, 1978) into what came to be called the 'instructional systems' approach to course design. Romiszowski, one of the chief proponents, identified an instructional systems approach thus:

> It is the presence of precise goals or objectives (however they are arrived at) and the presence of careful pre-planning and testing that are the main characteristics of our use of the term 'instructional system'. Instructional systems design is therefore, a three-phase process of establishing precise and useful objectives, planning study methods and testing them.
>
> (Romiszowski, 1984: 51)

With the instructional systems approach, learning objectives need to be clearly defined in advance and specified in behavioural terms so that it is possible to determine accurately whether they are being met. Where objectives are met, and the programme is successful, it can be easily replicated – thus bringing the advantages of well-planned and carefully evaluated education to very large groups of students who are not fortunate enough to have a talented and creative teacher. As a result, a well-designed curriculum is seen as a quality control mechanism which can compensate for less than excellent teaching. This approach to curriculum design has been particularly attractive to governments because it holds out the promise of accountability. If educational objectives are tightly specified and assessment is designed to determine whether they have been met, then the degree of effectiveness of the educational institution can be clearly demonstrated. Competency-based education provides the most recent example of the systems approach to course design.

The view of knowledge

Proponents of a systems approach would say that the only evidence that we have for knowledge and understanding is the kind of performance that an individual is capable of – what he or she is able to do or say. Understanding is exemplified in action, and the purpose of learning is to be able to expand one's repertoire of skills and ways of behaving. Knowledge is useful to the extent that it informs action. There is no split between theoretical and applied knowledge, as there can be in discipline-based programmes. Rather the opposite – theory is taught only in the context of the areas where it might be applied.

The process of learning and the roles of teachers and students

Inherent in this approach is the belief that learning is facilitated best when important learning tasks are analysed into their component knowledge and skills. The requisite knowledge and skills are then carefully structured and sequenced so that new learning builds upon previous learning until complex performances can be mastered. The role of the teacher will vary considerably according to whether or not he or she is the designer of the course or unit. Where teachers act as instructional designers, their role is complex. They should determine what kinds of performances will be the expected outcome of the unit, analyse those performances to determine what kinds of skills and knowledge will be required and in what sequence they should be introduced, plan appropriate learning tasks, and schedule frequent assessment so as to provide feedback on progress and identify any need for remedial action.

Where the teacher is not the instructional designer, which may be the case where a programme of study is being delivered largely through technologies such as computer-assisted instruction or other educational media, the teacher's role may be limited to facilitating group work, assisting individuals, answering questions and providing feedback on assessment tasks.

The students' role is comparatively straightforward: they follow the learning path that has been planned for them. Because the core skills have been determined through considerable research into the nature of practice, the systems approach allows little choice for students in terms of what they will learn. However, courses designed in this way can often allow considerable flexibility in timing if self-instructional materials are used. One of the virtues of this approach, from the student's point of view, is that expectations are much clearer. Explicit objectives with regular feedback on performance can increase students' confidence and sense of achievement.

The learning goals and how they are expressed

In the broadest terms the learning goal is to become a skilled performer. As you can imagine, this is a goal that seems particularly appropriate to many designers of professional preparatory programmes, although it is not limited to them. Language programmes and introductory science programmes aimed at helping students to acquire laboratory skills are often based on this approach. Under the broad learning goal of skilled performance, objectives are specified in terms of behaviour, and are often laid out for students in a map or learning hierarchy which shows how enabling objectives build upon each other and contribute to the final skilled performance.

How content is chosen and organized

In programmes which are planned from a performance viewpoint, content is not chosen according to teacher or student interests but on the basis of research into the nature of practice in the profession or by observation of skilled performers. Such research is designed to identify the skills which are most used, the kinds of knowledge most called upon and any factors which are critical to effective performance. This knowledge is used to plan a structured series of learning experiences, involving practice and feedback which should ultimately lead to competent performance.

What purpose does assessment serve and what methods are used?

Assessment in programmes based on this kind of approach will be frequent, in order to provide feedback to both teacher and student. Failure at any assessment point signifies a need for remedial action before further progress can be made. Final assessments are designed to certify a level of competence. They will be criterion-referenced (assessed against prespecified criteria rather than against others' performance). They may be marked on a satisfactory/not-yet-satisfactory basis, or may be graded for higher levels of performance.

What kinds of resources and infrastructure are needed?

The systems approach lends itself well to delivery through a range of educational media and thus to distance education. Projects involving large-scale development of interactive multimedia, other forms of computer-based instruction or educational videos are likely to employ instructional designers trained in this approach. As well as using media like video to demonstrate many aspects of performance, performance-based programmes are likely to need access to a wide range of equipment, materials and specialized work spaces like laboratories or simulated professional settings in which students can practise the requisite skills.

The following extracts from the course description of an articulated open learning programme in management suggest a predominantly systems- or performance-oriented approach to the design of the programme:

> The program design gives high potential managers access to leading edge management research and practice in a part-time format. The learning outcomes centre on the transfer of learning to the workplace to improve individual effectiveness and organisational efficiency ...
>
> The teaching and learning method of the Australian Open Learning Program is based on an approach which permits participants to remain at work while studying two subjects concurrently each semester. Study materials include: comprehensive self managed learning manuals, selected readings, audio cassettes, videos, computer software and case studies ...
>
> There is continuous feedback on performance, with instructor-marked assignments and national examinations monitored and centrally marked by the Australian Graduate School of Management ...
>
> Subject areas were nominated by potential users, both employers and participants. Subject contents were designed by leading Australian management academics, drawing on their research and consulting experience in the Australian environment. Senior AGSM faculty continue to have an important role as subject leaders overseeing and monitoring instructors and assessment. The development of the subject materials and delivery system is guided by open learning and instructional design professionals.
> (Australian Graduate School of Management Handbook, 1996)

What proponents of the systems approach often underestimate is the extent to which the performance orientation influences the values of the curriculum. On the surface it may be 'value free', but in practice it often translates into a position which conveys that values are not important. Consequently there is no place in the curriculum for examining ethical issues inherent in the way the profession interacts with society and the individual practitioner interacts with clients.

The cognitive approach

In the cognitive view the major functions of the school or university are to develop the mind, to help students learn how to learn and to provide them with opportunities to use and strengthen their intellectual faculties.

The concept of the curriculum focused on cognitive development originated in the nineteenth century with the idea that some subjects were important not for their content but because they developed specific faculties, such as the ability to reason. Mathematics was thought to develop logical thinking, and Latin a rigorous and precise mind.

This view assumed that the kind of logical thinking developed in mathematics would transfer easily to other areas of knowledge. Unfortunately for the cognitive position, Thorndike's research in the early twentieth century proved this to be false. Thorndike's subjects could only transfer what they had learned in one situation or task to very similar situations or tasks: general transfer across domains of knowledge did not exist.

The idea was revived with more recent psychological research on the structure of the intellect. Within educational psychology the dominant approach has moved from behaviourism to cognitivism, and the focus of research has moved from reproductive learning and memory to thinking, reasoning, understanding and meaning-making. Posner described the cognitive perspective as follows:

> Cognitive views derive directly from the ideas of the philosopher Immanuel Kant, who claimed that people may be born with certain capacities or 'structures' for acquiring language, concepts and skills. These innate structures develop as the individual develops. Furthermore, knowledge and beliefs the individuals acquire affect the way they perceive and think about subsequent ideas, objects and events. Thus people do not passively receive information from their senses; rather they actively construct ideas and generate meaning from sensory input by interpreting the input on the basis of existing ideas and previous experience.
>
> (Posner, 1995: 107)

With the swing to cognitivism among educational psychologists, the curriculum again began to be seen as a vehicle for helping students develop intellectual abilities, although now the focus was on acquiring the conceptual structures and thinking processes of a particular discipline. Resnick described the importance of both in the cognitive curriculum:

to understand something is to know relationships. Human knowledge is stored in clusters and organised into schemata that people use both to interpret familiar situations and to reason about new ones. Bits of information isolated from these structures are forgotten or become inaccessible to memory.

Good thinkers and problem solvers differ from poorer ones, not so much in the particular skills they possess as in their tendency to use them ... The habit or disposition to use the skills and strategies, and the knowledge of when they apply need to be developed as well.

(quoted in Posner, 1995: 108)

View of knowledge

In the cognitivist view, knowledge is personally constructed. But this does not imply that any one individual's views are as good as another's. Some explanations are better than others because they are based on stronger evidence and stand up to more rigorous examination. Poor understanding and misconceptions are also possible. Where the material to be learned is complex and seems to fly in the face of common sense and previous experience, then misunderstanding becomes highly likely. The conceptual structures of experts are far richer and more useful than those of novices; habits of rigorous thinking and analysis are not innate, but need to be cultivated and developed.

The process of learning and the roles of teachers and students

The constant refinement of ideas and intellectual abilities, and the development of a well-structured knowledge base, require teacher and students to work through a relatively limited amount of content in considerable depth.

Class work is likely to be focused on real-world examples and problems to ensure that students integrate new knowledge with previous experience. It is the teacher's responsibility to recognize areas where misunderstanding is likely to occur, to bring students' conceptions or misconceptions to light and to challenge them to come up with a better explanation in the light of all the evidence. Small-group work would seem to be a necessity because of the need to have students critically examine their own understanding and beliefs. This kind of critical examination is very difficult to undertake alone, and it is part of the cognitivist agenda to constantly model the process for students. The questioning skills of the teacher are particularly important, because the kinds of questions raised by the teacher should draw students to new levels of analysis which they would not have reached on their own.

The learning goals and how they are expressed

In contrast to the systems approach, which sees educational goals in terms of increasing the repertoire of skilled performances at students' disposal, in the cognitive view the development of the processes of thinking becomes the objective. The goal is higher-quality thinking, expressed in more rigorous analysis and argument, better problem identification and better problem solving. Thinking becomes both the purpose and the content of the curriculum. Learning goals are likely to be expressed in terms such as 'students will learn to think critically, become lifelong learners, solve problems'. Such objectives are of course about changes in students which are not immediately apparent. Come assessment time, they have to be translated into performance tasks through which students can demonstrate their increased intellectual capacities.

How content is chosen and organized

In the cognitive curriculum, content is not chosen for broad coverage of the field, but for the opportunities it provides for mastering important concepts and practising key intellectual abilities. According to Resnick and Klopfer, a cognitively based curriculum eliminates the competition between content and skills because 'concepts are continually at work in contexts of reasoning and problem solving . . . There is no choice to be made between a content emphasis and a thinking-skills emphasis. No depth in either is possible without the other' (quoted in Posner, 1995: 113). Given the time limitations on most degree programmes, depth usually comes at the expense of breadth, and the curriculum content may have to be pared back in order to emphasize cognitive development.

What purpose does assessment serve and what methods are used?

Assessment in a cognitively focused curriculum must allow students to demonstrate the complex understandings and increased intellectual abilities that they have developed through taking the course. Assessment tasks are likely to pose quite complex problems, often requiring students to take into consideration the features of a particular context in their response. Such assessment tasks are not easily evaluated, requiring high levels of judgement on the part of the marker. In line with the principles espoused in cognitivist programmes, students could reasonably expect markers to be able to articulate the evidence on which they make their judgements, and to defend their decisions. Because the learning objectives of cognitivist programmes often emphasize ill-defined abilities such as critical thinking or problem solving, it is particularly important to students that the assessment criteria be clearly articulated so that they have an understanding of what it means to be a critical thinker or a problem solver in this particular field. Perhaps because of the marking load, but certainly because of the emphasis on acquiring evaluative skills, cognitive programmes are more likely to include students in the assessment process through opportunities for self- and peer-assessment.

What kinds of resources and infrastructure are needed?

The chief learning requirements of cognitive programmes are opportunities for students to engage in active processing and questioning of ideas, and practise thinking skills. This will require a high degree of interactive small-group work, with guidance and challenge from an expert group leader. It is quite possible for students to organize themselves effectively to undertake many learning tasks, but it is difficult for them to challenge their own thinking. So the chief resource needs for cognitivist programmes are adequate student–teacher ratios for small-group work and appropriate accommodation, combined with adequate libraries and collections of other resources to support the level of independent investigation that is often involved.

Open learning and distance education programmes are becoming increasingly popular with governments, who see them reducing the need for capital investment in buildings. Higher education managers also welcome the possibility of expanding the student base and thereby income. Nevertheless distance education causes some problems for teachers with a cognitivist bent. The hardest thing for a distance programme to supply is the opportunity for extended interaction with others that allows the deep processing of ideas and the development of intellectual abilities. This is a problem that will be considered at more length in Chapter 6, when we discuss the possibilities for making access to learning more flexible.

A cognitivist approach is evident in the following description of a psychology unit. While much of the content will clearly be similar to other introductory courses in psychology, the emphasis here is on understanding key concepts and learning to think analytically and critically:

Psychology I: key concept of the course
This course is designed to help you learn the logic of psychology. Everything we do this semester will in some way, either broadly or narrowly, relate to improving your understanding of and thinking critically about psychological principles, theories, practice, and application. The primary goal is for you to come to think as a psychologist would think. This includes identifying and working through problems which psychologists address. The course will focus on the different types of psychologists, the different schools of psychological thought, the varying work that is done by psychologists. The course will also focus on psychological processes, both conscious and unconscious, which influence the behaviour and thinking of human beings.

To think deeply about the field of psychology, one must think clearly about the questions which face psychologists, one must gather relevant and valid information which relates to those questions, one must accurately analyze the value of information gathered and one must understand the complexity of human nature.

(Information for students on the Psychology I course
at the University of Sonoma, California)

The learning goals and how they are expressed

With a personal or experiential approach, learning goals may cover the full spectrum of learning but must involve learners in their formulation. Knowles suggests that learning goals should take the form of either 'a learning objective that describes the terminal behaviour to be achieved (which is appropriate for most basic skills learning) or the direction of improvement in ability (which is appropriate for more complex learning)' (Knowles *et al.*, 1984: 19).

How content is chosen and organized

The process of planning the knowledge and skills needed to meet learning goals, and the kinds of resources and experiences which might provide effective learning, is one of intense collaboration between teacher and students. In planning programmes with students, the teacher must provide sufficient guidance and structure for the experience to be educationally productive, without being prescriptive or coercive. The results may be formalized in a detailed learning contract which sets out what learning activities will be undertaken by the student, and how the results will be assessed.

What purpose does assessment serve and what methods are used?

An important goal of most personal or experientially based programmes is that students develop the ability to evaluate their own learning. Learners will generally be expected to select and present their own evidence of achievement and assess their own work, often in collaboration with teachers, peers and workplace supervisors or subject specialists. Recent work by Boud, Anderson and Sampson examines the issues involved in this kind of self assessment (Boud, 1995; Anderson *et al.*, 1996). Assessment in experientially based programmes often involves the evaluation of large and complex projects which have been undertaken for the learning opportunities they present rather than for ease of assessment. It can be a problem with programmes of this type, where students are working on large projects, that they receive little formative evaluation of the work in progress.

What kinds of resources and infrastructure are needed?

The chief resource need here is likely to be teacher time, combined with good access to libraries and professional contacts. The time spent by teachers working individually with students to negotiate learning contracts, or with groups to plan learning experiences, can be extensive and heavily weighted at the beginning of the process. Programmes of this type often try to incorporate 'real-world' experiences and so additional time may be needed to help students arrange placements or plan projects. Consequently, teacher–student ratios will need to be relatively low.

The personal or experiential approach values above all else the individual's freedom to choose and to become his or her own person. Considerable emphasis is given to helping individuals take responsibility for their own learning and develop their own judgement. This places considerable responsibility on the teacher, who must get to know students individually and establish rapport with them. In general it is easier to teach to a prescribed curriculum, and some teachers will lack the interpersonal skills and flexibility needed for the experiential approach.

Although costly in terms of teachers' time and effort, many variants of this approach are being adopted. Units and programmes based on 'learning contracts' or 'action learning projects' are often found in the fields of education and management. The problem-based learning curriculum, a hybrid which combines elements of both experiential and cognitive approaches, is becoming increasingly common in the health sciences.

The extract below, from the course information for a Graduate Certificate in Adult Education in Community Education exemplifies a personally relevant and experiential approach, with its emphasis on student-directed learning, individual projects designed and assessed through learning contracts, and reflection on personal experience through learning journals.

Graduate Certificate in Adult Education in Community Education Process
Some of the course is prescribed and some learner-directed. This means that there are opportunities for you to pool information and ideas with other participants and to tailor the study you do directly to your own professional, community and personal requirements.

Course components
Seminars are held on a weekday evening and are usually conducted as lectures/discussions. Sessions last two hours. The seminars are used to examine the theory that informs community adult education practice. In Autumn semester the seminars are entitled Adult Teaching and Learning. You will be encouraged to examine certain adult learning principles and a number of adult learning theories. This will lead to a study of teaching and learning techniques that place an emphasis on facilitation and dialogue, and draw on the theory and practice of educators with experience in the fields of community development and social action. In Spring semester the seminars are entitled Developing Community Adult Education Programmes. You will be encouraged to examine the theory and practice of designing and implementing a range of educational activities in differing kinds of community. By looking at the work of a number of adult educators you will be encouraged to develop your own theoretical framework to guide your practice.

Professional Skills is a composite activity requiring attendance on the same weekday evening as the seminars. Sessions last one and a half hours. On alternate weeks a member of staff will lead using lectures and exercises to help you develop your facilitation and teaching skills. On the other weeks participants will be allocated into semi-autonomous study groups and asked to work on a number of learning projects which within given parameters you will be able to choose and design yourselves.

Workshops are held on four Saturdays during the year. Each study group is required to help in the design of one workshop. The workshops enable participants to supplement the content of the course and to prac- tise planning, implementing and evaluating an educational activity.

Learning journals are kept by each participant throughout the course in order to record and reflect on their field work, community education practice and significant learning. The journals need to be completed according to a number of general criteria and sighted by a member of staff.

Assessment
Assessment is either pass or fail and is related to attendance, participation in all components of the course, the completion of the learning journal, and the completion of a number of learning contracts.

Learning contracts
These comprise the major written work for the course. They are negoti- ated by each participant with a member of staff. The idea is to get away from the set assignment and to make the coursework you do directly rele- vant to your own professional interests and work. You are required to complete four learning contracts during the course negotiated with your study group supervisor and with the seminar leaders.

The course places some emphasis on self-direction in learning. Staff are there to offer support and advice but the process of designing and plan- ning your own learning can be difficult at first and if you have not experi- enced this kind of learning program before you may need to be ready for an initial period of adjustment.

(Information for students in the Faculty of Education, University of Technology, Sydney)

The socially critical approach

A socially critical perspective seeks to develop a critical consciousness in stu- dents so that they become aware of the present ills of our society and are motiv- ated to alleviate them. A socially critical approach to curriculum draws upon the work of critical theorists who believe that the institutions of society, includ- ing educational institutions, are created and moulded by social elites. As a con- sequence the role of those institutions is to maintain and support the status quo. From the point of view of a critical theorist it is no accident that the children of minority and disadvantaged groups are not adequately represented in higher education – the system is designed by and for the socially advantaged. The role of the critical theorist and the socially critical curriculum is to examine society, its institutions and its cultural products and to expose the covert values that guide the way these work. The socially critical perspective has been particularly influential in the humanities and social sciences, but critical theorists have also begun to have an impact on the applied sciences, where they have raised questions concerning the usefulness and appropriateness of some technologically based solutions to fundamental social problems.

The view of knowledge

From a socially critical perspective, knowledge is constructed within our historical and cultural frameworks. We create our understanding through interactions with others who tend to be of similar background, culture and social class as ourselves. For instance, one's view of how the tax system ought to operate is likely to be highly influenced by whether one's friends and family are in business, in government service or unemployed. Each of these three different experiences of employment is likely to produce very different views about the tax system, but people who are more socially and economically powerful are far more likely to have their views taken into account when policy is formed or curriculum developed. Similarly, Western medicine has a 'scientific' explanation for how disease attacks the body, a powerful tradition of healing and an aggressive approach to the search for new remedies. Chinese medicine is the product of an even older culture, has a somewhat different explanation for how the body works, and focuses more on the maintenance of health than on the cure of disease. Which system you put your faith in depends on your ethnic background and current influences; which system gets taught in medical schools depends on where power and influence lie in the community.

In yet another example, there are many different views on the origin of the universe. Many scientists are proponents of the 'big bang' theory. Others prefer the concept of a constantly evolving system derived from the ideas of the philosopher Teilhard de Chardin, or the physicist Ilya Prigogine. Fundamentalist Christians offer their own explanation and have fought, with occasional success, to have it taught in the US school system. Whether the explanation that you favour becomes part of the curriculum depends on the power and influence of your particular group.

Thus knowledge, according to the critical theorists, is historically, socially, economically and politically conditioned.

The process of learning and the roles of teachers and students

The process of learning envisaged from a socially critical perspective is akin to the conceptual change model proposed by the cognitivists. Students and teacher engage together in understanding and critiquing social institutions or work on collaborative projects which have some social significance. The teacher's role is to help students understand where their own views have come from, to challenge preconceptions and to encourage them to consider other possibilities. Within a socially critical curriculum, a key question that students learn to ask is, 'Whose interests are being served here?'

The learning goals and how they are expressed

As with the experiential or personal relevance orientation, the overall goal is to produce a graduate capable of self-realization. The difference is that self-realization is seen in a social context rather than as a purely individual matter. Goals of individual units or subjects are likely to be written in terms like 'to understand . . .', 'to critique . . .', 'to be able to develop arguments and defend one's position'.

How content is chosen and organized

In a socially critical curriculum in the arts and social sciences, content is drawn from the pervasive and significant social problems of the day. In the sciences, socially critical aspects of courses might include consideration of the uses to which scientific research is put; the environmental and social impact of technical and engineering solutions; the distribution of health services; and the appropriateness of Western medical models for indigenous populations. Content is usually organized around investigations, themes or projects.

What purpose does assessment serve and what methods are used?

As with the personal or experiential approach, assessment is likely to involve a strong element of negotiation between students and teachers about the kinds of evidence of learning which will be put forward and the criteria for successful performance. Collaborative work and group projects are likely to be encouraged, as are self- and peer assessment. The assessment plan should support the goals of the socially critical curriculum: that students develop skills of critical inquiry, independent judgement and the ability to work effectively with others.

What kinds of resources and infrastructure are needed?

The most expensive aspect of the socially critical curriculum is the requirement for a high degree of interactive small-group work. The projects and investigations which form part of the course are likely to be community based.

In some senses the systems approach to curriculum and the socially critical approach are at opposite poles, but they do have a number of things in common. Both look beyond the structure of the discipline or the interests of the individual to society to inform decisions about educational goals. Where the systems approach looks to society to determine which skills are important and valued, the socially critical approach asks (among other things) whether other kinds of knowledge and skills might not be equally valuable to society. Both the systems and socially critical approaches place a premium on knowledge translated into action: the systems approach on skilled performance and the socially critical approach on social action.

The most famous of socially critical curricula are the literacy programmes developed by the South American educator Paolo Freire. In his work with illiterate peasants in Brazil, Freire devised a curriculum that not only addressed literacy needs but also helped his students develop a vocabulary that enabled them to question their working conditions and the political system which supported their exploitation. The programme that he devised was simultaneously an adult literacy programme and a political education (Freire, 1970).

Friere's work was much admired among educators. As a result, although higher education students are more likely to come from the privileged classes than from the ranks of the oppressed, many university and college teachers have tried to help them develop a more critical consciousness.

This subject description suggests a socially critical approach in an undergraduate law programme:

Feminist Legal Theory
Examines the complex role played by legal rules and practices in the construction and maintenance of inequality between women and men. Introduces students to feminist jurisprudence and significant debates within it, including the multiple meanings of 'equality' (for example, the sameness/difference debate and critiques of it); the public/private dichotomy; and the ways in which 'black letter' law is gendered. In addition to the broad theoretical material, topics covered may include the three part system by which women have access to financial support: viz, paid work, dependence on men, and dependence on the state; injuries to women and the ways in which women are distinctively harmed; the legal construction and regulation of women's connection with others: as wives, mothers etc: strategies for change (is the practice of law, in particular the adversary system, the only alternative for dealing with disputes; would gender neutral legal language change a gender specific world?).
(University of New South Wales: Faculty of Law Handbook, 1995)

Does one approach always predominate?

Each of these five philosophical approaches represents a different position on the purpose of higher education. Each has consequent implications for the way in which education should be carried out. To what extent can an individual hold to more than one approach? If asked, most teachers in higher education would say that they value all or most of the educational goals found in these different approaches: a broad knowledge of the discipline and the way know-ledge is structured within it, skilled performance, cognitive development and high levels of intellectual ability, personally meaningful learning which is strongly integrated into the individual's knowledge base, and ability to think critically about social issues.

Some examples exist of curricula which have been deliberately designed to encompass the best features of several approaches. Problem-based curricula usually place a high value on experiential learning alongside a cognitivist emphasis on the development of intellectual abilities.

Courses designed in association with the Higher Education for Capability Project combine elements of a systems approach: they focus on effective per-formance and knowledge exemplified in action, but broaden the learning goals with a much greater emphasis on personal development (suggesting an experi-ential approach) combined with effective thinking, reasoning and reflection (suggesting a cognitive approach) (Stephenson and Weil, 1992).

More common is the higher education curriculum which espouses a broad range of goals but fails to deliver. It is often instructive to examine the way in which the curriculum operates to determine which values take precedence. Time tends to be the factor that sorts out what is most valued – both the time available in the curriculum and the teacher's personal time for preparation and availability to students. With limited time available for classes, most teachers will face a choice between addressing all of the content they think is important and making time for the kinds of activities that promote higher levels of intel-lectual ability, independent learning, mastery of skills and critical thinking. Many teachers are still too wedded to the idea of 'coverage' to be able to bring themselves to cut some content in favour of different kinds of learning. They may also be constrained by the social frameworks in which they operate, par-ticularly where departments and professional accrediting bodies have certain expectations about what topics will be covered. Although many departments and faculties may pay lip service to a range of educational goals, the discipline approach, with its emphasis on breadth rather than depth, is still the dominant model.

Another factor which works in favour of the traditional approach is the gen-eral lack of knowledge about education in many academic departments. Those who are interested in pursuing other goals may lack knowledge of the most appropriate strategies to use and skill in carrying out different kinds of teaching roles. Although they have different aspirations, they are limited to reproducing the model of teaching that they experienced as students.

On the other hand, governments have recently favoured a competency approach because of its promise of increased accountability, and have attempted to influence universities and colleges to adopt it whenever possible. In both Australia and the UK, governments have imposed competency-based curricula (the latest variant of the systems approach) in the vocational educa-tion sector, which comes under direct government control. Considerable pres-sure has been exerted on universities and colleges of higher education to come into line and to adopt the same approach for their courses. Where professional bodies have also endorsed a competency-based approach, a number of departments have begun the process of re-educating their staff and redesigning their courses to follow a systems approach.

Within the humanities the socially critical model has become increasingly influential over the past two decades. This is probably attributable to the fact that this approach derives not from the work of educators but from the ideas of philosophers and social theorists such as Foucault, Gramsci, Marcuse and Habermas, who are significant figures within the humanities disciplines. The socially critical approach has led to a broadening of the content of humanities curricula, with a greater emphasis on the study of popular culture, as well as to less reverence for the work of many formerly important figures.

There is less overt pressure to adopt the cognitive or personal/experiential models in higher education, although they often have an intrinsic attraction for higher education teachers who encounter them. Examples of these approaches frequently show up in individual units or subjects and occasionally as the organizing concept for a whole curriculum.

Where higher education curricula have been created in a piecemeal fashion, with individual academics adding or remaking units in response to their own interests, the ensuing differences in approach among staff members may result in students having to meet a confusing array of expectations. Where academic departments are required to conduct regular reviews of courses, as is becoming common in many universities and colleges, differences are more likely to come to light in the planning stage. Course design workshops often expose great differences in perspective among academic staff teaching on the same programme.

Sometimes these differences can be resolved through the course development process, particularly where staff adopt one approach largely through ignorance of alternatives and may be quite open-minded about trying something new. At other times strongly held beliefs are involved and no agreement is possible.

How important is it to have some unity of approach throughout a curriculum? Obviously coherence has some advantages. Skills and abilities which are valued, whether they are technical skills, intellectual skills such as logical analysis and argument, or personal qualities such as the ability to manage one's own learning, can be developed over time. The course structure can offer appropriate learning tasks that are structured from the simple to the more complex.

That ideal is not always achievable, and students are reasonably adaptable. In my experience they adapt more easily if they understand what they are being asked to do and why. Where one part of the course holds to a very different approach from another part, students are likely to notice and challenge the differences. Where teachers can explain their rationale, students will usually accept the different approach, although acceptance may be grudging if the change involves distinctly different kinds of work practices and assessment. Where one part of the course takes a different approach and the teacher cannot or will not convince students that the different requirements are for a worthwhile purpose, then they are likely to prove resistant.

This resistance may affect innovators or traditionalists. In one department teaching French language and culture, the language side of the department adopted a strongly performance-oriented approach. Students were provided with specific objectives and assessment criteria which set out standards of performance for different grades. This worked well for the language subjects, but caused problems with that part of the department which taught literature and culture and continued to teach in the way that it had always done. Students began to demand of literature teachers that they make objectives explicit and provide assessment criteria. The literature teachers were unable to do so, but neither could they explain adequately why they took a different approach. The ongoing difficulties with students led to ill feeling between staff from different sections and ultimately to a demand for a complete curriculum review.

On the other hand, in an education department with a strong focus on curriculum design, almost all of the staff favoured a technological, performance-oriented approach with the exception of those who taught educational psychology. They were strongly cognitivist in orientation. Both groups could and did present well-argued explanations for their stance which treated the other position with respect. Because of the clarity with which both views were presented, most students found the opportunity to work from two very different perspectives more enriching than confusing.

Differences in beliefs about the purposes of education and the consequent design of courses may not be resolvable. There may be times when it is of benefit to students to experience different approaches. However, open discussion through the process of course design or review can help teachers define what is important to them and clarify what they believe in. If that clarity then helps teachers communicate with students, there is hope that both students and teacher will at least engage in the same endeavour.

4

Thinking about Goals and Content

If we believe that higher education amounts to more than the sum of the knowledge and skills which we acquire through studying different topics; if we subscribe to the idea that learning has the potential to transform our understanding of the way the world works and the way we operate within it; then we need to consider the larger goals of our programme of study. And to be of most value, programme goals need to be clarified very early in the course design process so that choices about content, structure and learning activities can be made with goals in mind.

Thinking about our beliefs about education and the outcomes which we value most highly is a starting point for determining what we might aim to achieve in a particular course. Discussion with colleagues who will teach on the course is invaluable, and input from current practitioners and community contacts can help in deciding whether one factor or another needs to be emphasized for this particular time or context.

The desirable qualities of graduates

A considerable amount of work has recently been done in different quarters in attempting to define what might be the expected outcomes of a university education, in whatever field. In the UK the Higher Education Quality Council (HEQC) has suggested that the award of a degree is likely to signify at least three kinds of achievement. These they characterize as:

- field-specific knowledge – the possession of a body of knowledge and other qualities particular to the field (or fields) studied;
- shared attributes – the possession of certain more general attributes that might be common to graduates from families of degrees, whether associated by cognate subject matter and/or approach (such as the life sciences or the performing arts);

- generic attributes – the possession of yet more general attributes, which might be common to all or most graduates.

(HEQC: Quality Enhancement Group, 1997)

In Australia, the National Board of Employment Education and Training (NBEET) of the Higher Education Council produced a somewhat more detailed list, describing desirable 'characteristics of quality' in graduates as a blend of the following:

- Generic skills
  These are skills that every graduate should be able to acquire regardless of their discipline or field of study. They would include knowing how to learn, to solve problems, to be able to think logically as well as laterally and independently, to be intellectually rigorous, to integrate information and to communicate effectively.
  There are also important socially-relevant qualities expected of graduates which relate to leadership, cooperation and team-work, ethical practice, and critical/evaluative skills; and personal skills such as intellectual liveliness and the willingness and capacity to learn and re-learn.
- A body of knowledge
  The knowledge that graduates acquire has two main purposes. It should provide the graduate with a knowledge of a discipline and its theoretical base at a depth and detail appropriate for the level of the award. It should also act as a vehicle to inculcate the generic skills . . .
- Professional/technical or other job-related skills
  The professional, occupational or practical skills which graduates can apply immediately to their employment. Some of these skills will be occupation specific; some will be more general such as an ability to work with minimum supervision in the specific field, to apply learning to the workplace and so on.

(NBEET: HEC, 1992: 9)

Academics themselves are likely to emphasize the so-called generic skills and abilities when they are asked about their goals for students. In many workshops with university teachers I have asked people to identify the goals that they have for graduates of their courses. Results are always similar and very close to the lists put out by the Higher Education Council and the UK body. Here is just one example of what one group of university teachers at such a workshop said that they wanted to achieve through their teaching:

Academics' goals for graduates

- to understand that knowledge is not fixed and that they can contribute to it
- to think, question and challenge
- to solve problems, both familiar and unfamiliar
- to make informed choices

- to have a rich cultural and intellectual life
- to be critical and to question their surroundings
- to be aware of their own values and beliefs in dealing with other people
- to treat others humanely
- to be able to interpret and evaluate research findings
- to be able to analyse increasingly complex problems and to work towards increasingly better-thought-out answers
- to be able to communicate effectively in all ways
- to be able to integrate personal experience and theory
- to work efficiently and safely
- to act with integrity
- to have confidence
- to have acquired the knowledge base of the discipline
- to continually seek out knowledge.

Harvey and Knight (1996) have observed that there is little disagreement between academics and employers on the desirability of developing the kinds of generic or transferable skills identified above. But academics are more likely to see such abilities as the natural by-product of a university education, whereas employers are more likely to hope that they will be explicitly developed and assessed. There is some evidence that a university education does develop such qualities: see, for example, the studies by Perry (1970) and by Belenky, Clinchy, Goldberger and Tarule (1986). However, there is also evidence that students develop those generic skills or abilities on which their teachers place a high value, but show little change in those areas which are not valued by staff.

Boyatzis' study of students and faculty at the Weatherhead School of Management at Case Western Reserve University in the United States showed that teaching staff placed greatest value on conceptual, analytical and planning skills when designing and conducting their classes. They placed least value on abilities concerned with managing people, interpersonal relationships and self-awareness. In a comparison between the entry-level abilities of their students and their skills on graduation, students were found to have made the greatest gains in the conceptual and analytical skills which were valued by their teachers. They showed little or no change in the leadership, self-awareness and inter-personal abilities which were least valued by their teachers in the design and conduct of classes. These findings were reflected in widespread criticisms of US MBA programmes for producing graduates who were overly analytical, not sufficiently action-oriented and who lacked interpersonal, communication and team-work skills (Boyatzis, 1995).

Boyatzis' study showed the powerful effect of teachers' goals on students' learning. Because teachers designed and conducted classes in accordance with their goals, students developed those abilities which teaching staff intended them to develop.

When course design teams develop programme goals as a starting point, choices about which goals to pursue are taken out of the realm of individual decision making and opened up for examination and critique. If staff can agree to work on developing the same set of attributes throughout the programme, the impact of their efforts will be increased.

Considering the significant abilities and attributes that we hope graduates will develop is only a preliminary step. As we think about these in the context of our course design yet more questions come to mind:

- Of the many desirable attributes or qualities that we would like to see in our graduates which are most important? Can we identify a manageable number which might serve as a nucleus around which the course can be designed?
- What constitutes the necessary content that makes up the 'body of knowledge'?
- How can we ensure that in teaching that content we develop the generic skills, dispositions and patterns of thinking that should characterize our graduates?

Some of the most interesting higher education programmes in the past decade have been focused around a limited number of core attributes which are consciously developed through all stages of the programme. Such an approach has the advantage of keeping attention on a limited, and therefore memorable, number of goals. It allows these attributes and skills to be developed in a coherent way over the duration of the course so that students can move from simple applications to more complex ones. Lastly, it requires all teachers on the programme to take some responsibility for developing these attributes in the context of their individual subjects and does not allow them to be lost in the drive to master content and technical skills.

Master-performer analysis

One way of getting at these core attributes is through the concept of the master performer. This idea of a master performer can be used not just for analysing purely vocational roles but in any discipline – philosopher, historian, economist, physicist, choreographer, physician and so forth. Sometimes it is possible to recognize real role models, but more often we are likely to envisage a composite performer, an imaginary figure who exemplifies the kinds of skills and knowledge, values and attributes which are characteristic of an expert – or perhaps just a competent performer in the discipline.

In thinking about what constitutes this kind of performance we need to ask questions like:

- What roles do master performers undertake?
- What sorts of problems do they tackle?
- What sorts of methods do they use for solving problems?
- What kinds of evidence do they collect and how do they assess it?
- How do they present their findings?

- How do they communicate with peers and with wider audiences?
- What distinguishes excellent performers from the merely average?

This sort of analysis can bring to light the important skills and methodologies of the discipline – which will of course be already evident to most practitioners. It can also highlight the less obvious domains of practice, ways of thinking and dispositions (such as the willingness and capacity to continually evaluate one's own performance) that may characterize the master performer.

At one level a master-performance analysis might be carried out by asking a group of experienced practitioners and academics how they envisage a skilled performer. Georgine Loacker and her colleagues have described this process in the development of the abilities-based curriculum at Alverno College in the US. Having determined the eight core abilities they want their graduates to have, the teaching staff then analyse what those abilities mean to scholars in each discipline:

> we agreed that we would 'break open' analytic ability into a sequence for emphasis in learning – observing, inferring, making relationships, integrating . . . Third, we agreed that we would spell out the specific manner in which scholars and students in different disciplines do their analysis . . . What does it mean to observe in biology? What does it mean to make inferences in psychology? How do students in literature make relationships? How do students in history integrate to make sense of their learning?
>
> (Loacker *et al.*, 1984: 4)

At another level the identification and analysis of the characteristics of master performers may involve a more elaborate research study. A fascinating account of one such research project is that by Spencer (1984), who described an elaborate study to identify master performers among US diplomats. The characteristics of the master performers were to be used in developing a selection strategy for graduates applying to enter the foreign service, and were to form the basis of in-service professional development. Master performers were identified by their colleagues, who were also asked to provide examples of *critical incidents* which exemplified the way they handled demanding situations and which singled them out as experts. Interestingly, the characteristics which distinguished master performers turned out not to be related at all to the academic results which had previously been used in selection. Instead they were abilities like 'political networking' – being able to identify and use the power relationships in any context; communication skills like 'accurate empathy' – being able to understand and deal with the emotional as well as the factual content of any communication; and 'openness to different cultures'. Spencer maintains that although such skills are not usually part of the curriculum in formal education, they are quite teachable and important in many human service professions.

Deciding on broad goals for the programme of study

The outcomes of exercises like the analysis of the master performer and the desired qualities of graduates need to be formulated into general goals for the programme of study. Of course these will be useful only if they are used to shape teaching and learning activities down the track. But this application is most likely to happen where those involved in teaching on the programme have spent time exploring options and thinking about what is most valued. One of the difficulties in maintaining the impetus and direction of a unique programme of study is that those who come later to teach on the course have not shared the experience of formulating its goals.

The University of Newcastle in New South Wales introduced a radically different approach to medical education when it instituted its problem-based learning course in 1978. The 'integrated curriculum' in medicine comprised five domains: professional skills; critical reasoning; identification, prevention and management of illness; population medicine; and self-directed learning.

The medical programme has five objectives which relate to these domains and aims to ensure that at the conclusion of the course the graduate has the ability to:

- engage in productive professional relationships and maintain those relationships to acquire, evaluate and communicate information;
- apply the process of critical reasoning to medical care;
- apply his or her understanding of illness to its prevention, identification and management and to the promotion and maintenance of health;
- apply his or her understanding of medicine in a community or population context; and
- take responsibility for evaluating his or her own performance and implementing his or her own education.

(Candy *et al.*, 1994: 262)

Getting agreement on programme goals and educational approach: a case study

Jenny Bygrave was one of the key people who recently developed an innovative four-year business degree at Auckland Institute of Technology. It has three distinctive features. The first one is that the curriculum takes a capability approach: all units encompass the 'personal and professional capabilities' of communication (oral and written), the ability to work as part of a team, critical thinking, problem solving, ability to use technology, research skills and technical competence.

The second feature of the programme is that for the first three semesters out of eight, students do an interdisciplinary course in business. Instead of learning subjects such as accounting, economics and business law as separate units, they study business problems and themes under headings like 'The New

Zealand Business Environment', 'Information and Business', and 'Managing Organizations'. These interdisciplinary themes bring together the foundational business disciplines and at the same time provide a context for developing the capabilities.

The third feature is that all of the business students do one semester of co-operative education, during which they work in industry. For students specializing in international business this will mean at least one semester overseas.

Jenny Bygrave sums up the philosophy of the programme: 'Our whole approach is – if you want to be a professional you've got to understand the theoretical frameworks, you've got to understand how they are applied and you've got to be able to manage yourself and be effective as part of a team.'

Designing the programme

The design process for a fairly radical programme like this was not straightforward. There were two early attempts which failed. Bygrave described the process of trying to get agreement within the Faculty about the shape of the new degree:

> In 1990 a new piece of legislation was passed that enabled polytechnics to grant degrees. We had this wonderful opportunity to design something from scratch. Our very first question was – What is a degree? What makes a degree different from a certificate or a diploma? And we discussed that in terms of student capabilities. The graduate from a degree programme looks like *this* and does *these* sorts of things.
>
> The Institute of Chartered Accountants suggested to us that we should offer an accounting degree. We started talking to other polytechnics and began developing a model for an accounting degree. It was what you might call a vanilla-flavoured one, in other words it was just like a university degree. You do your subjects and they're fragmented. You do accounting in year 1 and then you do some more accounting in year 2 and then you do some economics. It looked as if it could have been offered by Auckland University or Melbourne University or anyone. The faculty was highly departmentalized then, and so the accounting department was considering it and the people in the other departments like marketing and management were aware of developments but we weren't encouraged to get involved.
>
> Then there were some people like me who were very interested in looking at problem-based learning, enquiry-based approaches: we were reading people like Schön on reflective learning and effective practice. John Stephenson from the Higher Education for Capability Project came out and we talked to him about capabilities and we really liked that approach. It fitted with our view that a degree was about development and transformation of students in the context of disciplines and subjects.
>
> So then we started having discussions across the faculty, and I and one or two others proposed that we should have a business degree. We insisted

that it shouldn't be like a conventional university degree – why would a student come to a polytechnic to do a business degree that was exactly the same as a university offered, when they could go to a high-status institution and do it? We started to say that we had to differentiate ourselves and we needed to build on our strengths, which are our commitment to teaching and learning and our vocational orientation.

At that point, some of us put forward an idea about an integrated curriculum. I had first come across such a thing at Newcastle Medical School in Australia, and in about 1987 I wrote a note to the dean of our faculty and suggested an integrated curriculum and he said, 'Not now, go away!' Well, we brought it up again and a few of us, heads of department and one or two other principal lecturers who are interested in teaching and learning, started to put together this idea about a degree curriculum that was interdisciplinary, that had cooperative education, and that had a capability focus. But it got left to one person to lead that team and she wasn't terribly effective and consequently the work didn't get done.

As the project appeared to be failing for the second time, Bygrave was asked to take over as leader of a new course design team. I asked her what enabled the project to succeed on this third attempt. She highlighted the commitment of team members, the value of expert advice on educational design, the importance of continual communication about the project and the support for staff as they learned about this new way of teaching:

You need passion and enthusiasm. I had been reading the educational material for two, three, four years and I was very interested in that. I was passionate about wanting our graduates to be the best in the world, and I didn't believe that a traditional university delivery mode was the best one on the basis of the research that I'd been reading. There were a few other people who believed with me and were trying different things in the faculty, but we were all doing it independently. In a traditional curriculum you end up with burn-out when you get people working on their own. We used to talk to each other about what we were doing, but what we wanted was a whole curriculum.

Another very important factor was that we now had support from the top. The dean was very much on our side and he said, 'Go for it', and he released six of us from most of our teaching to work on the curriculum.

Most of these people [on the team] were very strong on the educational side; the others were brought in for political reasons so we that we had a spread of disciplines from across the faculty. We set up a project management approach. We used all sorts of strategies to try and get involvement and commitment, communicating across the faculty as much as we could, making sure people knew what was going on, sending out newsletters, trying to keep the heads of school on side, having faculty forums.

There was a huge amount of flack at times because the accounting department had previously envisaged this wonderful accounting degree that looked like all the other degrees where students specialized in accounting from day one. They couldn't see how you could possibly bring students into an accounting degree and not teach them accounting from the beginning. So there was all this opposition from people with a very functionalist, traditional model of education.

We worked our way through it and we managed to find out about a professor of education at Massey University who was involved in integrated and interdisciplinary curricula at secondary school level. We brought him up to see us and he was so pleased by the idea of anyone doing this in business education at tertiary level, which he thought was the most boring, traditional kind of education you could have, that he immediately started to work with us on a consulting basis and as a mentor. He helped us with the models of integration and interdisciplinary work. He wasn't strong on capability, we really did that ourselves through reading and debating issues with each other.

Because it was such a different model of a business curriculum we had to be really strong, and we had to have the backing and the authority so that we could actually convince the panel of university professors and industry people [the accrediting body] that we could do it and that it was worth doing.

Once we had designed that curriculum then we developed our teaching team: it was an encouraging and an enforcing role at the same time. We said to everyone, 'There is a capability approach in this degree, wherever you teach and learn and assess in this degree, that must be explicit.' We taught people about what capabilities were, we worked with everyone about how you teach, learn and assess in that way. We've gradually increased the number of people who can do it, and who can help other people do it, and it is just part of the way we do things now. We talk about it all the time, if you ask any of our teachers now it is the same for them as it was for the original team. When it comes to the quality of the programme everybody knows that the quality of the programme starts with the undergraduate profile and the capability approach and everything must reflect that. We don't let anyone get away with a technical approach.

Jenny Bygrave is now working on another course design project – this time a master's degree in business. I asked her what she had learned from her experience of leading the first project and what advice she would have for someone taking on a similar project for the first time.

The first thing we do now, which I think reflects what we have learned, is to develop a graduate profile. By that we mean the capability statement for graduates. We negotiate that among a small team. We send it out to all sorts of people and get their comments and that's our starting point. Once we're happy with our graduate profile we start to think about what sort of structure we will need, the teaching and learning components, the assessment, the whole student experience which is going to get us to those graduate outcomes. At the moment with the master's, we've developed our graduate profile and we've got our draft structure. Our draft structure is a huge matrix of the subject components, the teaching and learning and assessment strategies which shows how they link and build towards the graduate profile. We build this huge matrix so that we're sure we've got it coherent, that it fits together and that we're not leaving anything out.

Choosing content

Once some progress has been made on defining the course goals it is usually necessary to make some preliminary decisions about content. The list of topics produced at this stage will later be refined, elaborated, rethought and reduced as units are designed in more detail, but at this stage it is necessary to get some idea of the pieces which will ultimately fit together to form a whole.

What sources of information might be considered in deciding on the content of a course? The usefulness of different sources and research techniques will vary considerably according to the discipline, but some possibilities include:

- published educational materials such as textbooks and curriculum documents;
- information from academics teaching in the field;
- information on current professional practice;
- information from students and recent graduates.

Published educational materials

Analysis of the curricula of similar courses at other institutions, as well as analysis of textbooks and recent literature, provide a view on what others involved in teaching the subject think is important. Curriculum documents from other institutions occasionally incite unstinting admiration, but are more likely to prompt questions about the importance given to some topics and the inclusion or non-inclusion of others. Curriculum documents from institutions outside the local area have often been difficult to obtain. However, the World Wide Web is proving an increasingly useful source of curriculum outlines. A general literature review, as would be undertaken at the beginning of any research project, will also provide a useful starting point for the curriculum team.

Information from academic staff

Academics who teach in the discipline will usually have the best understanding of foundation concepts and will also be able to identify concepts which cause students most difficulty. They may also be well placed to comment on future directions for their discipline. Their views can be obtained through techniques such as surveys, individual and group interviews, or concept analysis or concept mapping.

Sometimes the starting place for planning a new course (or reviewing an existing one) is a re-examination and redefinition of the fundamental concepts of the discipline. Here is an extract from the curriculum documents of a degree in nursing which sets out the faculty's understanding of the concept of health:

> To begin with, health as a state is relative and is reflected in an individual's capacity to engage in the activities of daily living in an integrated way, which in turn contributes to survival and fulfilment as a human being. As a process, health is dynamic and is characterised by adaptive and maladaptive responses which may or may not help maintain the desired state of equilibrium necessary to sustain a high level of wellness in each of the major domains, that is, biological, psychological, spiritual, environmental and social.
>
> (University of Western Sydney, Macarthur: Faculty of Health,
> Bachelor of Nursing Course Assessment Document, 1991: 5)

With this definition of health the faculty has already made clear that the course which they offer will involve nursing students in the study of all aspects of patient welfare and not just physical needs.

Concept mapping

Concept mapping is a graphic technique which can provide a useful way of analysing the key concepts in a course and their relationships. Mapping can help in identifying the hierarchy of concepts in a course and any prerequisite knowledge or skills.

The benefit in using a concept map is that it helps in identifying the relationships between concepts. This can be particularly useful when decisions are being made about how subject matter should be divided and sequenced into subjects and units.

Concept analysis for curriculum development is usually best carried out as a small-group activity. The stimulus of more than one mind at work can bring about a richer result. Different understandings of the concepts involved are likely to be revealed in the discussion of definitions and examples. Rowntree provides a detailed guide to concept analysis for curriculum development (Rowntree, 1981).

Considering future directions for the field

The other area where academic staff can be particularly useful is in forecasting the directions which the discipline may take, and the impact that changes are likely to have on the preparation of students. It may be desirable to go beyond the staff of one's own department in order to consider the probable impact of change.

A possible mechanism for exploring future directions is to conduct a search conference, a technique that has been used both for curriculum planning and for strategic planning in organizations. It can be particularly useful in curriculum planning if the discipline is undergoing major change or there is tension over the direction that change should take. Leaders in the discipline from higher education and from the professional community are invited to participate. The search conference usually begins with an examination of the economic, social, technological and other forces which are bearing on society and then moves to a closer examination of the effects of these on the educational needs of the profession or discipline (Crombie, 1985).

A search conference may highlight needs for different areas of content to be taught, or for students to develop new skills and different abilities. These may be new technical skills, specific to the discipline or profession, or they may be more generic abilities. If, for example, one of the trends identified is that graduates are more likely to work as independent practitioners or contractors rather than as employees of large organizations, then students may need to develop business management skills. If the discipline or profession is undergoing rapid changes in its knowledge base, then there will be a need for students to acquire the disposition and skills of self-directed learning during their undergraduate education in order to take responsibility for their own professional development as graduates.

Information on professional practice

Information on the current requirements of professional practice can be sought in a number of ways including:

- reviewing information published by professional bodies on requirements for registration or practice, as well as published reports on future directions for the profession;
- functional analysis of professional roles;
- surveys and interviews with professional practitioners on the current nature of practice and predicted directions;
- surveys and interviews with major employers concerning their perceptions of graduates.

Those preparing students for professional practice often need to take account of strong opinion from professional bodies on what content ought to be included in the qualifying programme. In recent years some professional bodies have invested in considerable research to establish the tasks and roles in which new practitioners need to be competent. These sets of 'competence standards' are not necessarily intended to dictate the higher education curriculum. Often they have been developed as part of the registration process for overseas qualified professionals. But clearly it would be foolish not to pay close attention to competence standards where they have been developed.

While professional competence standards can be very useful sources of information to course designers, it is as well to be aware that their most common weakness is a tendency to focus on the technical performance of specific tasks and roles and to neglect aspects such as the way professionals must integrate and manage different tasks simultaneously with other aspects of the job – the way in which they interact with colleagues and clients and the approach that they take to solving unfamiliar problems (Toohey *et al.*, 1995).

In cases where a professional association acts as an accrediting body its expectations may not be set out as standards of competence, but as lists of topics which ought to be included in the degree programme, sometimes with suggestions for the number of hours which ought to be given to each topic.

Where such requirements on the part of professional bodies exist they are likely to be well known to those preparing students for the profession. There is often a strong incentive to meet such requirements, because without compliance the degree programme may not be endorsed by the professional body. However, guidelines and requirements specified by professional bodies should be treated with some caution. At best they may represent an investment in research into the current nature of professional practice which a faculty could not afford the time or money to conduct on its own behalf. Some of the examples of the development of competence standards have been carried out in close association with academics involved in preparing students for the profession. At worst, the requirements of a professional body may represent an overly conservative view of the nature of the profession which will inhibit students from developing the skills and abilities they will need for future practice.

Guidelines and registration requirements of professional bodies should not be accepted as a given if the faculty believes that they will have a damaging effect on the curriculum. Development or major revision of a curriculum is often challenging for the academic staff involved as they are forced to examine their beliefs about their discipline and the way it should be taught and learned. Sometimes that process needs to be extended to the professional body as well.

Where no current research exists on the nature of professional practice, it may be desirable for the course development team to commission such research or to carry it out themselves. Such research is most likely to be needed where the field is a relatively new one, is changing rapidly or is cross-disciplinary in nature. The most common research techniques employed for this purpose include:

- surveys;
- structured or semi-structured interviews;
- observation of practitioners;
- functional analysis;
- DACUM (Developing a Curriculum);
- Delphi technique; and
- critical incident analysis.

Surveying, interviewing and observation are research techniques which are widely used in the social sciences, and many academics will be familiar with them. Any introductory textbook on research methods will include guidelines for using these techniques. Here, I will limit myself to identifying a few disadvantages. Surveys may appeal initially because they seem to offer a relatively straightforward method of gathering information. However, they are often quite expensive to produce, distribute and analyse in large enough numbers to ensure an adequate response rate and a representative sample. And then, because responses are generally either fixed or limited in length, they may not produce detailed enough information to be really useful. Some research has indicated that a handful of experts can generate essentially the same information as a survey of thousands of practitioners (Gonczi *et al.*, 1990).

Interviewing, on the other hand, can be a useful technique for developing detailed information. If necessary, unstructured or semi-structured, wide-ranging interviews can be carried out initially with a handful of participants in order to identify topics to be explored in more structured interviews with a larger group of interviewees. Interviewing can be time-consuming and expensive, particularly if interviewers need to be trained. However, interviews can often be carried out within a shorter time than a large-scale survey.

Observation of practitioners at work can be a useful source of detailed information about practice, but its chief disadvantage is usually the time involved, particularly as researchers may need to do follow-up interviews to confirm their observations. Training of observers may be necessary to improve objectivity and reliability. Observation is most likely to be used to validate findings from other methods of investigation, and to provide more detailed information on the demands and impact of the environment in which the practitioner works.

We will look in a little more detail at those techniques which have been developed or used extensively in curriculum research.

Functional analysis

Functional analysis has been the main technique used for the development of competence standards for vocational training, but it has also been used in a number of projects related to professional work and higher education. The functional analysis and development of competence standards has usually been carried out by industry 'lead bodies' or professional associations, usually with the guidance of a consultant. Functional analysis is a top-down process which begins by identifying the key purpose of the occupation under study and continues by asking the question, 'What needs to be done for this key purpose to be achieved?' In this way all of the important activities and tasks involved are identified.

For example, the Dietitians' Association of Australia, in the process of carrying out a functional analysis, determined the key purpose of the profession to be 'the promotion of health, and prevention and treatment of disease, by optimizing the nutrition of populations and individuals . . .' In answering the next question, 'What needs to be done for this key purpose to be achieved?', tasks were organized under three headings, 'Routine', 'Organizational' and 'Non-routine'. Routine tasks which a dietitian could be expected to undertake included collecting food-intake data, translating technical information into practical advice and writing meal plans. Organizational tasks included working with other staff, managing the workload and preparing and managing budgets. The less frequent but equally important non-routine tasks included policy development and public relations (Ash *et al.*, 1992).

Once significant activities such as these have been identified, they are further broken down by continuing to ask the same question: 'What needs to be done for this to be achieved?' The rule of thumb for when to stop is: 'Stop when the task that has been identified would be clearly understood by any practitioner in the discipline.' The group will then go on to develop performance standards for each task, define the range of contexts under which beginners might be expected to perform and identify the kinds of assessment evidence which might be sought to show that competence has been achieved.

Functional analysis has been criticized for underestimating the complexity of many occupations by focusing too narrowly on tasks and ignoring the underlying knowledge base and personal attributes and dispositions which are required for true competence (Gonczi *et al.*, 1990; Scott, 1991). However, it has been used by some professional groups, such as the Institute of Chartered Accountants in England and Wales and the Australian Veterinary Association, to develop competence standards for those professions.

DACUM (Developing a Curriculum)

Developed in North America in the 1960s, the group method known as DACUM offers a less limiting and more comprehensive form of occupational analysis than the functional analysis technique. It has been widely used in higher education. For the purposes of a DACUM a dozen or so experts are brought together with a skilled facilitator. The participants are usually a mix of educators and expert practitioners representing different locations, size, level and variety of practice. Their first task is to identify the principal roles or duties of the occupation being analysed. These are usually displayed on a wall, on cards or sheets of butchers' paper. The next step is to analyse the tasks that are involved in each role and the knowledge, skills and attitudes which are required for effective performance. Participants may also be asked to sort knowledge and skills into those which are essential for entry level practitioners to possess, those which are desirable but not essential and those which are required for specialist areas of practice. They may also be asked to comment on the frequency with which beginners are likely to undertake particular tasks.

A well-conducted DACUM has the advantages of being fast (usually conducted over a day), systematic, thorough and relatively inexpensive.

The Delphi technique

Originally developed for forecasting, the Delphi technique has been used for a wide variety of planning needs. Essentially involving two or more rounds of a particular kind of survey to the same group of experts, its advantage lies in bringing a degree of consensus to a situation where certainty is not possible and experts are likely to disagree.

As with the DACUM, participants in the Delphi are chosen to represent a range of different educational interests and practice situations. There are usually considerably more participants though, often somewhere between 30 to 50. The Delphi is most often used to predict future educational needs. In the first round of the survey participants will be asked to comment on changing areas of practice, needs for new knowledge and skills and, possibly, the expected demand for new graduates. After the first round of the survey has been returned, the results are analysed and summarized. These form the basis for the second round of surveys, in which the findings from the first round are fed back to the participants and they are asked to draw their final conclusions about future educational needs, this time taking into account the opinions of their expert colleagues. The second survey is usually more structured than the first, requiring participants to rank priorities or to select the response closest to their own view. Responses to the second round are then analysed and reported to the participants and the course design team.

The Delphi is likely to be most useful when an occupation is undergoing significant change and the trends are not yet clear. It allows opinion to be consolidated from experts who are widely dispersed geographically. And it keeps disagreement to a civilized level. Until now the Delphi has usually been conducted by mail, which can make it a slow process. Where e-mail use is feasible the time frame could be greatly reduced. See Delbecq *et al.* (1975) for detailed guidelines on carrying out a Delphi survey.

Critical incident analysis

The critical incident technique can be a useful supplementary source of information in a course development project. It cannot provide such a systematic overview of the skills and knowledge of a profession as some other techniques can, but it can help in identifying the knowledge, thought patterns and personal attributes which distinguish the excellent performer. It can also provide a wealth of case material which can be used at later stages of the course design process in the development of teaching materials.

The process requires practising professionals to identify incidents in their professional work which might be classified as 'critical', using a number of criteria. The outcome may have been notably successful or unsuccessful; the incident may have been crucial to the success of a larger venture – a defining moment or turning point; or it may typify one aspect of work in the profession. Respondents are then led through a series of questions regarding the incident, either in an interview or in a self-report workbook. Typical questions include:

- What happened?
- What was the outcome?
- What factors in the situation did you take into consideration when you decided on your course of action?

- What were you thinking or feeling? What were your concerns during the incident?
- What knowledge, skill or training did you call upon in this situation?
- With hindsight, what, if anything, would you have done differently?

The critical incident technique has been used to identify the distinguishing characteristics of experts in the following ways. Spencer asked diplomats to identify high performers among their colleagues and to describe the incidents which caused them to stand out. Once the list of those who were consistently identified by their colleagues had been established, the incidents were analysed to determine the particular blend of knowledge, skills and attitudes which distinguished high performers from the merely competent (Spencer, 1984). Benner (1984) used pairs of novice and expert nurses in her study of nursing practice and analysed their different versions of the same incident.

Subjectivity in analysis is obviously a potential weakness of the critical incident technique, and too much should not be made of a single incident. For this reason it is best used with another technique such as DACUM. Critical incident investigations can be time-consuming and expensive to carry out and analyse, but may pay off in the richness of the data which result.

It is always preferable to use two or more of the methods suggested here in combination, as this increases the validity of results considerably.

Research conducted to inform course design may be more or less formal – rigorously designed so that the results are publishable, or planned and carried out by members of the course design team as part of the development process. While at first glance it may seem easier to do an informal investigation, in practice it may be more effective to commission a formal project, particularly if research funds can be obtained so that the course design team do not have to carry out all of the work themselves. The example below shows the use of a number of different research methods in a fairly elaborate curriculum development project.

A case study in research into professional practice for curriculum development in a combined social work–law degree

A combined social work–law degree which had been offered for five years was to undergo review. During the first five years of operation the programme essentially operated as two separate degree courses; there was little attempt at integration. Students undertaking the joint degree expressed difficulty in reconciling the different approaches of the two disciplines. They commented that law subjects focused on the rights of individuals and on technical questions, whereas in social work they were encouraged to see the community at large as the client. While students found the law subjects more academically demanding, they found the social work subjects more challenging to their personal values. There was some evidence that these tensions and conflicts were replicated in the working relationships of practising lawyers and social workers.

As the first step in the curriculum review, the relevant social work department sought and obtained research funds and commissioned two researchers,
Mick Hillman and Jane Hargreaves, to investigate the current status of socio-
legal practice. The intention of the project was to produce background information which might influence a redesign of the current curriculum, and to
produce detailed descriptions of current practice which would ultimately form
the basis of teaching materials.

The specific objectives of the research project were to:

- locate areas of practice in which law and social work overlap, or where practice requires significant cross-disciplinary knowledge;
- identify the respective roles undertaken by social workers and lawyers and
  the clarity of mutual understanding in this respect;
- identify ethical and professional values which may produce differing stances
  or proposed action between the two professions and investigate how such
  situations might be resolved;
- articulate and publicize positive models and strategies for collaboration
  between social workers and lawyers;
- utilize information obtained from the research to develop ways in which
  cross-disciplinary learning can occur (where, for instance, legal knowledge
  and skills can be incorporated into existing social work practice);
- develop 'linking themes' specifically aimed at students in the social work–law
  degree to assist in the integration of material from the two courses.

(Hillman and Hargreaves, 1994: 2)

The first stage of the project involved a literature review and extensive
interviews with 13 experienced social workers and six legal practitioners in a
range of practice contexts. These interviews provided sufficient information to
establish:

- a definition of socio-legal practice;
- the key tasks of practitioners in socio-legal practice;
- the purposes of socio-legal practice;
- the context of interaction in socio-legal practice.

Hillman and Hargreaves felt, however, that the interview material did not
provide sufficient detail on what practitioners actually did, or how real
examples of practice might differ from the ideal. One thing that had come out
of the interviews was that differences in values were likely to result in tensions
between the two professional groups. The researchers wanted examples of how
this might occur. They also wanted more concrete material which could be
translated into teaching materials.

The second stage of the project therefore involved observation of the social
workers and lawyers at work. The researchers made detailed notes of examples
of practice; actions were documented and skills and values inferred. Inferences
were checked for accuracy with practitioners. In addition, the critical incident
technique was used to generate more examples. Participants were given

workbooks and asked to document, over a number of days, significant incidents in their practice which involved cross-disciplinary knowledge or professional interaction. Through answering a number of questions the practitioners then reflected on the incident, identifying the factors that they took into consideration in decision making, the relevant knowledge and skills which they called upon, the attitudes of the protagonists and the tensions between them.

The data that resulted from this project allowed the researchers to make a number of recommendations relevant to both the social work and the law components of the course. They also identified a number of units (such as family law, juvenile justice, alternative dispute resolution and social policy) which they recommended should be team taught by teachers from both disciplines. In addition, the project produced a wealth of critical incident and case material to be used as teaching material in both the degree course and continuing professional education programmes.

Using research to set priorities for content

Research into the nature of contemporary practice can also be useful when hard decisions have to be made about what content to omit. One lecturer in medical radiation at a regional university with whom I worked was concerned to cut back what he believed was an overloaded curriculum which discouraged students from taking a deep approach to learning. Students on the programme were expected to be able to identify a very wide range of conditions through diagnostic imaging. It was decided that the number of conditions they were expected to recognize needed to be reduced, but that the reduction should be done on a rational basis. It was agreed that this basis should be the most frequently occurring conditions which arose in local practices. The list of frequently occurring conditions was produced from a telephone survey of all the practitioners in the region. The content of the programme could then focus on the most common conditions, allowing students to become very well informed about these.

Information from students and graduates

This might consist of:

- evaluation data;
- surveys and interviews with students and graduates;
- analysis of data on employment destinations of graduates.

Information from prospective students (or from current students if the programme involved is under review) can be helpful to course designers if it is available. A preliminary step to a course review may be an evaluation process in which current students and recent graduates are interviewed or surveyed about their perceptions of the course. In some cases data are already available from regular end-of-session student evaluations. Frequently, though, this information is too general to be of any real use in redesigning the course. Students have responded to questions such as 'How would you rate the teaching, the course materials, the workload?' Responses to such questions can highlight areas where there are problems, but do not provide much help as to what changes need to be made.

In rethinking the content of a course the most useful opinions will often come from final-year students or recent graduates who have just begun to practise. The most revealing questions to ask are ones like, 'Are there areas or tasks for which you feel inadequately prepared? Are there areas of knowledge or skills which should have been included in the course or given greater emphasis? Were there topics that you would have liked the opportunity to study in more depth?'

Another source of data which can throw a new light on the content of the course is the employment destination of graduates – information which many universities and colleges now collect routinely. Such information may reveal that many students undertaking a professional degree such as law are not going on to practise as barristers or solicitors. In fact they may be regarding a law degree as a general education which will be of value in a very wide range of occupations. Conversely, programmes of study which have been assumed to be for general education rather than professional preparation may in fact produce graduates who tend to end up in particular kinds of employment. Recognizing this, some arts faculties have put together structured programmes for arts graduates who are aiming at research or policy work in the public sector. Similarly, some fine arts programmes have introduced a 'professional studies' strand for those students who will enter curatorial work or arts administration.

In thinking about the choice of content, student input can be enlightening. Diamond (1989) describes using surveys of potential students to identify the topics that they would find most interesting in an introductory course in religion. The results showed no pattern or clear trends but a wide variety of preferences for both topics and teaching formats. In my experience this kind of result is typical of such surveys. The faculty which commissioned the survey initially believed that it had failed to produce any useful information. However as Diamond reports,

> What we later came to see was that the concern for diversity, for flexibility, for variety of instructional formats was specifically the pattern that was common to the sample population. The test instrument clearly suggested modular construction and a flexible selection procedure. It also became apparent that a common base of meaning and of definitions had to be developed before the course could be effectively taught.
>
> (Diamond, 1989: 54)

In practice it may often be difficult to identify potential students at an early enough stage for their preferences to be able to influence the course content and structure. But if sufficient flexibility is built in at the unit level, then introductory sessions with students who are about to begin studying a new unit often provide a different perspective on the topics to be chosen and the weighting to be given to different aspects. Gibbs (quoted by Rowntree, 1981) describes asking a first-year class how they envisaged the psychologist's role. While they identified some valid conceptions of the psychologist's role, not one of these incorporated 'the objective, systematic, experimental, scientific aspects that would normally be given prominence in most courses on psychology' (p. 39). Here is a major dimension of the subject of which beginners are unaware and which is likely to need special attention.

Similarly, in a unit on curriculum development which I teach to academic staff, I ask participants to recall their previous experience with course development and to identify the aspects of the process that give them the most difficulty. Interestingly, it is not the technical aspects of the design process, or questions of resources, which people find most difficult, but concerns about how to manage the people involved in the process. This has been a significant factor in shaping the design of the unit.

Of course, finding out this sort of information on the first day of class means that adjustments to the teaching plan have to be made 'on the run', and sometimes it is impossible to adjust as much as one would like at this stage. But no course design or unit plan should ever be fixed, and these kinds of initial student concerns and perceptions provide a very useful basis for continuing development.

In this section I have suggested a range of different research techniques for gathering information about content decisions. Some, such as concept analysis, are more likely to be useful in general education programmes, while others are clearly more appropriate in planning professional education. Some information will be readily available and need only be brought together and analysed for what it can reveal. Other information needs to be generated especially for the purpose and may require more extensive and thorough research. No course design or review team is likely to collect information from all the sources identified here. But it is important not to skip over this stage too lightly. If considerable change is envisaged which may lead to existing units being dropped, or to people having to take on new units or teach in different ways, it is important that these decisions be made on the best available information. It is also important that the people who will be affected by the changes have the opportunity to help plan what information and opinions will be sought and what methods will be used. They need to be assured that the process used is a valid one. They also need sufficient time to think about the implications of the data and the changes in direction which they might suggest.

5

The Structure of the Course

The way in which a course or a unit of a course is structured may be the most obvious feature which students encounter – or it may remain a mystery to the end. Where the structure is an unfamiliar one for students it becomes the first thing that has to be dealt with. Candy quotes a student describing how she came to terms with her degree course, which was structured around independent and contract learning:

> I was unfamiliar with this unstructured method of learning whereby you identify what it is you want to learn and take responsibility for your own learning. It was totally new to me, and I felt uncomfortable with it in the beginning because I expected something to be clearly black or white, 'This is the way to go', 'This is what you need to do', and so on. But it all started to fit into place in the first year and subsequently it has been wonderful having that opportunity to identify what *I* want to learn, rather than someone setting a curriculum and me just having to pass various subjects to get a qualification at the end. I could see what was required for my personal development as well as for my professional development, and the course helped me structure my goals more clearly.
>
> (Candy *et al.*, 1994: 132)

On the other hand there are many situations like that recounted by the part-time lecturer in Chapter 1, who found that she could not understand the structure of the course on which she was one of the lecturers and felt unable to provide much guidance to students. Decisions to give a course a very different structure are going to require more thought and more preparation on the part of course designers and teachers and are likely to give students more pause for thought. More traditional structures require less effort because everyone is familiar with the kind of track they are going down. But that familiarity may lead to less creativity on the part of teachers and less involvement on the part of students.

Under the heading of 'structure' many different kinds of decisions have to be made: about the logic that will be used in dividing the subject matter into manageable units and how those units will be related to each other and sequenced; about the way in which concepts, facts and skills will be organized and presented to students within units; about the ways in which students will be able to gain access to the learning offered in this course and where learning needs to take place; about the timing of the whole venture and the significant events within it. All of these decisions will ultimately affect the kinds of learning that will take place and the effectiveness of that learning.

Consequently, when making decisions about course structure we constantly need to ask ourselves: 'Will this structure support the kinds of learning that we want on this course? Does the structure help to achieve the course goals? If not, how can it be modified?' The same process will occur again when thinking about the structure of individual units. Their structure will in many respects follow that of the whole course, but in some respects may be quite different. In any case the structure needs to support students in attaining the learning objectives, not undermine them.

In thinking about questions of structure we will attempt to sort them into three different aspects:

- the structure of ideas and knowledge;
- the way in which access to the course is structured; and
- the way in which the events of the course are structured.

The ways in which access to the course might be structured will be discussed in the next chapter. Here we will look at how the contents and events of the course might be structured.

The structure of ideas and knowledge

The way in which concepts, facts and skills are organized in a course is usually closely related to the beliefs about knowledge and learning that we discussed in Chapter 2. In higher education courses, by far the most common way of organizing the knowledge in the course is according to the logic of the subject matter.

Course structure based on the logic of the subject matter

Here the content is sequenced or structured according to the organization of the subject matter. The organizing principle may be *time*, as in a history course organized according to chronological development; *spatial relationships*, as in a geography curriculum organized by country; *species*, as in a biology course sequenced from the simplest forms of life to the more complex; *forms of expression*, as in an art course divided into drawing, painting and sculpture or a literature course based on poetry, prose and drama; *functional systems*, such as the human body's respiratory system and digestive system. Sometimes the course follows significant *processes*, such as a human resources management course which is built around the life cycle of an employee from recruitment to dismissal or retirement. Alternatively the organizing principle may be *simple to complex* whereby the later knowledge depends on the elements introduced earlier.

Frequently, course designs use more than one of these subject-related organizers. So the literature course may look at forms of expression in terms of their development over time and the biology course may look at species on a regional basis. Once the organizing principle has been established there may still be decisions to be made about sequence and depth or degree of specialization. Should students simply begin at the beginning and work their way to the end, or is it desirable to examine two or more systems, forms or processes in parallel? An introductory survey unit might be considered desirable, to introduce students to the major strands of the discipline before they pursue one or more parallel strands in depth.

The advantage of using an organizing system like this is that the student gets a picture of the way knowledge has developed or is currently organized in the discipline. On the other hand, when knowledge is organized and presented in this way it does not necessarily relate to any needs or interests of students. Because it gives the impression that the territory has already been mapped, it may not encourage students to challenge existing conceptions of knowledge or even to readily identify new areas for investigation.

Performance-, role- and competency-based structures

Instead of building the course according to some internal logic of the subject matter, an alternative is to identify the ultimate roles, or performances, for which the student is being educated and build the course around those. This structure is most commonly referred to as 'competency based' because it attempts to develop competent performance in the specified roles. In vocational training competence may be conceived in terms of ability to perform specific tasks, but in higher education it is usually conceptualized far more broadly. As an example, in one competency-based nursing curriculum, the roles which a nurse undertakes were identified as those of clinician (providing both preventative and therapeutic health care), manager, communicator and educator. Once defined, these roles must be analysed to determine what knowledge, skills, attributes and dispositions students will need to acquire in order to perform them. Knowledge and skills are then sequenced from the most elementary, prerequisite ones to the more complex, sophisticated final performances.

The educational psychologists who proposed this method of curriculum organization, as an alternative to those which were organized around the structure of knowledge in a particular discipline, believed in a 'psychological' rather than a 'logical' structure of knowledge. Robert Gagne (1977), one of the most important theorists concerned with this method of curriculum organization, emphasized the importance of identifying and teaching prerequisite skills. In considering the kinds of roles or performances for which the student is being prepared, the curriculum designer must ask, 'What are all the things a student must know or be able to do in order to carry out this role?' This question is repeated until all of the prerequisite knowledge and skills are uncovered and can be laid out in a *learning hierarchy*.

One of the strengths of this method is that it often identifies areas of knowledge or skill which are overlooked in more traditional courses because they do not form part of the structure of the main discipline. For instance, if one were thinking about the competences required by a doctor, one of them might be that he or she is able to establish good communication with a patient so that the patient is prepared to speak honestly. Gagne would insist that this ability be analysed into its component skills such as establishing rapport, questioning and listening, and that these should then be taught and assessed. Similar abilities that need to be thought about in terms of prerequisites might include levels of reading and numeracy skills, particularly the ability to analyse and evaluate certain kinds of academic writing or the ability to write in specific forms or genres, for example. All the dimensions of a performance or role or competence should be analysed, sequenced from simple to complex, and consciously developed.

Performance or competency-based curricula are most likely to be found in those courses which offer some kind of vocational preparation. But there are examples of this approach being used in general education courses. Alverno College in the United States, a liberal education college for women, offers the best example of a general education built around competences. Founded by Franciscans, Alverno is a small college of around 2500 students. In addition to its BA degree, it offers professional preparation in a number of areas including business and management, nursing and engineering. As is the norm in the United States, all students undertake at least two years of liberal and general education before moving into specialization in a discipline or professional preparation.

In the early 1970s, the college decided to re-examine its operations. When re-evaluating its purpose and goals the faculty spent a considerable amount of time considering what should be the outcomes for students of a liberal education, rather than the more usual question of what should be the inputs from staff. Initially four goals for students were identified and over the next three years these were expanded to eight. Given the religious background of the college and the fact that its focus was on liberal and general education, these goals for students (initially called competences, now referred to as abilities) were quite broad. Alverno College was always interested in developing the whole person and not just a set of technical skills. Its definition of competence required students to develop not just knowledge and skill but certain values and dispositions:

> Working through this was one of many experiences that helped us to discover the notion of *competence* as a characteristic of the individual person, rather than a skill or an enumeration of tasks. A competent

student demonstrates certain abilities; she is also committed to using them. Not only can she analyze or communicate effectively, she habitually does so.

(Alverno College, 1981: Liberal Learning at Alverno
College, quoted in Heywood, 1989)

Within the eight domains of competence which were initially identified, six levels of performance were specified. Students are expected to develop competence in each of the eight domains up to the fourth level during the first two years of their general education programme. The fifth and sixth levels of competence are developed in the last two years of the programme, when students concentrate on their area of academic or professional specialization. Competence at the fifth and sixth levels takes longer to acquire and is more difficult to demonstrate.

The College has a commitment to consistently re-evaluating its programme and so the way in which the abilities are expressed may change. Here is the version currently offered to students in materials introducing the College:

Alverno's eight abilities

Communication
Make connections that create meaning between yourself and your audience. Learn to speak, read, write, and listen effectively, using graphics, electronic media, computers, and quantified data.

Analysis
Think clearly and critically. Fuse experience, reason, and training into considered judgment.

Problem solving
Figure out what the problem is and what is causing it. With others or alone, form strategies that work in different situations. Then, get done what needs to be done, evaluating effectiveness.

Valuing
Recognize different value systems while holding strongly to your own ethic. Recognize the moral dimensions of your decisions and accept responsibility for the consequences of your actions.

Social interaction
Know how to get things done in committees, task forces, team projects, and other group efforts. Elicit the views of others and help reach conclusions.

Global perspectives
Act with an understanding of and respect for the economic, social, and biological interdependence of global life.

Effective citizenship
Be involved and responsible in the community. Act with an informed awareness of contemporary issues and their historical contexts. Develop leadership abilities.

Aesthetic response
Appreciate the various forms of art and the contexts from which they emerge. Make and defend judgments about the quality of artistic expressions.

Much of the student assessment at Alverno is conducted through its assessment centre. Assessors are often brought in from outside the College, or are drawn from staff who are not directly engaged in teaching the students who are being assessed. Students must demonstrate their competence at the designated level which is being evaluated in a number of different contexts. At the higher levels the College requires that the competences become more integrated. Students must demonstrate ability in a number of different areas by carrying out quite complex tasks. These may take the form of extended simulations.

In order to assess the effectiveness of its radical curriculum, the College has set up its own office of research and evaluation. Since 1976 it has carried out many studies, including a number financed by the National Institute of Education. A considerable amount of data has been produced, documenting and comparing the achievements of full-time and part-time students, school leavers and mature-age-entry students, in intellectual development as well as many other areas such as moral development, professional performance following graduation and lifelong learning ability.

The studies that have been done with Alverno students and graduates demonstrate a significant positive effect of their college education on their intellectual and emotional development. But how different this is from more conventional programmes is more difficult to say. John Heywood from Trinity College Dublin, who has written extensively on assessment in higher education, visited Alverno in the 1980s to study its assessment methods. He commented that in the classes which he observed the content was at a similar level and breadth to his own classes. Students he spoke to believed that there was a greater focus on memory work in other universities that they had attended. This was not the case at Alverno and the students preferred the latter for that reason. Heywood comments that his own and other traditional universities obviously aim for a high level of competence, and clearly many students achieve at a high standard. But he believes that those students who only achieve minimal passes in traditionally structured courses might have gained more from a competency-based system. And it is worth noting that Alverno attracts and graduates very high proportions of minority group students and others whose family backgrounds have not included university education. However, as Heywood points out, the Alverno curriculum also demands more intensive teaching and smaller class sizes, more educational support and development for teaching staff and in general a greater investment of resources (Heywood, 1989).

Since the 1970s, when competency-based programmes were first developed in higher education in the United States, this method of structuring a course has waxed and waned in popularity; but it has recently enjoyed a resurgence in the United Kingdom and Australia. Considerable government support has been given to efforts to convert curricula in the technical and vocational areas to a competency basis. Government councils and boards have been created to bring together representatives from technical colleges and industry, to support the work of occupational analysis and to accredit new competency-based curricula. Why this very large investment in promoting a particular kind of curriculum structure?

Governments have seized upon the competency-based vocational curriculum as one more weapon in the struggle for economic survival and domination. It holds out a number of promises. One is inherent in the name itself. A curriculum which promises competence appears to offer a guarantee that a more conventional curriculum does not. The implied promise is that all those who pass the course will be fit to practise – there will be no more dodgy operators. A more rigorous and comprehensive form of assessment, which covers all of the essential skills of the occupation, will ensure that newly qualified workers know what they are doing. A second implied promise concerns relevance. The occupational and task analyses which are used to develop competence standards must be carried out in concert with industry to ensure that they cover all the necessary aspects of the job and are up to date. Indeed, in some cases development of industry competence standards has been undertaken with no input from educators at all. From the government point of view this ensures that vocational programmes will be relevant and prevents educators from diverting students into interesting but less fundamental areas of study.

Lastly, competency-based curricula offer the promise of more flexibility, recognition for learning acquired informally or through workplace training, and ease of articulation between different levels of courses. Savings are possible if students do not have to undergo training in educational institutions in order to receive recognition for skills they have already acquired through work. And when competence standards with prerequisite knowledge and skills are laid out for all courses it will not be possible for institutions to deny students credit for that prerequisite knowledge and those skills when they want to move on to a higher level of qualification.

These are the arguments which have been used to force competency-based curriculum into technical and vocational education. There has been less pressure on institutions of higher education to adopt competency-based curricula, although developments such as modularized courses in the UK contain some similar features. In 1994 I carried out with colleagues a major literature review of the work that had been done to that date on competency-based curricula in technical and vocational education. One of the most widespread concerns that we found was that many competency-based curricula were focused almost exclusively on narrowly defined technical skills and that students were not being given sufficient opportunity to integrate those skills or to develop other abilities, such as being able to work effectively in groups or plan and manage one's own learning (Toohey *et al.*, 1995).

These criticisms were not true of all competency-based vocational education programmes, and they seem to be less true of those designed in higher education. Those who have developed competency-based higher education programmes, whether in professional education or in general education, have usually been careful to specify broad outcomes and to integrate general educational outcomes with technical knowledge and skills. Of course, when a school or department decides to structure a new curriculum in a very different way it is often because members of the faculty have a strong commitment to education. In addition, the course designers are likely to put a great deal of thought and effort into planning because their work will come under considerable scrutiny.

If we had to sum up the known advantages and disadvantages of this form of course structure they might look like this.

Advantages and disadvantages

Probably the greatest advantage of a course structured around competence, or professional roles, is the effect that it has on students. Because students can always see the connection between what they are studying at any time and the course goals of personal or professional capability, they are usually more motivated. The clarity of the goals and objectives, the logic with which the units of the course fit together and the relevance to professional practice all help to encourage a sense of purpose and desire for progress in students. This sense of knowing what they are about and where they are going can be particularly important for students from non-traditional backgrounds whose families and friends have no experience of higher education. In a conventional programme where the goals and structure of the course are not made explicit, it can take a long time for such students to work out what it is that they are expected to achieve, and what forms of discourse are acceptable.

Another factor which contributes to student success is the careful sequencing of prerequisite knowledge and skills which is part of a competency-based course. If this is done carefully then students are far less likely to encounter steps beyond their capacity and more likely to meet success along the way.

Another strength can lie in the wider definition of what constitutes valuable knowledge. Some of the elements brought to light in a comprehensive task analysis (such as the interpersonal skills) have been overlooked in traditional discipline-based courses, but research into professional practice has shown that here, they are crucial to successful performance (Spencer, 1984). Their acquisition should not be left to chance.

On the other hand, one of the disadvantages of the competency-based curriculum is its relative inability to cater for any individual student interests. There tends to be little flexibility in a curriculum like this, because it is tightly specified and because many additional areas of learning have been identified. The development of the specified skills and abilities may require that students spend a high number of hours in classes, laboratories or supervised practice. Competency- or performance-based courses usually require students to carry out complex tasks in real-life or simulated environments. Where it is intended to offer the course in more flexible modes, particular ingenuity will be required to ensure that students who do not have regular contact with teaching staff or campus facilities are able to get sufficient practice and the feedback they need to make progress.

In a performance- or competency-based course, the trade-off for a better understanding of the professional role may be a weaker discipline base. Students who have focused all of their learning on professional roles, drawing on knowledge from the disciplines only as it affects each role or task, will not have the same picture of the discipline and its structure as students on discipline-based courses. This may be of little significance to graduates who become professional practitioners, but may mean that this course is less effective at preparing future academics and researchers. Writers like Barnett have identified the lack of immersion into a particular discipline, and identification with its modes of investigation and discourse, as a potential loss with competency-based courses (Barnett, 1994). However, it needs to be recognized that in many cases what the course developers are hoping to achieve is the same kind of identification with a profession – usually one which calls on a number of disciplines for its foundation knowledge.

A more telling criticism may be that because of this strong identification with a profession there may be little or no opportunity within the course to critique and evaluate the professional role as it is currently conceived. It is accepted as a given. Of course, it does not necessarily follow that more traditional courses are better at critiquing the role of the profession and its practitioners in society. As Barnett also points out there are many traditional courses which are primarily focused on passing on established knowledge. But it is equally true to say that most competency-based courses aim to equip students to function effectively in the world as it is and not to challenge the status quo.

With the wholesale move of technical and vocational education to a competency-based framework, higher education has also felt some pressure, if not to adopt the whole competence structure, then at least to make expected student outcomes and assessment criteria more explicit. This has been somewhat difficult and embarrassing for those higher education teachers who have never given the matter much thought. There is also concern that the not-so-hidden agenda is to make teachers accountable for the performance of their students. As a result there have been attacks on the idea of competency-based curricula from many academic sources. The argument is put forward that there are valuable outcomes of higher education which cannot be expressed as goals or objectives; that there are some aspects of a discipline which can only be 'caught, not taught'; that competency-based courses will not allow deep exploration of areas of interest or encourage a mentor relationship between students and their teachers.

In the anxiety over where changes in higher education may be leading, I think there is a tendency to compare present developments with a golden age of university education which never actually existed for many students. Traditionally structured university courses served a percentage of students well. But as the research by Biggs showed, for the majority of students their tertiary education was more likely to encourage a surface approach to learning than a deep involvement with the discipline (Biggs, 1987). In an earlier study, Ramsden found that polytechnics, where there was a greater integration between knowledge and performance, were more likely to promote a deep approach to learning (Ramsden, 1983). So there is certainly some evidence which suggests that alternatives to traditionally structured courses have something to offer. Many well-designed courses structured around goals of student performance already exist in higher education, from those mentioned earlier in this chapter to many of the courses offered by the Open University. It is a model which deserves consideration.

Project-, inquiry- or problem-based structures

Another framework for structuring a course which also aims for a greater integration of theoretical knowledge and practical application is the problem-based or project-centred course. While many conventionally structured courses include problems and projects, a course which describes itself as 'problem-based' or 'centred on inquiry learning' uses problems and projects in a different way. Rather than using problems as an opportunity to apply the knowledge that they have gained through learning activities like lectures and tutorials, the problem-based course uses everyday problems or situations as a way of stimulating students to discover and explore the key concepts and skills of the discipline. From the first day of the course, students are presented with the kind of situation which they will meet in professional practice. The subject of 'the problem' may be a patient who presents with certain symptoms to a health-care professional, a product or solution to be designed, a client in need of legal advice or an issue of social concern (e.g. 'How can we reduce pollution?', 'How might we fund higher education?).

Typically working in small groups with a facilitator, students analyse the problem or situation and identify those aspects about which they need to know more before they can make further progress towards a solution. These learning issues become the subject of independent or group study and may be approached through resource materials, lectures provided by academic staff or resource people in the community. Once initial learning needs have been addressed, the group reconvenes with its facilitator to address the next stage or aspect of the problem. Although problems are eventually 'solved' by students and facilitator agreeing that a particular design or course of action seems the best available from the range of possibilities, the aim of the course is not to find solutions. It is to use the problem to decide what one needs to learn.

Southern Illinois University School of Medicine, which operates a long established problem-based course, describes the process like this (1998):

The first phase

In the first phase, students reason their way through the patient problem, bringing out prior knowledge they may possess to: 1) understand the basic pathophysiological mechanisms responsible for the patient problem and how these problems might be managed and, 2) identify the additional knowledge and skills they need to better understand and manage the problem.

When the students have gone as far as they can with the problem, they determine what resources they will use (faculty experts, library, computerized data bases, on-line information sources, etc.) to gain the knowledge and skills needed.

The second phase

The second phase is a period of self-directed study during which the students, independent of the tutor, consult resources and work collaboratively. The length of this phase is negotiated by the student group, depending on the extent and depth of issues they have elected to pursue. Each group has a study room that is their home base available 24 hours a day.

The third phase

In the third phase students apply the newly gained knowledge back to the problem, critique their prior thinking and knowledge, and refine their understanding of the problem and its management. They also synthesize what they have learned, relate it to prior problems and anticipate how it might help with future problems. In doing this they try to develop overarching concepts and abstractions, enhancing transfer to other problems.

Initially the tutor's role is to stimulate and guide student learning but always with the aim that students must take responsibility for their own learning. As the group becomes proficient, the tutor withdraws more and more, allowing the group increasing independence.

As the last step in the third phase, the students assess themselves individually in the following areas: problem-solving skills, knowledge acquisition, self-directed learning, and support of the group. Each self-assessment is followed by comments from their peers and the tutor. This process, carried out at the end of every problem, becomes a formal assessment for the members of the group at the end of each curricular unit.

Problems or projects must be carefully chosen so that students continually extend their knowledge and skill, building on what they have learned with previous projects. Although the problems or projects selected may appear to students as a random collection of real issues, they must enable all of the essential concepts and skills to be addressed. Donald Woods, from McMaster University in Canada, another centre for problem-based learning, has identified a range of different kinds of knowledge that the student in a problem-based course must learn. These different kinds of knowledge include:

- fundamental principles about subjects such as we would find in a text; example, the conservation of mass;

- tacit information about the subject; this is usually not given in texts but it is known by the experts in the discipline. However the experts are usually unaware of that knowledge and cannot easily describe it. Usually we acquire that tacit knowledge 'by experience'. For example, an experienced professional 'just knows' when a decision sounds wrong yet he/she cannot explain why. Alternatively, they might intuitively know what to do in a complex situation, yet when asked why, they might answer 'experience!'
- procedural knowledge that describes processes and things to do in different situations;
- episodic knowledge or information and recollections about experiences and events that have occurred in our lives;
- skill at problem solving, communicating, evaluating, interacting with people, learning how to learn, and working in groups.

(Woods, 1985: 26)

A problem-based or project-centred course structure is usually chosen because those responsible place a high value on experiential learning. Learning in such a course does not consist of information handed on by experts but results from interaction between the situation that students are confronted with and their interests, needs and previous experiences. Thus the base for learning is broadened and Woods can claim that students on problem-based courses will need to develop the range of different kinds of learning that he identifies above. Although learning from experience provides opportunities for developing this wider range of knowledge and abilities, it does not necessarily facilitate the development of the 'well-structured knowledge base' that distinguishes experts from novices. In real life, learning experiences present themselves randomly and the opportunity to expand and deepen knowledge from one experience to the next does not necessarily occur. If today I deal with one sort of problem and tomorrow quite another sort of problem presents itself, then I may collect quite a lot of different experiences. But this will provide little chance to compare problem situations and identify differences and similarities, or to develop further the knowledge and skills I have acquired to date.

So developers of problem-based or project-based courses usually select or develop the problems or projects for students within a clearly structured framework that will help them consistently develop their abilities. The frameworks most likely to be used are those provided by a performance analysis of the discipline or profession such as would be done in developing a competency-based course or a framework based on the logic of the subject material.

Here are some examples of how that might work. Hurley and Dare (1985) have described a graduate diploma in management which is problem and project based but is also built on a model of managerial competence developed by the American Management Associations. The AMA, after extensive research, identified six clusters of competences and these became, in effect, the learning objectives of the programme. Students work on a combination of problems presented to them by teaching staff and problems (or projects) which they identify for themselves and which are related to their own or their organization's needs. Where students work on their own problems and projects, the specific knowledge and skills to be learned are formalized in an individual learning contract. Students can choose the areas of competence on which they wish to focus, based on workplace assessment and their own self-assessment.

In this case a number of different factors caused the staff involved to re-evaluate their existing programme and institute a new educational design using a problem/project-based approach. Predominant among them was the dissatisfaction expressed by employers both locally and internationally with existing formal management education courses. This was coupled with the fact that recent research into managerial effectiveness had revealed that specialized knowledge, the basis of most traditional management programmes, was not necessarily related to effectiveness as a manager. Those qualities which did distinguish effective managers were very similar to the abilities which problem-based learning claimed to be able to develop, including self direction and ability to manage human relations.

The problem-based medical curriculum at Newcastle University in Australia derives its learning objectives from 'domains' of medical practice, developed by the faculty, which are used as the basis of student assessment. The selection of content for the problems which students tackle is based on 'a spiral curriculum where areas and concepts are revisited to enable the development of complexity from organ to system, from single symptom to multi-system problems' (Wallis, 1985: 102). Woods described the criteria for selecting problems for the McMaster medical course as follows:

> For the choice of problems, the faculty prepare problem situations that (a) include all the fundamental knowledge and necessary psychomotor skills, (b) occur frequently, (c) are potentially serious and life-threatening and (d) are currently being poorly handled by physicians. The content is organised as *systems* – rather than as textbook topics like biochemistry. For example, for the neurosciences system, the faculty prepared 22 problems. Experience has shown that the groups use typically six or seven of these to satisfy their objectives.
>
> (Woods, 1985: 34)

One of the claims made for courses structured around problems or projects is that they develop students' abilities in problem solving, self-directed learning, self evaluation, and group work. Obviously in a problem-based programme students will participate in these activities, but programmes differ in the extent to which they make ability in these areas a formal part of the learning objectives and the assessment and consciously help students to develop these skills. Woods commented in 1985 that the McMaster medical programme provided many opportunities for students to develop these abilities, but little actual instruction. He believed more class time devoted specifically to developing these abilities would have been beneficial to students. In contrast, the medical programme at Newcastle makes these abilities part of the learning objectives and students must pass formal assessments in them to complete the programme.

Simulation exercises, role plays and communication exercises are used in the small-group sessions to help students understand how groups operate, and to evaluate their own skills and performance. Similarly students might be introduced to different strategies for problem solving, and be encouraged to experiment with them and critique their own performance in solving problems.

Advantages and disadvantages

Courses structured around problem-based learning (PBL) have now been operating for more than 20 years, and considerable research has been undertaken on their effectiveness. Albanese and Mitchell (1993) provide the best meta-analysis of the studies that have been carried out comparing medical students from conventional and problem-based programmes. They found that while PBL graduates are slightly more likely to score lower on tests of basic science, they are more likely to be highly rated on clinical performance. PBL students are likely to spend more time in studying and to use study methods which emphasize understanding rather than memorization. Students in PBL programmes tended to enjoy their studies more, as did the faculty who taught them. But not surprisingly, when large numbers of students were involved (class sizes larger than 100), conventional programmes were less costly.

The problem/project-based approach is usually more motivating for students because it is seen to be dealing with problems of significance which are highly relevant to future practice. It clearly encourages integration of theory and practice, which can be a problem in traditional courses. Because problem- or project-based courses usually involve a heavy emphasis on abilities other than knowledge and technical skills, such as acquiring skills for lifelong learning and working in groups, the time available within the curriculum for its traditional content may be reduced. Albanese and Mitchell noted that problem-based courses covered the traditional content at 82 per cent of the speed of a conventional programme. And initially at least, students may find it difficult to extract general principles from particular tasks or problems.

While students often experience initial difficulties in adjusting to the demands of problem-based or project-based curricula, these are usually resolved in the first year or two of the course. The adjustment required of staff members often proves more difficult. The teacher's role changes from that of the expert and authority, who provides the information which students need, to that of supporter and facilitator, who lets students make the running and intervenes only by asking questions which may help to redirect inquiries. For many academics this shift proves very difficult. Evaluation reports from the Southern Illinois medical programme revealed one case of a student group who asked their tutor not to attend group session for four weeks because he could not be prevented from constantly revealing the 'answers' that students were looking for.

The change in teaching role also requires different skills. Group facilitators need to feel comfortable working in areas in which they are not expert.

Questioning skills are all-important, as is the ability to establish good working relationships within a group, and being able to help students resolve conflicts. Many staff members will require training to help them develop their skills in these areas.

A great deal of work goes into the preparation of learning and resource materials for problem- and project-based courses. Feletti and Wallis suggest that where a school is developing a whole new problem-based course (not just one or two units) it is essential for that school to employ its own educational development staff for the duration of the project. Not only can educational development staff assist with the development of materials, planning of learning sessions and design of assessment, they are also available for the ongoing educational development and support of the faculty (Feletti and Wallis, 1985: 99).

Cognitive structure based on key (overarching) concepts, themes or intellectual abilities

Yet another possibility in structuring a course is to select and organize the content and activities around key concepts. Examples of such concepts might include the idea of revolution in history, hegemony in political science, natural selection or ecosystem in biological science. Similarly, the course may be organized around certain intellectual abilities, such as critical thinking, reflective practice or lifelong learning.

Joseph Schwab, writing about the structures of the disciplines, asserted that concepts formed the substantive structures of a discipline. Not only are they fundamental ideas which subsume more specific facts, but they also provide a framework within which researchers can begin to propose their research questions. As one example he took the situation that prevailed in the study of animal behaviour some 60 years ago. At that time, biologists' understanding of the behaviour of small aquatic animals such as tadpoles and small fish was no greater than any child could have attained by observing pond life. The darting movements of small fish could be observed, but the reasons for those movements were completely unknown. Schwab described the researchers' dilemma:

> What then, should we investigate about these dartings, movements and plays? Should we ask what needs they serve? Perhaps. Yet we do not even know that needs are involved. Shall we ask what purposes the animals have in mind? We do not know whether they have purposes or not. Shall we then try to discover the patterns of these motions, the order in which they occur? The trouble with this is that when a vast number of movements are involved, we must suppose, by analogy to ourselves, that they do not all belong together. Hence the overall order of them would be meaningless. Yet we cannot determine each coherent sub-group of motions because we do not yet know either the beginnings ('wants', 'needs', 'stimuli') or their terminations ('goals', 'needs satisfied', 'terminal response').

This frustration of enquiry was resolved by appealing to the then popular view that all things, including living things, were no more than simple machines, the pattern of which was the simple one known to nineteenth century physics. This idea of a simple machinery was applied to the study of behaviour by supposing that every movement through space of an animal was a response to some single specific stimulating factor in the environment. It was further supposed that each such stimulated response could be one of only two possible kinds – a movement toward the stimulus or away from it. Such a movement was dubbed a 'tropism', 'taxis': movements towards the stimulus being called positive, those away from the stimulus, negative.

This naive and now obsolete conception removed the frustration of enquiry by giving us questions to ask. We were to determine for each organism what stimuli it responded to and whether it responded in the positive or negative sense.

(Schwab, 1964: 26)

A curriculum organized around cognitive structures will present many examples of the key concepts so that students can establish what are the essential elements by comparison and contrast. Courses structured around key concepts may be concerned with a single discipline or they may be cross-disciplinary. Sometimes only part of the course may be structured around concepts and that may be the foundation year/s, the core studies or the electives.

In the business degree which Jenny Bygrave described in the previous chapter, the first three semesters of an eight-semester course are devoted to 'integrated studies'. (In the later part of the programme, students specialize in accounting, business computing, management or marketing.) Each semester's work in integrated studies is built around a particular theme, with different perspectives provided by a range of disciplines including social sciences, law, economics, computing and so forth. In semester one, the theme is *the business environment*, in semester two it is *information in business* and in semester three it is *managing the organization*. Before students start to specialize they must have a good understanding of the whole business environment, from the individual organization to the political and social environment and an understanding of how their future specialization contributes.

The course designers describe the integrated studies modules in the following way:

The structure of the integrated studies modules can be envisaged as a wheel of learning. The theme of the semester forms the central hub. The spokes of the wheel represent the disciplines. Surrounding the hub is an inner circle that represents the group sessions [where students begin to develop the capabilities required by the programme]. In those sessions, students examine the theme from many different perspectives, teasing out issues that relate to disciplines. The outer circle represents the disciplines which provide the students with ways of dealing with those issues.

(Auckland Institute of Technology, 1995: 22)

Figure 5.1 Map of integrated studies programme

Alternatively, a course may be structured around concepts and abilities which are not specific to a particular discipline, like critical thinking or reflective practice. The content and learning activities chosen will present many opportunities to practise and refine the key abilities, usually working from simple examples to more complex ones. Sonoma University on the United States is the home of the Center for Critical Thinking and staff from the Center also teach on the University's undergraduate programmes. The box shows extracts from the syllabus of an introductory undergraduate unit in psychology which is offered by the Center, as an example of a course which has been structured around the idea of critical thinking.

Syllabus: Psychology I

Instructor: Linda Elder

Key concept of course
This course is designed to help you learn the logic of psychology. Everything we do this semester will in some way, either broadly or narrowly, relate to improving your understanding of and thinking critically about psychological principles, theories, practice, and application. The primary goal is for you to come to think as a psychologist would think. This includes identifying and working through problems which psychologists address. The course will focus on the different types of psychologists, the different schools of psychological thought, the varying work that is done by psychologists. The course will also focus on psychological processes,

---

both conscious and unconscious, which influence the behaviour and thinking of human beings.

To think deeply about the field of psychology, one must think clearly about the questions which face psychologists, one must gather relevant and valid information which relates to those questions, one must accurately analyze the value of information gathered and one must understand the complexity of human nature.

General course plan

This course is designed much differently from most others you have been exposed to because you will be asked to think critically about the subject matter throughout the semester. All of our activities will focus on helping you to better understand the logic of psychology, and to come to think like a rational psychologist. You will be asked to continually engage your mind during class and while preparing for class. The textbook will be used as a general resource for the course. You will learn to connect the logic of psychology to the logic of your own thinking so that the subject becomes relevant to you. While you will learn some 'facts' about psychology, they will be learned in the context of learning about the logic of psychology, rather than being memorized for test time.

You will be asked to bring some assignment to each class period, and each class period will build upon work done in the previous class period. Each student will actively participate in class sessions, as you are asked to continually process information by restating information, giving examples, offering alternate points of view, etc. You will also be involved in daily group work, self-assessment, and peer assessment. The ultimate goal is for you to learn to think critically about your thinking, so that you are able to accurately assess your strengths and weaknesses and to take charge of your thinking.

Questions

For each class session, you will be required to write the answer to a question posed at the end of each class period. The question may result from the class discussion or may be prepared in advance by the instructor. These questions will be discussed at the beginning of each class period in small groups. Your written answers/papers will often be assessed by your peers . . . Students who have not written the assignment will not be allowed to participate in the activity until they complete it.

First written assignment:

You are to choose a psychology related article in which you are interested. You may either chose one from a collection I will bring to class, or from a journal. If you choose an article not from my collection, I need to approve it. Read the article so that you thoroughly understand it. Then write a paper that includes:

1. The main issue or problem the author is focusing on in this article
2. The main purpose of the article

3. The information being used by the author and its relationship to the main issue
4. The conclusion(s) being drawn by the author
5. The implications of the conclusion(s)
6. The main concepts being used in the article which relate to the main issue
7. The point of view of the author
8. The author's assumptions
9. Once you have clearly established the author's logic as detailed in one through eight above, add the following to your paper:
10. Discuss the significance of the issue which is the focus of the article. Why is it important? On what do you base your assertions regarding its significance?
11. What potential problems do you see in the author's reasoning? What potential problems are there with the author's use of information? Does the information used appear relevant, significant, valid, and sufficient for the conclusions being drawn? Do you have enough information to determine whether the information is relevant, significant, valid?
12. What point of view is ignored by this author, or has not been considered in dealing with the issue?

Student assessment of papers
On the day the paper is due, students will be assigned to groups of three or four. Each group will receive the same number of papers as they have members in their group, to be assessed (but they will receive none of their own papers). Each group will assess the papers they are assigned, providing commentary on each criteria point listed below. The paper will then be returned to the students, with comments.

Assessment criteria
Papers of the highest quality in this assignment will include the following:

1. Questions outlined above are answered clearly and precisely, with detail and/or examples to support each point appropriately
2. The main issue and purpose are clearly stated
3. A clear connection between the information used and the author's main issue is drawn. The author's use of information is made clear
4. The concepts being used are made clear
5. The implications actually follow from the conclusions, or any fallacies in the author's reasoning about the implications are clearly described
6. The point of view and the author's assumptions are clearly stated. The assumptions described are all inclusive. In other words, the student writer has clearly and completely stated all the assumptions on which the author has based his reasoning
7. The importance of the issue is clearly stated and well thought

through, and supported with implications which accurately follow from conclusions

8. Problems regarding the author's reasoning are clearly and accurately stated. All potential problems with the author's reasoning are included

9. Opposing points of view are accurately included.

Second written assignment
Once the papers are assessed in groups, they will be returned to the writers to be rewritten. You will rewrite the paper, taking into account the group assessment, and modifying the paper for ultimate clarity and precision. You will submit this paper to me, along with the original paper and its assessment, for grading. I will use the same assessment criteria for grading as used in the group assessment process.

Advantages and disadvantages of a course structure focused on concepts or modes of thinking

The great advantage of a course structured like this is that the most powerful ideas of the discipline, or important modes of thinking, are practised and established. Students have many opportunities to explore key concepts and to use them to predict and analyse. Fundamental misconceptions or weaknesses in thinking are more likely to be exposed in this kind of course design than in more traditional ones. University teachers operating from a cognitive perspective usually believe that mastering these significant and powerful ideas and habits of thinking is the most important outcome of tertiary education and deserves to be the focus of the course.

Obviously, students in a course structured in this way do not get the same 'map' of knowledge of the discipline as is presented in a discipline-based course. The key ideas may be presented out of the context in which they were developed and students may not understand how they came into being. The content material which is used to explore the key concepts may be more or less relevant to students' interests and purposes and so more or less motivating. As with problem-based courses, group work is usually an essential feature of concept-based courses. Students need the opportunity to explore with others and test what is or is not an example of the concept and whether the application is valid. Group facilitation and questioning become important skills for teachers if all students are to be encouraged to participate and stretch their understanding.

Hybrid structures

We have discussed four quite different models for structuring a course; but it is important to realize that a complete programme of study built around one approach is comparatively rare. Medicine and the other health sciences offer a number of examples of full degree programmes which are completely problem based. But it is far more usual to find combinations of different approaches in the same course of study. This can be a matter of chance, resulting from individual staff members pursuing their own beliefs and interests in designing the units they teach without much consultation with other staff on the course. Or it can be a matter of conscious choice, if staff have chosen to combine what they hope will be the best features of two different kinds of structures or to structure units in different ways because of the nature of their content and learning goals.

A number of examples exist, including several in engineering, where the main part of the course is structured along traditional disciplinary lines, but a parallel strand is included which is structured around problems or projects. This strand is often called something like 'Professional Studies' and students are expected to draw on the knowledge they have acquired in the traditional part of the course to solve problems and resolve professional issues. This has the advantage of providing an arena for students to integrate and apply knowledge from other parts of the course. However, because students are applying knowledge that has been fed to them in other parts of the course, it does not necessarily develop the same ability in self-directed learning as fully problem-based courses. If students *are* expected to go out and research new topics and acquire new skills which are not taught in other parts of the course, there is a serious risk that the curriculum will be overloaded and students will not have time to learn anything in depth.

Another combination which can work quite well is where the goals of a course are expressed as competence in professional roles and tasks, but rather than those roles being analysed and the necessary knowledge and skills being presented in a carefully ordered sequence, the students may have to acquire the necessary knowledge and skill through a problem- or project-based format. The competence standards serve as a reference point for learning, allowing students to pull back from the detail of individual cases and recognize the abilities that they are acquiring which can be applied to the next case. The competence statements also serve as the basis for assessment.

As was mentioned above, quite often the core sections of a course may be structured along cognitive lines, while the electives are left to the individuals responsible to structure as they prefer.

Sometimes these hybrid structures turn out to have particular strengths, but there is always a risk when a minority of units in a course are structured in a significantly different way from others. Students are likely to be reluctant to change the working patterns and habits of thinking, which serve them quite well in most of the course, to meet the demands of one or two units. For this reason, staff on one faculty of adult education, teaching in a programme which is structured around student projects formalized through learning contracts, advised a whole-hearted commitment:

> Start right at the beginning, don't just, as many courses do, have some kind of open-ended project in the last semester of final year. If you are

going to develop some of these practices and skills then you need to do them in modest and not so modest ways very early on . . .

Studies we have done suggest that almost all the problems our students meet are problems that they have with their first two learning contracts. Once they have got through that then they are flying and none of them want to go back to any other system. So if you are only going to use one or two learning contracts in your course, all you are going to see are the problems and you are going to get far less of the benefits.

(quoted in Candy *et al.*, 1994: 259)

6
Making Learning Opportunities More Flexible

What I'm trying to do is change my curriculum – get away from the rigidity of the course as it is structured at present . . . and pick up subjects that I need . . . I want to reach into another faculty and bring the subjects into my programme . . . I'm trying to get the two faculties to liaise on this but they don't see it – that there's an opportunity here for students to construct more flexible programmes that engage them.

(Mature student quoted in Cartwright, 1997: 113)

Until recently there was one path to obtaining a tertiary qualification. Students passed their matriculation examinations with satisfactory results, enrolled in the university or college of their choice (or the one which would have them) and attended lectures, tutorials and meetings with supervisors according to the timetable laid down by the institution. Many students lived on campus in colleges or halls of residence, allowing ease of access to classes and libraries and ensuring maximum availability for study. Few programmes were available on a part-time basis and even fewer classes were scheduled out of normal working hours.

In the past ten years this notion of the student as someone fully available to the university or college has changed considerably, along with the idea that one dose of tertiary education, gained immediately after leaving school, was enough to last a lifetime. The explosion of professional knowledge, the need for many people to change careers during their working lives and a generally more fluid society has sent many more people in search of initial or continuing higher education. But these are students who are already far too committed to work and family obligations to make themselves available for education full time. They have begun to access the distance programmes initially designed for geographically isolated students and then to ask why the universities in their local area cannot be more flexible in their provision.

At the same time increasing competition for funding has forced many higher education institutions to seek a wider pool of potential students. This has meant reconsidering entry requirements as well as the ways in which education can be delivered to students. Even exit points have been reconsidered, allowing those students who wanted to focus on a highly specific area to leave with a certificate or diploma rather than being forced to choose between committing themselves to a full degree or dropping out early.

Governments have also become interested in more flexible delivery arrangements for higher education, as they see the potential for developing a more highly skilled workforce while reducing investment in infrastructure like classrooms and laboratories. At the same time that the nature of the demand for higher education has been changing, technologies which can deliver educational programmes have also been undergoing rapid development. Information resources available via the Internet have increased rapidly. But potentially the most exciting change has come with increased options for group work and collaborative learning at a distance. Previously these have been limited to teleconferencing or video conferencing, both fairly cumbersome operations to set up and not always easy for students to access. Now it begins to be possible to create – via e-mail and the Internet – the kinds of interactions between whole groups of people that were previously only feasible in a classroom.

As a result, many universities and colleges are now looking closely at what has come to be called 'flexible or open learning', or have already committed themselves to it. Certainly the degree of flexibility which might be offered to students is a factor that any design team working on a new programme would want to consider.

Before we go any further it is important to distinguish at least two different aspects to flexible learning. One is concerned with increasing flexibility of access to higher education, and the other is concerned with increasing students' control over what and how they learn. It is possible to increase access to a course by making all or part of it available by distance learning and/or by easing entry requirements. The same course may remain absolutely rigid in format, with students having little or no say in what subjects they must take, what order they take them in, what learning activities are required, and what assignments must be done. Alternatively, a course which has only one mode of access may offer considerable flexibility to students in the choice of how and what they learn. Both aspects need to be considered when the structure of the course is being determined.

Flexibility of entry and exit

What kinds of qualifications or experience might be required to enter your course? Course designers usually begin with an assumption that their course will be at either undergraduate or postgraduate level. However it may be worth reconsidering the level of the course. In the UK and other British-influenced systems, most professional training has been offered at the undergraduate level. But some providers of professional qualifications are now considering the US pattern and beginning to offer professional courses as postgraduate degrees.

The decision to offer a course at postgraduate level might be considered for a number of reasons. For example, some medical degrees in Australia are now being converted from undergraduate to postgraduate. Prerequisites are usually a generalist degree with certain content in the sciences. Teaching staff hope that making the medical course postgraduate will ensure a greater level of maturity on the part of the students entering medicine, and a more considered choice of medicine as a career. Personal maturity is considered particularly important for medical practice. Making the medical degree postgraduate allows much of the base scientific knowledge to be acquired in the first degree, although this need not be purely a science degree. Or a postgraduate course might be offered because the target population for a new programme may consist largely of employed people who are likely to have already acquired a first degree. A postgraduate degree may be more attractive to this target group than another bachelor's degree. This is frequently the case with areas such as management qualifications, which are more likely to be of interest to mid-career professionals than school leavers. If you choose to offer a postgraduate programme to entrants who will come with first degrees from a range of different disciplines but where the subject matter will be largely new to students, you do need to think about what capacities students will bring from their first degrees that will enable this course to be run at postgraduate level. What will you expect of these students that you would not necessarily expect of undergraduates? It might be useful to consider some of the lists of expected qualities of graduates that we discussed in Chapter 4 to prompt thinking here. It will be important to plan the new course so that students are consistently required to do the kind of work that demands high levels of critical analysis, synthesis and independent thought. If students are not dealing with advanced disciplinary knowledge and are not required to think rigorously and use independent judgement, it is difficult to see in what sense the course could be justified as postgraduate.

Alternative entry routes

Whether the course is at undergraduate or postgraduate level, will there be an alternative entry route for potential students who do not possess the formal entry qualification (matriculation or first degree)? One of the possibilities for alternative entry is the assessment and accreditation of previous informal learning through systems like learning portfolios. A number of useful guides have been published on accreditation of prior learning and it is worth looking at Cohen *et al.* (1993) and Simosko (1991) for guidelines on the process. Another possibility is to set up an entry course, which both helps develop the skills which students will need for further tertiary education and also gives teachers a chance to assess the ability of individual students. Often these kinds of alternative entry programmes are run on an institution-wide basis. But if your course is aimed at a particular target group which has many members lacking the formal entry qualifications, it may be worth building a component like this into the faculty's course offerings.

I know at first hand of two departments which have structured programmes in this way. One is located in a faculty of adult education which offers both undergraduate and postgraduate degree programmes in areas like training and development, community education and adult literacy. Entry to these programmes is by the usual routes. But the faculty also offers an Associate Diploma in Aboriginal Studies which requires no formal educational entry requirements. The associate diploma acts as an entry point for indigenous students who may not have completed secondary education. Successful completion of the diploma allows students to enter any of the first-degree programmes.

Similarly, at another university, a graduate school of management offers postgraduate diploma and master's degree programmes. However, would-be students who are employed in managerial positions but do not hold a first degree may enter a certificate programme. Successful completion of the course brings a certificate in management; excellent results throughout this initial course allow the certificate holder to continue into the postgraduate programmes.

Options for exit

As well as entry routes, exit points for the new course need to be considered. Maybe students must complete all three or four years of a degree to achieve anything of value, but maybe they can also be given credit for learning in smaller chunks. Nested courses, which allow students to exit with either a certificate, a diploma or a degree, are becoming more popular. They may be particularly appropriate where the student target group is largely made up of working adults. The limited initial commitment to a certificate course is attractive to many adults who are uncertain how they will be able to balance work, family and study. Modularized programmes have been criticized on the grounds that they will not encourage deep engagement with a discipline as did more traditionally structured courses. In my experience of teaching on a nested postgraduate programme of the kind I have just described, the case is almost the opposite. Many students who initially enrol in the certificate choose to continue studying to master's level because they become fascinated by what they are learning. Few decide to leave the programme earlier than they had planned.

Although colleges in the United States have long offered an undergraduate study pattern whereby a two-year associate degree can be easily converted to a four-year bachelor's degree, this pattern is relatively unknown in British-influenced systems.

But it may well have something to offer undergraduates, particularly those who have not yet decided which direction their career should take. The challenge is to design a coherent programme at each level. There are a number of models that could be considered. One is the common US model where the first years of a programme are devoted to broad general education before discipline or professional specializations are taken up in the later years or for the second degree. This has the advantage of allowing students more time and a broader educational experience before they must settle for one discipline or profession. It also has the disadvantage that preprofessional studies, particularly in the sciences, are divorced from any professional context, which may lessen their perceived relevance and actually make it more difficult for students to call on that knowledge in professional study and practice.

There seems to be little enthusiasm for this model at present, outside the US, but there is more support for a pattern of tertiary education which would provide technical skills first and general education later. In this model students might undertake an initial qualification which was designed to allow them to practise, usually not at a full professional level of independent practice but perhaps at a technician level. This training might be undertaken at a university but it might also be provided by a technical or vocational college. Graduation from the first programme would enable entry into the second stage of the programme, which would provide a degree qualification. It is to be expected, however, that many students would not progress automatically but would take the opportunity to work for a number of years before enrolling for further study. This may not seem very different from the situation which exists now, where a technical college graduate goes on to further study for a degree, getting some credit for previous study. The difference proposed in this model is that the two parts of the programme are designed to fit together. At present, universities which are willing to accredit previous study in technical and vocational colleges often find the process difficult because skills and knowledge have been taught in different combinations and performance contexts. The idea instead is that these two courses would be designed as two parts of a whole.

Despite the enthusiasm with which this idea is being pushed by governments – which tends to make academics automatically suspicious – this idea has points which recommend it, although not necessarily for all students. It does fit with the way in which interest in learning develops in many people. For many students in their late teens and early twenties there is a strong motivation to acquire skills which will make them employable, useful, respected and generally able to establish themselves as independent adults. To ask students at this stage of their development to critically appraise the values and practices of their profession or discipline may be difficult because at this stage of their lives they do not want to stand aside from the profession, they want to be part of it. The experience of practising a discipline or profession, however, raises many of the questions which academic teachers were unsuccessful at raising earlier. Older students who have both work and life experience are often motivated to study in their profession or discipline in a way that they were not ten years earlier. At present we see many of these students coming into postgraduate course work programmes and they are usually a delight to teach. Surely it ought to be possible to offer a similar opportunity for broader education to people who didn't want or couldn't afford to undertake a full degree programme at the beginning of their adult lives.

Flexible delivery – where can this course be studied?

The next question to consider might be how students will get access to your course. Will it be necessary for them to come to classes on campus or might they be able to study all or part of this course at a distance, in their homes or workplaces? Some courses offer students the choice of different delivery modes – they can enrol in classes on campus or study by distance education. A handful of universities have made arrangements with large organizations to deliver classes in their workplaces. Many universities are considering whether the use of more resource-based learning for on-campus students might enable face-to-face teaching to be limited or at least used more effectively. The extent to which courses can be delivered through materials (print, audio, video and computer based) rather than through interactions between teachers and students can only really be decided by looking at the kinds of learning that the course requires.

Higher education courses are usually intended to develop specialist knowledge of a discipline. This will include the particular ways of thinking and problem solving which characterize the discipline as well as the acquisition of a considerable amount of detailed, factual knowledge.

Although this specialist knowledge is important it is by no means all and when planning for more flexible provision we also need to think about how to provide for:

- conceptual change – deep understanding of complex concepts which often run counter to what is learned from common experience;
- development of intellectual abilities like critical thinking, logical argument, selection and use of appropriate evidence and so forth;
- skilled performance – not simple motor skills but the combination of mastery of procedures, physical dexterity, responsiveness to the situation, knowledge and judgement which makes up much professional and specialist practice;
- development of dispositions – such as the disposition to take responsibility for one's own learning; to self-evaluate regularly; to work cooperatively with others; to take account of ethical considerations. (There is definitely a knowledge and skill component to these, but probably more important is the willingness and commitment to carry them through.)

I would now like to look at the kinds of activities, materials and conditions that have been found to be most important in developing each of these different kinds of learning so that we can take them into consideration in planning for more flexible learning.

Acquiring technical and conventional knowledge through resource-based learning

Much straightforward information can be acquired relatively easily from print materials. In fact research suggests that print is at least as efficient as lectures in transmitting information (Bligh, 1975). Print material can of course take various forms. It can be the standard textbook which students are often instructed to read a chapter at a time. The unit of study based on a standard textbook seems to be a common pattern in the sciences, pretty much unheard-of in the humanities and used to varying degrees in the social sciences and professional courses. The advantage of a good textbook is that most of the information that students need is collected in one source; it is clearly organized, with key information highlighted, and may include exercises in which students can test their understanding and immediate retention of the material. The disadvantage of basing a unit of study on a textbook is that students rely on that one source, do not encounter alternative views and do not develop any skills in seeking out and organizing information for themselves.

Other possibilities include packages of readings taken from the current literature which have both the advantage of offering a much wider range of views, which can be updated and modified with comparative ease, and the disadvantage that students will be required to interpret materials which are not specifically written for instruction.

Where all or part of a unit of study is designed to be offered as resource-based learning, textbooks and/or packages of readings are usually combined with instructional materials written specifically for each unit of study. These can be designed to present information to students in the sequence and to the level of detail required by the particular course and unit. They are usually designed to be easy to read and to understand, and are presented in an informal tone and style, so that students are introduced to important concepts in an easily understandable way rather than having to struggle to understand new concepts and an unfamiliar academic language in the professional literature. Most open learning materials will contain frequent self-assessment questions and exercises to encourage students to monitor their understanding and progress. Race (1989) provides useful guidelines for writing self-instructional materials.

These text-based methods of presenting information can be supplemented by visuals such as illustrations, graphs, charts, film and video. They can be provided directly to students as packages of materials or students can access the same kinds of materials via computer on the World Wide Web. Providing the materials in the form of a package allows students to work on them wherever they are in the world. Packages may be relatively expensive to produce, but probably less so than building more lecture halls. If the instructional materials are accessed via computer, students will be tied to the computer wherever it is located, to a greater or lesser extent depending on whether they have the facility to download and print some of the material. However, a compensating factor is that the computer also provides, via e-mail, the means for students to ask questions of the teacher and of fellow students as they come to grips with the materials and to get feedback reasonably promptly.

What am I suggesting here about learning from print materials, computer-based materials, audio and video that is in any way different? After all university courses have always supplemented lectures with readings and other resources. What I'm suggesting is that in order to increase flexibility in learning we should start thinking about these kinds of resources as the primary means and the starting point from which students access knowledge. There doesn't seem to be much point any longer in bringing students together in mass lecture halls to supply them with information. We know from the research that they can usually acquire information more effectively from print. Whether students are officially 'on-campus' or 'off-campus', contact time with teachers is becoming increasingly precious and we need to use it for those kinds of learning which are difficult to achieve by other means. The kinds of learning most difficult to achieve by learning from resource materials are those which most of us would like to think best typify higher education: conceptual change, intellectual development, and the ability to carry out complex tasks requiring high levels of judgement.

Conceptual change, intellectual development and flexible delivery

I have included conceptual change and intellectual development together in the same section because they are related, conceptual change being just one aspect of intellectual development. Certainly, similar conditions are required to develop these kinds of abilities.

Helping students to understand and master concepts which run contrary to their own everyday experience is one of the most difficult tasks of higher education and one in which we do not always succeed. As examples of these kinds of fundamental concepts, Brumby used the concept of natural selection in biology while Dahlgren used the economic law of supply and demand and its role in price setting. Their research showed that students who had successfully passed their courses could still hold basic misunderstandings about these fundamental principles (Brumby, 1984; Dahlgren, 1984). Roth and Anderson's research with middle-school students showed that the great majority of students in their study did *not* change their experience-based misconceptions about photosynthesis after reading their textbooks (Roth and Anderson, 1988). How can students be induced to absorb ideas like these and use them correctly?

Firstly, of course, students need definitions and explanations. But this on its own is not sufficient. I am sure that all of the students in Dahlgren's and Brumby's research would have received definitions and explanations as part of their course work. They may well have been able to repeat those definitions and explanations at exam times. On their own, definitions and explanations are not enough. Students need to see many examples of the concept in action, both straightforward examples and more complex ones. Then they need to practise applying the concept to predict, analyse and explain in a range of situations with different variables. And they need feedback on their responses.

The development of other kinds of intellectual abilities, such as critical inquiry or building and defending an argument, demands a similar process. Students need the opportunity to try out the process and to get feedback on their efforts. This kind of work is well suited to small groups where students can work on problems alone or with others, discuss their results with the group and the group leader, make adjustments and try again. Through the discussion, common misunderstandings, the impact of different variables and different approaches can all be explored. It is important to remember, however, that group work that doesn't challenge students' thinking in these ways can leave misconceptions unchanged. Group work can be so useful for concept change and intellectual development that most course designers will want to make provision for it in flexible learning programmes, even though having to participate in a group at a specific time makes the programme somewhat less flexible for students.

There are various options for including group work in flexible learning courses. *Workshops can be offered on a daily attendance or residential basis* usually lasting several days, which may be offered at the beginning of a session's work to help students develop the most important concepts of the course, and/or towards the end of a unit of work to give them the opportunity to discuss problems and questions they have encountered in their study and assignments and to practise some of the skills which the course is supposed to develop. Block arrangements like this tend to be very intensive. They require considerable preparation of activities and materials on the part of teachers. There needs to be a wider variety of activities than there might be if the same number of teaching hours was distributed in weekly tutorials across a whole session. Changes in the pace and the demands of activities are important if students are to be able to maintain concentration and involvement over a number of very intensive days. This different kind of teaching may require staff members to develop new skills, and they may need help and support in planning for this kind of workshop teaching. Attendance at workshops will obviously make demands on students, who may have to travel and/or to arrange accommodation, child care and leave from their jobs. In some cases, the university or college may be able to offer accommodation and/or child care, which will be more convenient for students but will entail more administrative work for departmental staff. Alternatively, the workshop block may be held at a location convenient for the majority of students, in which case it is the teaching staff who travel and arrange accommodation and child care. But for both students and staff, the block of workshop days may be easier to arrange and offer more flexibility than regular meetings.

A 'real group' of students can meet regularly in a location convenient for them. The group may be led by a 'real' tutor, usually a local person with some expertise in the subject area who has been hired by the university or college specifically to facilitate such groups. The local tutor may be responsible for all or part of the marking of student assignments and may be responsible for planning what happens at each meeting. Alternatively, he or she may be expected to follow a teaching plan provided as part of the syllabus and designed to ensure that students in all locations receive similar instruction. Obviously this option relies on enrolling sufficient students within commuting distance of a meeting point, who can make themselves available at the time scheduled. Requirements for meetings will need to be made known to students at the time of enrolment, just as class schedules are available to on-campus students. The recruitment and support of local tutors is also a matter that needs to be given thought. What will be the criteria on which they are selected? Do they need to be qualified in a particular area? Is it more important that they have good teaching skills? What support could be offered to local tutors to make up for deficiencies? Generally, the less knowledgeable and skilled the local group leaders are, the more detail will be required in lesson guidelines, both as to the content and its interpretation and in the way group sessions should be structured and activities managed. Sometimes, the employing department decides to focus on either subject expertise or teaching ability in recruitment, planning to compensate with either detailed and thorough materials or by developing the tutors' skills. Recruiting, paying for and monitoring the work of a considerable number of local tutors can add a considerable administrative burden to a department.

A 'real group' of students can have a 'virtual' tutor. A third option is to link the student group with a leader from the department's teaching staff, via teleconferencing or video conferencing. This method of linking two or more groups with a single group leader has been referred to as a 'distributed classroom'. This option avoids all of the problems of hiring local tutors, at the cost of some loss of the personal relationship between teacher and students. Video conferencing has tended to be very expensive to set up and the quality of the image transmitted has often been poor; in addition it is highly desirable to have technical support on hand. Teleconferencing is much simpler to set up, but the important visual element of the communication is missing. The teacher cannot read the body language of the group, and discussion can be difficult if all parties are not sharing the same view of the materials, figures, diagrams or objects under discussion.

Students and tutor can form a 'virtual' group. An option that has only recently become available is the possibility of linking students and tutor in different locations through an e-mail group or a World Wide Web bulletin board. Groups such as these can 'meet' to discuss a topic in real time – that is, the discussion session is convened for a particular date and time and the participants submit their ideas and comments within a specified time frame. Alternatively the discussion topic can be nominated and the discussion can run over a period of weeks, with students and tutor logging on at times convenient for them and submitting contributions at any time. Further discussion of the issues involved in using interactive bulletin boards and e-mail discussion groups can be found in Hewson and Hughes (in press) and Hughes and Hewson (1998).

Although educators are still exploring the potential uses and difficulties with computer-mediated groups, they seem to offer the possibility of interactive learning for isolated students in a way that has not previously been feasible.

From the experience that my colleagues and I have had in using them to date I would offer the following suggestions for running such a group.

Indicate the need for computer access before enrolment. Let students know how they will access the system (e-mail, World Wide Web, other), what kinds of computing power will be required, and what are the possibilities for access if the students do not own their own computer. (Is it possible, for instance, to arrange access through a local college or university or through a public library system?)

Provide clear written guidelines about all the technical details of getting on and off the system, including the use of passwords, what to do if you forget your password, how to submit comments, times when the system will be down for maintenance and so forth. It is not sufficient to put this information on the computer: students need the users' manual for the times when they are having trouble making the system work for them. The level of stress that can be induced in students who are required to participate in a course by computer but cannot make the system work for them could lead to the disappearance of many.

Require participation. My experience of using computer-mediated group discussion with adult learners is that while most will willingly visit the site or the bulletin board and observe what's going on, they may be very reluctant to launch into the debate themselves without a great deal of encouragement. This may not be an issue if your potential group consists of young computer enthusiasts, but it does seem to be a problem which is not just about a lack of familiarity with the technology. Many of my students are highly computer literate but are still reluctant to participate. My feeling is that this problem is more related to the differences between spoken and written communication. Students who feel quite comfortable joining in a vigorous discussion in the classroom will hesitate before setting down opinions which they are still in the process of forming. This is particularly the case when the discussion will run over weeks and their early statements will be open to scrutiny for that period of time. In contrast, opinions offered in class, no matter how naive, rarely come back to haunt you.

Because I feel that it is so important that students test out and develop their ideas and their reasoning with others throughout the course, I now require students to contribute at least once to each of the Web discussion groups that form part of the subject. Contributions are not evaluated in any way, but the requirement pushes students to overcome their discomfort with a new medium of expression and begin to use it to explore ideas.

Monitor the tone of the discussion. It is important to set the tone of a computer-mediated discussion group from the beginning, just as you might establish ground rules with any group. I find it is important to emphasize that the discussion is intended to be informal and developmental and not a formal debate with well-rehearsed presentations. It is also important to monitor the ongoing discussion for these tendencies. Colleagues have found that it only needs one student to post a highly abstruse and theoretical contribution for all of the other students to fall silent and withdraw from the discussion. It may need the teacher to step in here and make a contribution which brings the debate back to a more down-to-earth level. It is equally important to watch for a tendency to be overly critical of other's contributions. The relative anonymity of computer mediated discussion groups can encourage some participants to be more brutal than they would be if the discussion were taking place face to face and the group leader needs to make it clear that abuse is not acceptable.

Of course the kinds of interactive learning that support intellectual development need not occur in groups, but there usually does need to be opportunity to work with another person. It is very difficult to challenge one's own conceptions, to criticize one's own reasoning, to think laterally and explore a broader range of options without the prompting of dialogue and questioning. We can, of course, raise questions in the texts and articles that we give students to study, but we can't explore or challenge the student's response. Assessment exercises provide some opportunities for teachers to identify misconceptions and inadequate reasoning. We can provide feedback which highlights common misconceptions. But in general the opportunities to do this are limited, and there is not enough feedback for students to feel comfortable with a new way of thinking. The discomfort involved in conceptual change may mean that students retreat to older and more comfortable ideas and ways of thinking as soon as that topic or unit is completed.

Skilled performance and flexible delivery

It is important to be clear what we are talking about when we refer to 'skills'. Romiszowski (1981) provides a useful way of thinking about skilled performance. He puts skills on a continuum ranging from 'reproductive' skills to 'productive' skills. With a reproductive skill, the student is required to reproduce a set performance to a prespecified standard; at the other end of the continuum students must apply their knowledge and skills to a new situation to produce a response that may be unique to that context. Between the reproductive and productive ends of the continuum, tasks vary in the degree of planning and creative problem solving that they require. In higher education we are mainly concerned with productive skills, but it is important to recognize that productive skills subsume reproductive skills and these still have to be learned and practised.

If we look more closely at productive skills, or as I prefer to call it, skilled performance, there are four stages which students must master in order to be able to perform in a skilful fashion:

- The first involves *interpreting situations* and recognizing characteristics of typical problems.
- The second involves *calling up one's knowledge* of the full range of strategies and procedures which could be considered.
- The third involves *planning a response* – evaluating the options and choosing one strategy or procedure or a combination.
- The fourth involves *performing* – carrying out the planned actions with the necessary degree of dexterity, strength, fluidity, self control, sensitivity to others or whatever may be the characteristics of skilled performance in this particular situation.

Some kinds of skilled performances, such as interpreting a literary work or solving a mathematical problem, have no physical element and require no interaction with others. The only limitation on developing these kinds of skills is the capacity for providing feedback on students' attempts. But developing skilled performance which does have a physical aspect, or requires the performer to interact with others, poses more of a problem. How can we bring greater flexibility to this kind of learning so that students do not always have to be in the classroom or laboratory at set times?

Once we look at the four stages in skilled performance set out above it is easy to see that the first three stages can be practised in a number of ways. Students can respond to trigger situations presented on film or video, as written cases, as design briefs, or just as problems to solve. Either alone or in groups they can evaluate options and plan a response. They can usually submit the plan for assessment and feedback to the teacher or their peers.

More difficult is finding ways for students to develop the skills that they need to perform at the fourth stage. The development of skills has always been something of a problem area for universities, even with students who are on campus full time. The amount of time and attention that students need for individual practice and feedback on their performance has usually not been a consideration in planning teaching schedules and staff–student ratios. So some of the suggestions here might apply equally to traditional on-campus programmes:

- Self-instruction: a great deal can be accomplished by getting students to practise on their own. You may need to provide them with written step-by-step instructions, illustrated charts of procedures, examples of performance on video or audio tapes to be used as a model. Students need to be encouraged to assess their own performance and to be given checklists, specific criteria and models to assess against. It is helpful if you can provide some indication of how many hours of practice or how many repetitions or opportunities to perform the skill are likely to be needed to develop an adequate standard of performance. There is some evidence which suggests that students are poor at predicting how much practice will be needed to master a skill.
- Intensive workshops: many distance programmes require students to attend campus once or twice a year for workshops of several days. These on-campus workshops are used for skill development and group work. This approach may be the only one feasible when the skills to be developed require tools and equipment that students may not otherwise have access to. It can have a significant disadvantage, though, if the skills are taught in isolation from the more theoretical parts of the programme.
- Workplace learning and clinical placements: work placements have been used in many professional programmes for some time, but not always with the aim of skill development. Frequently the aims of the work placement are of a more nebulous nature and relate to areas like 'giving students insight into the world of work' and 'helping them to integrate into the work environment' (Ryan *et al.*, 1996). In order for the clinical placement to be used for the systematic development of skills, as it has been used in many of the health

professions, a far higher degree of organization is required. The skills which students are expected to develop must be identified, and negotiations undertaken with participating organizations to ensure that students can be offered adequate opportunities to develop them. Workplace supervisors who will work with students need to be identified and carefully briefed about what will be expected of them, particularly if they are to be involved in assessment. Supervisors may require some training, and will almost certainly require ongoing contact and support. Clinical placements in the health sciences have achieved this level of structure and organization largely through conjoint appointments of staff, but work placements in other disciplines are rarely structured well enough to enable systematic development of skilled performance (Ryan *et al.*, 1996). The difficulties in finding appropriate organizations which can offer adequate learning opportunities and supervision to students become even greater if the students are geographically dispersed. Still, the effort may be worth it because of the richness of the experience associated with working in real settings.

Limitations of resource-based learning

Simply by looking at these three different aspects of learning we can see some of the issues which have to be faced in trying to make access to higher education more flexible and open to a wider population of students. There is a real danger that as universities and colleges which are pressed for funds seek more students by converting courses to 'flexible' delivery, what will be delivered is simply packages of learning materials. In effect, this means more and more information and too few of the transformative educational experiences which higher education can and should offer. My one experience of distance learning as a student bears this out.

The course I enrolled in several years ago was a certificate course in management. Having held a management position for a couple of years I decided that it might be useful to study the subject formally. Work commitments made it difficult to get to any of the classes on offer, and so a distance programme seemed the only viable option. On paper the course seemed well designed. There were lesson materials in print, built around a standard fat textbook and supplemented by a telecourse which would be broadcast on national television. In practice it didn't work out so well. The print materials and the textbook were basic: they concentrated on the functions of management which anyone already in a management position would know only too well. With no provision for regular contact with teachers and no opportunities to raise questions or discussion, there was no possibility of going beyond the basics. The television series was more interesting, as it included many interviews with prominent managers. However, I missed several episodes through forgetting to program the video late at night. (The series was broadcast very early in the morning.) I would have preferred video tapes to broadcast, though I suppose that the course providers thought that broadcast provided wider access.

At the end of each topic there was a written test which was submitted for assessment, and other suggested activities which were not assessable. The written test was short-answer or multiple-choice and referred mostly to the textbook and not the broadcast material. The questions were factual and easy so that I had no trouble achieving almost perfect scores. The other suggested activities were far more imaginative. They often involved finding and interviewing a specific type of manager about a specific issue, such as a McDonald's manager about staff training. Unfortunately, I did few of these activities – because of both the pressures on my own time and the fact that I knew that the managers that I had to find and interview would face similar pressures. I know that I would have carried out the interviews if I had had to submit any assessable work related to them or had even had to discuss my findings with others. In the end I got the certificate but felt that I had learned almost nothing. It was a real experience of surface learning for me. You could say that it was my own fault, that I had the opportunity to make this a much richer experience than I did. That's true up to a point. But one of the reasons that adult learners enrol in formal courses is that they hope that the structure provided by the course requirements will give them the impetus they need to make learning a priority. In this case the course requirements did not demand any real engagement with the subject matter. All that the assessment required was some simple factual knowledge. When there are many competing demands for students' time the focus of the course has to be on significant learning and not on what is easiest to assess.

Flexibility in making up a programme of study

Recently, governments and universities have pushed faculties and departments to increase flexibility for students when making up their programme of study, by promoting modular courses and credit transfer. Modular courses offer students the chance to structure their own courses, choosing the particular combinations of units that they are interested in, the sequence that suits them and the time frame in which they want to study. Credit transfer assists students in making up a programme from the units offered by different departments or even different institutions. Once again the reason for so much heavyweight support comes back to finances. Costs to both funding bodies and students can be reduced by ensuring that students receive full credit for previous study when they change courses. Standardizing credit points for units across departments simplifies administrative systems and procedures.

Modular programmes have been introduced without much drama in many general education areas, but have met with considerable resistance in areas of professional preparation. Professional education still tends to be very highly structured, with few electives, driven by a need to produce graduates who can safely be allowed to practise on the general public. Innovations like problem-based courses tend to reduce flexibility in choice of units even further, as foundation disciplines and practice units are integrated into a single learning experience built around the exploration of carefully structured and sequenced professional problems. On the other hand, they may require fewer hours of class attendance than conventional programmes and so offer students more flexibility about where and when they study. Even in those disciplines which have retained fairly rigid programmes with few electives, there are debates about whether students should be given a general preparation for all areas of professional work or whether they might be allowed to choose to specialize in one aspect of professional work during their undergraduate degree. As an example, some civil engineers would argue that students ought to be allowed to specialize in areas like structural, geomatic or transport engineering, and some programmes have been redesigned to allow students the flexibility to do this.

Some writers have seen student choice in making up their programme of study as virtually guaranteeing a deep approach to learning, but this is too simplistic. For those students (often mature, employed, with well-defined interests) who know what they want, flexible, modularized programmes are ideal. Many course-work postgraduate programmes are designed in this way to cater for these characteristics in their target student group. Modularized programmes may be less ideal for entry-level students who are still learning about their own interests and the possibilities within their discipline or profession. They may need individual advice if they are to put together a coherent and sensible programme, and they can be helped by laying out the links between units in programme maps which show recommended routes to a qualification.

Preparation of materials for resource-based learning

The move towards more flexible delivery usually involves a greater reliance on resource materials. When the decision is made to redesign a course to make access more flexible, whether this involves packaging the course for distance learning or redesigning it to make more effective use of the teaching time on campus, one of the issues to be resolved is who will do the work. What kinds of materials will be needed? Who will write them, design them, produce them, send them to students, and who will students approach over mistakes and problems with materials and equipment?

The preparation of materials for resource-based learning requires a much longer time frame than most academics are used to, and it usually needs input from specialist staff for design and production. With many departments seeing a shift to resource-based learning as a cost-saving measure, there is often a tendency for all of the writing and design of materials to be pushed onto academic staff while administrative staff are forced to take on production and distribution. This often represents a poor use of staff resources and the end product suffers. Universities which specialize in distance education have long since realized the necessity of employing educational designers, graphic designers, specialist producers for audio, visual and computer-based materials and technical support staff. As more traditional institutions move into different delivery modes they also need to accept that different kinds of staff will be needed if they are to produce high-quality programmes and materials which can compete with the best in the field.

What do flexible learning and flexible delivery have to offer?

To many departments, faculties and universities, flexible access, flexible delivery modes and flexible programmes have come to seem the only feasible way out of relentless funding pressures. Easing entry requirements, and reducing or eliminating the need to study on campus can open up much wider student markets, both at home and overseas. Rationalization of teaching and a shift to more resource-based learning may reduce infrastructure costs and salary costs. Such resource gains may turn out to be more illusory than real.

But greater flexibility does offer some real advantages. It makes it possible for students who have not met conventional entry requirements for whatever reason to enter higher education. Since many of these students are likely to be from different cultural backgrounds, they bring a range of different viewpoints and experiences which enrich the educational experience for everyone. Greater flexibility also enables students with work and family commitments to enrol, enabling them to keep up to date and forcing their teachers to grapple with the realities of practice in the workplace. Greater flexibility in programmes of study enables students to pursue individual academic and professional interests. Not every student wants or needs this freedom, but those that do are often among the most creative and most highly motivated. Another point in favour of the push for greater flexibility is that it frequently leads to a significant review of the whole curriculum and a more carefully considered choice of content and teaching methods. Content may be reviewed to avoid overlap, conventional lectures replaced by resource-based learning and face-to-face teaching reserved for work on challenging questions and problems.

The risks, though, are also significant. At worst, we may see a proliferation of distance education courses, expensive for students but cheaply produced, which rely on packages of printed lectures with little or no opportunity for engaging in questioning, discussion or challenging projects. Courses like this lack most of the opportunities for intellectual development which we would like to think characterize higher education. But there are already a number of examples to be found, just as there are examples of poorly designed and taught courses among conventional programmes. The lesson is that a mediocre programme is not improved by being offered in more flexible ways, and even a well-thought-out conventional programme will have to be reconceptualized and redesigned for different students and different delivery methods.

7

Deciding on Goals and Objectives for Units of Study

How do students decide what to study in any given subject or module? How do they decide what kind of learning will be valued by this teacher? How do they determine what they want for themselves from any educational endeavour?

The factors that help students decide what is required

Considerable research work has been done on how students conceive of learning in higher education (Säljö, 1979; Van Rossum and Schenk, 1984; Van Rossum *et al.*, 1985; Marton *et al.*, 1993). In a number of studies which asked students to talk or write about their conceptions of learning in their university studies, the researchers found that five different views on learning could be distinguished. These were:

- Learning as acquiring knowledge. Knowledge is viewed quantitatively – one knows a little or a lot; understanding consists in being able to reproduce what one has learned.
- Learning as memorizing and long term retention. While learning is still focused on acquiring detail, there is recognition that some points are more important than others (main and side issues).
- Learning as application (particularly algorithmical applications of this knowledge). Two kinds of application are sometimes recognized – being able to apply the knowledge in an exam and practical applications.
- Learning as insight or understanding – being able to understand an author's intention and being able to relate new ideas to what one has already learned. Application of learning is not seen as a technical activity but as the ability to use one's new knowledge to interpret and understand new material and

situations. Learning *is* seen however, as subject matter oriented and a purely cognitive activity.

• Learning as personal development. Learning comes to have an emotional as well as a cognitive aspect. It is oriented to problem-solving and developing a personal philosophy. At the same time learners become better able to make interpretations based on views not their own.

(Van Rossum *et al.*, 1985)

In 1993, Marton and his colleagues added a sixth conception in which learning is seen as transformational – the key to changing and developing as a person (Marton *et al.*, 1993).

This schema has many parallels to that found in the work of Perry, who studied the intellectual and ethical development of male American college students (Perry, 1970, 1988), and to that of Belenky and her colleagues, who looked for similarities and differences in the ways that women conceptualize their learning (Belenky *et al.*, 1986).

As Säljö pointed out, these conceptions of learning form a hierarchy, in that the later ones necessarily encompass the earlier ones. Students who are capable of seeing learning as the development of a personal philosophy are also able to see that on some occasions learning also consists in increasing one's store of factual knowledge and applying that knowledge in routine and predictable ways. However, those who are at the earlier stages of development see learning only as something external to themselves, a piece of information or a skill to be acquired, and not as a fundamental change in their way of thinking and being in the world.

There is a distinct difference between the first three conceptions, which are essentially reproductive in character, and the later categories, which require learners to construct a more personal understanding. The first three also differ quite significantly from the kinds of outcomes that most university teachers say that they want for their students. When lecturers are asked what kinds of learning they want, most tend to talk about critical analysis, solving complex problems, building logical arguments based on evidence, as well as knowing when and how to use the tools and techniques of their discipline. Clearly there is often a mismatch of expectations between many teachers and students which is bound to result in disappointment on both sides.

In the absence of other signals, where do students get their ideas of what kinds of learning will be valued in a particular subject or unit? Research into student learning has shown that one of the strongest factors in determining what and how students learn is the form of assessment that they expect. Miller and Parlett's research identified the 'cue seekers', trawling for any hints as to what topics and types of questions might appear on the exam, while the 'cue-deaf' remained oblivious (Miller and Parlett, 1974: 52). Van Rossum and his colleagues showed that those students whose conception of learning fits with categories 4 or 5 often prepare quite differently for the different types of questions they expect, as evidenced by this quote from 'Emmy':

> When only knowledge questions will be asked I learn all sorts of defini-
> tions by heart – 'drumming things into my head'. When I expect insight
> questions at an exam, I don't learn definitions by heart but I try to fathom
> the main lines of the matter to be studied and to form as many interrela-
> tionships as possible.
>
> (Van Rossum *et al.*, 1985: 631)

Many students are not able to make this distinction between 'knowledge'
and 'insight' questions for themselves, however. Hanne Bock's research (1983)
shows first-year students struggling to understand the different modes of reasoning and conceptualizing which are required, and struggling to find a personal voice in their writing which will be acceptable in academia. When I was
an undergraduate, majoring in English, I was never clear about exactly what
my teachers wanted from me. Was it sufficient to show that I was familiar with
the full range of critical opinion on the writer under study? Was I expected to
include my personal response to the writer's work? What if I disagreed with the
major critics? Safer really, to leave my own opinions out of it and stick to a
technical analysis. I had always attributed my uncertainty to stupidity, until
this year when I read a memoir by the American literary critic, Jane Tompkins
(1996: 66–84), who confessed that she had also felt the same confusion as a student and come to similar conclusions.

All of these factors – differences in conceptions of learning, uncertainty
about what is expected and reliance on assessment to indicate the kinds of
learning to be undertaken – highlight the need to spend some time with students examining the educational purpose of any unit of study.

The question of educational purpose – the objectives of learning – is
absolutely central to the idea of curriculum design, but the question of what
those purposes ought to be and how objectives ought to be expressed continues
to be one of contentious debate. Partly this is because many of the models for
formulating learning objectives have been drawn from industrial training and
seem inappropriate for higher education. But sometimes it also appears that
the reluctance to talk about learning goals and objectives reflects an unwilling-
ness on the part of some teachers to have their 'espoused theory' compared to
their 'theory in action'. Virtually all teachers in higher education espouse high-
level goals. As we have seen, they talk about teaching for understanding, developing critical thinking and problem-solving abilities. But these broad goals do
not contain direct implications for decision making in the classroom. They do
not suggest particular activities on the part of teacher or students or particular
kinds of assessment. As a consequence, many teachers simply replicate the kind
of teaching that they themselves received, maintaining an ancient tradition of
teaching as the provision of information and learning as the reproduction of
information received.

If we are to make any advance in educational decision making, to put our
choices about teaching and learning activities on a rational and strategic basis,
it will be necessary to think much more rigorously about how a particular unit
of study might contribute to those broad educational goals of thinking sceptic-

ally, logically, analytically and creatively. It will involve being able to tell students what kinds of things they will need to do to demonstrate the progress that they make towards those goals.

Being explicit about goals for student learning invites students to challenge the appropriateness of those goals and also the means for arriving at them. Such challenges are rare, most students being only too aware of the dangers of antagonizing the teacher/examiner, but the possibility may still be discomforting. Teachers who are not particularly confident about leading discussion may wonder how they would handle a potentially difficult discussion of goals and objectives at the very beginning of the semester before they have even begun to know the students.

On the other hand, not to be as explicit as possible about what you would like students to achieve sends a message that is distinctly anti-educational. Unless there are clear goals in front of students and teachers, students are asked to take the whole process on trust – 'Trust me, I can't say where we are going but it will be worth it.' An attitude of unquestioning faith in authority figures is not generally considered to be a desirable outcome of higher education. It fits only with the earliest level in Säljö's conceptions of learning hierarchy or the first stage of Perry's intellectual development scheme, yet it is an attitude that is sometimes unwittingly endorsed by teachers' actions.

The value in giving time and thought to what we might expect students to achieve within a semester's work does not only lie in having a solid basis for discussing the purpose of the subject. It is also the beginning for many teachers of a different way of thinking about what might go into a unit. Instead of asking themselves, 'What do I need to say about this topic?' the question becomes 'If that is what I want them to achieve, then what might they best do in order to achieve it?' In other words, the whole teaching and learning exchange can become focused on what students need instead of what teachers have to offer.

The development of the idea of objectives for learning

The idea of formulating objectives which would specify what the student was intended to achieve, and using these as a basis for designing the educational programme, was first put forward by the American curriculum theorist Ralph Tyler in 1949. According to Tyler:

> If an educational program is to be planned and if efforts for continued improvement are to be made, it is very necessary to have some conception of the goals that are being aimed at. These educational objectives become the criteria by which materials are selected, content is outlined, instructional procedures are developed and tests and examinations are prepared.
> (Tyler, 1949: 3)

Tyler believed that educational objectives should not be expressed in terms of the content which the course would cover, because this would give no indication of what students should be able to do with that content. Nor should educational objectives be written in terms of general attributes such as 'to develop critical thinking' because this gives no idea of the kind of context or content to which such attributes are to be applied. The most useful way of thinking about educational objectives, according to Tyler, was to identify 'both the kind of behaviour to be developed in the student and the content or area of life in which this behaviour is to operate' (pp. 46–7).

In speaking of behaviour, Tyler did not intend that it should be interpreted in a narrow sense. Behaviours might include patterns of thinking and feeling as well as those actions which could be openly observed (p. 6). Thus his concept of 'educational objectives' was quite broad and to Tyler their value lay in identifying 'general modes of reaction to be developed rather than highly specific habits to be acquired' (p. 37).

However, the direction in which Tyler's ideas were developed by subsequent writers led to a much narrower focus on student 'behaviour'. Tyler was an educator, and his book represents the content of his course in curriculum development at the University of Chicago. Robert Mager, who took up his idea of objectives, did much of his work in the area of industrial training. In his influential book first published in 1962, Mager dropped the term 'educational objectives' and substituted 'instructional objectives'. Although the use of the term 'instructional' might seem to imply a focus on the role of the teacher, this was not so. Mager continued to emphasize the importance of specifying what students were to achieve rather than what teachers planned to do or what topics were to be covered. Indeed, he argued that if students understood clearly what the results of their learning ought to be, they would be better able to decide what activities on their part would help them get the desired results (Mager, 1975: 6).

But Mager was far more prescriptive than Tyler about how student achievement ought to be specified. He believed that the words used to describe student achievements must be clear and unambiguous, so clear that an observer (such as the teacher) would be in no doubt as to whether the objective had been achieved or not. To achieve this kind of clarity, terms which might admit many interpretations, such as *to know, to understand, to appreciate, to be familiar with*, were to be avoided. Instead, teachers were to ask themselves how understanding, appreciation or familiarity might be demonstrated in observable ways and then substitute concrete performances like being able *to describe, to identify, to solve . . .*

Mager was not only concerned with achieving greater clarity and specificity about the kinds of behaviour which would provide evidence of student achievement. In the interests of precision, any *conditions* which applied to the performance must also be specified. These might include such points as whether the student would have to perform with or without aids like a calculator, or be able to complete the task within a given time limit. And finally, the objective was to include the *criterion*, 'the quality or level of performance that will be considered acceptable' (p. 23).

Here are two of the examples which Mager gives of instructional objectives which meet his own criteria of completeness and specificity

Example 1
Given access to any sources available, be able to prepare and present a videotaped talk intended to inform a group of your superiors, colleagues or the public of the merits of criterion-referenced instruction [CRI]. You are expected to specify the group to which your talk is directed. The talk will:

- describe at least five characteristics in which CRI differs from conventional instruction;
- anticipate at least three common misconceptions about CRI and offer suitable rebuttals; and
- describe at least two benefits that might accrue to your specified audience from the use of CRI.

The talk should not last more than ten minutes.

(p. 84)

This particular objective, which Mager tells us is one that he wrote for one of his own teaching programmes, typifies the kind of learning objective which I and many others would have problems with. What is described in this objective is not the learning goal, but one possible assessment task which might be used to evaluate how much students have learned about criterion-referenced instruction and incidentally, whether they can make an effective presentation. The real goal of learning about criterion-referenced instruction is much wider and more significant than being able to give a talk. If we are teaching students about criterion-referenced instruction it is probably because we want students to know what distinguishes it from other kinds of teaching approaches, what its particular strengths and weaknesses might be, and in what contexts it is appropriately used. This knowledge might be assessed in a number of ways including writing about CRI, talking about it, and even designing a programme which uses CRI appropriately and presenting a convincing rationale for the design. In contrast, Mager's objective focuses students on the specific assessment requirements for this unit of study rather than the more significant, real-life applications of this knowledge. Narrowing the goal to the assessment requirements in this way seems more likely to discourage students from taking a deep approach.

Example 2
Given all available engineering data regarding a proposed product, be able to write a product profile. The profile must describe and define all of the commercial characteristics of the product when introduced to the market, including descriptions of at least three major product uses.

(p. 25)

As can be seen from both the examples above, the writing of objectives with this degree of specificity requires performances to be analysed into their component parts. Although Mager defined the criterion as the 'quality of performance' which would be deemed acceptable, in practice such criteria are often limited to those which could be measured quantitatively, as can be seen in both of these examples.

Mager's work on objectives formed the basis for much of the thinking on curriculum design that went on in the 1960s and 1970s. The term 'instructional objectives' which Mager used was dropped in favour of 'behavioural' or 'performance' objectives. Elliot Eisner maintains that these changes were not accidental. They represent 'an increased emphasis on the manifest behaviour of the student and on discrete forms of student activity' (Eisner, 1994: 120) and a move away from 'education', with its positive social connotations, to a kind of 'value-free' training. Certainly, they represent a highly technical approach to education which was dominant at that time – a belief that rigorous and logical analysis could remove the uncertainty from curriculum design and transform it from an art into a science; that courses could be designed which were 'teacher proof'; and that by following the prescription exactly the promise of the objectives would be delivered.

The more tightly the behaviourists tried to tie down the definition of objectives in their quest for clarity and specificity, the more strongly many educators reacted against them. The perceived shortcomings of behavioural objectives are many. Two of their most prominent critics were Elliott Eisner (1994) and Lawrence Stenhouse (1975). Their objections could be summarized as follows:

- To expect that all our educational aspirations will be measurable is to expect too little. Eisner points out that many of the performances that we require of students, such as the analysis and synthesis of information from different sources, aesthetic appreciation, creativity in expression and problem solving, are not measurable. Informed judgements can certainly be made about them, but success in these kinds of performances cannot be evaluated with the certainty which the behaviourist would like to see.
- Because it is easier to formulate specific, measurable objectives for relatively trivial kinds of learning, such as remembering information, more complex kinds of intellectual performances, which are harder to measure, will be underemphasized. Stenhouse acknowledges that in some fields, particularly the sciences and language learning, there is much information to be acquired. Even so, acquiring such information is usually subordinate to a larger goal of developing the knowledge structures used for thinking, problem solving and creative work in the discipline.
- Prespecification of objectives may prevent teachers from taking advantage of educational opportunities which occur unexpectedly in the classroom. With continuing pressure to include more and more information in the higher education curriculum, the possibility of interesting but non-essential side-trips may seem a thing of the past. However, Stenhouse points out that much broader objectives may still fulfil the function of keeping teachers and students on track while avoiding the narrowness of the behavioural model.

- The analytic approach used in developing behavioural objectives, which involves breaking down significant performances or tasks into their component knowledge and skills and then teaching each component separately, undermines the real goal of synthesis – being able to bring together different kinds of knowledge in order to think about new situations.
- Not all productive activities are goal directed. Particularly when we are concerned to develop qualities like creativity, insight, integrity and self esteem, there is a need to engage in activities which are not assessable but are purely exploratory and even playful.

What are we to learn from these arguments over the appropriateness of behavioural objectives that might help us in formulating objectives for our own teaching? The great contribution which the behaviourists made was to move the focus from the content of the curriculum and the activities planned by teachers to the students and their learning. Their influence forced teachers to think about what they wanted students to achieve, and to express this in ways which make it clear to the students themselves. I think it is clear from the research that has gone into the ways in which students conceive learning that students' expectations of what is required may be quite different from the kinds of changes in thinking and behaving that their teachers want. And ultimately it is what the students do, rather than what the teachers do, that determines whether those changes come about.

Alternatives to the behavioural model of objectives

In light of the criticisms above, a number of suggestions have been made about how objectives for learning might be expressed without the limitations of the behavioural model. Both Elliot Eisner and Lawrence Stenhouse put forward alternative models which are worth examination.

As his way around the limitations of behavioural objectives, Eisner suggested expanding the concept by adding two additional kinds of objectives. He retained what he called *instructional objectives*, which were essentially very much the same as behavioural objectives, for all of the knowledge and skills that could be adequately encompassed in this framework. And he suggested adding *problem-solving objectives* and *expressive objectives* or *expressive outcomes*. Problem-solving objectives would provide students with the opportunity to work on real problems – typically the kind of design project which students in engineering, architecture or design might be given. Expressive outcomes would encompass the learning acquired through creative and appreciative activities for which it would be difficult to specify results in advance.

I have reservations about Eisner's concept of problem-solving and expressive objectives (or outcomes), at least as the idea might be applied in higher education. (Eisner's critique of objectives was set in the context of primary and secondary schooling.) My concern is that the reason why teachers set problems is often far from clear to students.

Many disciplines in higher education regularly require students to engage in problem-solving activities. Sometimes (as Woods pointed out) what is presented as a 'problem' is really an 'exercise' – that is, there already exists a well-defined route to the solution and students must simply follow the formula (Woods, 1985: 20). Many teachers, however, spend considerable energy in finding real problems for students to work on. What is the point of these kinds of activities?

Sometimes teachers set problems which require students to use certain kinds of materials, certain media, certain technologies or research methods. The real object of the exercise is that students should become very familiar with the particular material or technology, its properties, strengths and weaknesses for different applications. Sometimes the aim is broader: teachers want students to develop problem-solving skills which will be transferable to new situations. These would include being able to analyse problems, to generate a range of possible solutions, to evaluate the alternatives systematically before choosing and implementing the best. In this case the emphasis is on the process. Students will need to evaluate the effectiveness of the process that they have used, and its potential for application in other contexts.

However, teachers often complain that students miss the point of problem-solving activities, that they are focused on getting an acceptable solution rather than looking at what they are learning in the process. Eisner's proposal that we set problem-solving objectives does not really lead students to a better understanding of why they are being asked to work on a particular problem. If the problem is a means to an end, as in education it usually is, it is better to clarify, for ourselves and our students, the kinds of knowledge or skill or understanding we are hoping to develop through working on the problem. In doing so, we are more likely to build in time and opportunity for students to analyse and reflect on what they have learned.

My reservations about Eisner's expressive objectives or outcomes are similar. Eisner is perfectly right in saying that there is a need in the curriculum for exploratory and expressive activities – activities which allow students to explore media, materials and forms, to develop responses and ideas. Expressive activities are there not as an end in themselves, but because teachers and students want to develop certain kinds of abilities: the ability to use language more powerfully, to generate more creative solutions to design problems, to conceive of problems in science in new ways. It is not necessary to create objectives for particular expressive activities, but it is important to be able to express the reason for including them in a particular unit of study.

The English curriculum writer Lawrence Stenhouse proposed what he called a process model, as a guide to educational decision making. Rather than proposing objectives in the form of prespecified behaviours which students must master, Stenhouse suggested that in planning courses of study we should focus on the process of learning rather than the product. Significant learning would emphasize the processes which students should master, such as the development and testing of hypotheses, use of first-hand sources as evidence, reflection on experience, as well as the ability to listen to others and discuss different positions with an open mind. Classes would be planned to allow students many opportunities to experience these processes while working with the kinds of content and problems which typified the particular discipline.

Stenhouse readily admitted that assessing the gains made in a process-based curriculum was far more difficult than assessment in a course designed around specific behavioural objectives. Because the process-based curriculum aimed to help students understand the deep structures of the discipline and the concerns of scholars, it would not allow teachers to 'teach for the test' nor students to pass their exams by last-minute cramming. Inevitably, assessment decisions would rely to a far greater extent on the professional judgement of individual teachers. And as Stenhouse also conceded, far from its being 'teacher proof', both the strength and the weakness of his process model was that it relied very heavily on the expertise of the individual teacher.

The open-ended nature of the outcomes of the process model does not sit comfortably with notions of certification of professional competence and accountability held in many professional schools. But his proposition that the curriculum in any discipline should focus on the processes by which knowledge is discovered and understanding deepened is potentially a very powerful one for higher education. It fits with a need that many higher education teachers would acknowledge: the need to prepare students to cope with continual changes in their field and with a glut of information. Unfortunately, because of Stenhouse's belief that curriculum change should not be imposed on teachers and students by 'experts', his process approach provides little practical guidance beyond the central idea.

A more recent attempt which tries to retain the clarity of purpose possible through setting clear objectives, while acknowledging the educational importance of non-behavioural goals, is that developed by Derek Rowntree. Rowntree proposed that teachers and course designers needed to set objectives in three distinct domains – life skill objectives, methodological objectives and content objectives.

Life skill objectives encompass those personal attributes often held to be the outcome of higher education, but which are not usually specified as goals at the level of individual units nor consciously developed through the teaching/learning strategy. In the current jargon they are usually referred to as generic or transferable skills. They might include attributes like being able to be autonomous and self-directing, questioning and critical, open-minded and flexible. An element of most of these life skill objectives is cognitive, involving thought processes. But there is also a significant affective element, involving the understanding and management of feelings and emotions. Rowntree recognized that while life skill objectives could be formulated without any reference to subject matter, in fact they could be developed only in dealing with a specific body of knowledge. Different subject areas may demand different kinds of critical thinking or problem solving – which provides a sound reason for translating what are often suggested as broad course goals into more specific objectives at the unit level.

Methodological and content objectives are more self-explanatory. Methodological objectives correspond with the technical skills and the inquiry processes of the discipline – the 'knowing how'. Rowntree acknowledges that they can often be difficult to distinguish from life skill objectives, as in many cases they may appear to be special applications of generally useful abilities. Content objectives represent the 'concepts, generalizations and principles that make up the substance and structure' of the subject area (Rowntree, 1981: 51).

This can be a generally useful model for helping teachers in higher education plan what they want to achieve with their students. But Rowntree also drew another distinction which is particularly useful in understanding the role of objectives in higher education. In relation to his life skill objectives, he pointed out that such objectives did not allow of mastery but implied 'infinite improvability'. This qualification is also true of many methodological and content objectives. It is quite common to have a working knowledge of a concept which is extended and deepened with experience; similarly application of a process or skill can be refined. This is particularly likely to be the case with the kinds of complex knowledge and skills which are the stuff of higher education. We may have to set a minimum level of understanding or performance for assessment purposes, but neither students nor teachers accept that this is all there is to know. Much of the criticism of objectives has been based on the assumption that the achievement of an objective must imply complete mastery and that only relatively trivial knowledge and skills are capable of being mastered in this way. Rowntree pointed out that while it is useful to both students and teachers to set objectives for learning in higher education, many different kinds of performances can provide evidence of different levels of acceptable achievement.

Recently, more emphasis has been placed on those areas of knowledge which Rowntree described using the terms 'life skills' and 'methodologies'. In the UK, groups like the Education for Capability movement and the Enterprise in Higher Education Initiative have criticized higher education for its focus on propositional knowledge and pushed for greater attention to process knowledge, experiential knowledge and 'know-how'. Allan (1996) suggests that higher education can encompass all of these, plus more traditional kinds of academic learning, under the term *learning outcomes*. Different kinds of learning outcomes will include subject-specific outcomes (which would cover the same ground as Rowntree's content and methodological objectives), personal transferable outcomes (such as the ability to communicate effectively, organize, gather information, use information technology, work independently and be numerate) and generic academic outcomes (including being able to make use of information, analyse, think critically and synthesize ideas and information (pp. 107–8).

This schema has the disadvantage of throwing together all of the discipline-based information, theories and concepts which a student must acquire, along with the technical skills and abilities needed to practise the discipline, while making a rather dubious distinction between generic academic and personal transferable skills. It is difficult to see, for instance, why 'communication', 'numeracy' and 'use of information technology' should be considered personal transferable skills rather than generic academic skills, and why 'gathering information' is a personal transferable skill while 'making use of information' is a generic academic one.

How helpful have all these developments been in helping teachers clarify what they are about and communicate their intentions to students? Tyler's ground-breaking work argued for the importance of placing students and their learning at the centre of educational design and planning. His suggestion that the curriculum ought to be planned to give students the best chance of achieving specific educational goals has had a profound impact on educational practice. The behaviourists who followed him demonstrated the gains which students could make when they were clear about what they were expected to achieve and the path which they needed to follow (see, for example, Cohen, 1987). Unfortunately, the gains made through greater specificity were often at the cost of ignoring more complex kinds of understanding and reduced ability to transfer learning to new contexts (Salomon and Globerson, 1987).

While acknowledging the importance of clear goals for educators, both Stenhouse and Eisner pushed for a broader conception of learning than could be contained within the behaviourist model. They pointed out that important educational goals such as developing creativity, flexibility, open-mindedness and understanding of complex ideas could not be achieved through the behaviourist formula of demonstrating particular behaviour, under defined conditions, to a specific performance standard.

Rowntree suggested that teachers and course designers might encompass the desired breadth of purpose by planning courses around content objectives, methodological objectives and life skill objectives, and by acknowledging that what was aimed for was more in the nature of continuous improvement than mastery.

Recent developments have continued to emphasize the need to develop and acknowledge a wider range of learning and ability, including propositional knowledge, personal experiential learning, technical and intellectual skills. It is recognized that students might present evidence of their achievement through many different kinds of performances, which although assessable against a set of criteria, will not meet a single specified standard of performance as the behaviourist model required (Allan, 1996; Biggs, 1996).

Another way of thinking about learning goals

In trying to make sense of the different prescriptions for defining educational purposes, a conceptual framework which I have found particularly useful is that developed by Lovat and Smith (1995), based on the work of Jurgen Habermas. Habermas, in one of his earlier works (1972), proposed that people seek knowledge in response to different interests. The three important interests which he identifies are:

- the interest in controlling the world in which we live;
- the interest in communicating with others and understanding different points of view;
- the interest in freedom and autonomy.

The drive to satisfy these interests produces different kinds of knowledge, each with implications for teaching and assessment.

Setting objectives for empirical, technical and conventional knowledge

The kind of knowledge that enables us to control and manipulate our environment is empirical or technical knowledge. Empirical knowledge is that which is obtained through observation and experimentation – knowing, for example, the temperature at which water will boil. Conventional knowledge – knowledge of the conventions of language, vocabulary, rules of operation– also falls into this category of knowledge, which contributes to control. Knowledge about temperature scales is one example; knowing the specialist vocabulary of a discipline or particular formulae are others. Also included in this category are many techniques and skills – those procedures where there is a well-established and agreed method of operation.

In the area of empirical, technical and conventional knowledge most teachers want their students to attain mastery. There is very little room for error and much of this knowledge is crucial to successful performance. This kind of knowledge may form a small or large part of the knowledge that the student is expected to acquire, depending on the discipline. In some disciplines the amount of conventional knowledge to be acquired is very large – I have a biologist colleague who tells me that the amount of vocabulary that a first-year biology student must master is greater than that of a first-year French student. First-year students are expected to acquire and use this vocabulary with pretty much 100 per cent accuracy.

Empirical, technical or conventional knowledge, however, never constitutes the whole of a discipline. Where it plays a significant part, as it does in much of the sciences and in language learning, teachers will want to formulate learning objectives for it and those objectives will tend to look much like classic behavioural objectives. They will specify exactly what the students must be able to do – apply the formulae, use specified terms correctly, carry out the procedure accurately – and they will specify a standard of performance, usually one which allows for few errors. In those disciplines where empirical, technical or conventional knowledge plays a less important role, teachers may not make it the focus of specific objectives, but they will still expect students to have mastered the technical or conventional knowledge which is necessary. Thus a higher education syllabus in English literature will not normally contain learning objectives about terminology, but students will still be expected to use technical terms like 'sonnet', 'ballad' and 'lyric' correctly.

The following examples of learning objectives from a unit on linguistics and another on anatomy are typical of objectives for this kind of knowledge. The objectives cited here are not the only learning objectives for these courses.

Examples of learning objectives for technical and conventional knowledge from a linguistics course

- use the International Phonetic Alphabet to do simple transcriptions of simple English words;
- differentiate between phonetics and phonology;
- demonstrate understanding of phonological notation by writing a plain English version of the technical notations;
- write phonological rules of English using technical notation;
- use terminology related to morphemic analysis appropriately;
- analyse morphological units of English words;
- identify the different types of morphemes;
- analyse morphological units of a simple language data base.

(Clampitt, 1998)

Examples of objectives from a unit on the anatomy of the face and cranial contents

Objectives: At the completion of this laboratory assignment, you should be able to perform the following in a written or lab exam or in a laboratory demonstration:

- Identify the bones of the cranium and face. Indicate the foramina in each bone.
- Follow the course of the major sensory and motor nerves and their branches to the face and scalp. Indicate the source (cranial) of each and predict the deficit which would to be expected to follow injury to each.
- Trace the flow of blood, arterial and venous, of the face and scalp. Indicate the major supply and drainage of this vascular network and identify known vascular interconnections.
- Trace the flow of blood into and out of the cranial cavity. Indicate known vascular interconnections. Follow the flow of blood through the cerebral arterial circle indicating the region of brain supplied by each major branch and known vascular interconnections.
- Identify the three layers of meninges surrounding the brain and spinal cord and the folds of dura mater which subdivide the cranium.
- Identify the cranial nerves that pass through the cavernous sinus and indicate their relationship within the sinus.

(School of Medicine: Emory University, 1998)

Learning goals and interpretive understanding

Habermas's second area of cognitive interest relates to the interest that humans have in understanding – in finding meaning, in understanding different viewpoints and in communicating interpretations. Such knowledge might be called 'communicative' or 'interpretive' knowledge. It is usually established through the negotiation of meaning in dialogue or group discussion. As an example, if we want students to understand the reasons for the collapse of the Soviet Union, we are not talking about an area of knowledge that can be empirically tested. Students can only consider a range of views, come to some tentative conclusions, and test those ideas in conversation or by putting them into writing. Teachers and other students may attempt to influence those understandings by suggesting other interpretations of the evidence. In the attempt to understand the collapse of the Soviet Union there are elements of conventional knowledge – the names of key players, dates of specific events – that students need to use correctly. Ultimately, the understanding that each student comes to will be individual, and the only way that teachers can assess exactly what it is that students understand and believe to be true will be to ask them to put their knowledge into their own words in some kind of oral or written account.

When we set objectives for this kind of learning we are essentially hoping that students will learn a process, a methodology, a way of thinking and arguing. We readily acknowledge that students may come to different understandings about events in the Soviet Union. What we hope is that they have learned where and how to find information, how to evaluate their sources, to consider different points of view with an open mind, to argue logically, drawing only those conclusions which are warranted from the evidence. We can write objectives for these kinds of learning in the sense that we can identify the processes that we wish students to learn and to use. We can also identify the kinds of evidence that students might present that would satisfy us that they had been more or less successful.

This exercise is valuable to us as teachers because it helps us to clarify our thinking. It is even more valuable to students because it highlights goals for learning that may not be otherwise apparent to them, especially if their conception of learning is currently limited to acquiring more information and useable skills.

The extent to which students meet such process objectives can be assessed against sets of criteria, but such assessment will always be subject to the judgement of the assessor(s). Learning objectives about generating understanding, and the processes or methodologies for doing so, can never be subject to a single standard of performance. Neither would we want to define strictly the conditions under which students must perform, precisely because we want them to make these processes part of their habitual way of operating and to begin to use them under a wide range of conditions.

The following examples of learning objectives from units on literature and statistics emphasize understanding as the goal. The scope and depth of understanding which students achieve can be assessed in a wide range of tasks. But it is important to note that those assessment tasks will need to be accompanied by clear criteria because these learning objectives do not spell out the kinds of performances which will be required.

Example of learning objectives from a unit on 'The Storyteller's Art'

- To strengthen your literary vocabulary which will enable you to analyse and to read, write and speak about fiction more effectively.
- To understand and articulate how fiction can serve as a form of communication between writer and reader.
- To respond to literature as an aesthetic organization of human experience and to understand how aesthetic organization relates to response.
- To recognize the relationship between the historical context in which fiction is written and the development of the short story form.

(Alverno College Faculty, 1994: 128)

Examples of objectives from a unit on 'Economic Reasoning Using Statistics'

The student will:

- Understand basic statistical reasoning. Statistical methods provide powerful analytic tools for almost every human enterprise that can state its observations in numbers. A critical understanding of statistics – its limitations as well as its potentials – is almost as essential for living as is the ability to read and write
- Gain access to existing knowledge by:
  - locating published research in economics and statistics and related fields
  - locating information on particular topics and issues in economics
  - searching out economic data as well as information about the meaning of the data and how they are derived
- Display command of existing knowledge by:
  - summarizing the principal ideas of an eminent living economist
  - summarizing a current controversy in the economics literature
  - stating succinctly the dimensions of a current economic policy issue
  - explaining key economic and statistical concepts and describing how they can be used
- Display ability to draw out existing knowledge by:
  - writing a precise summary of a published journal article
  - reading and interpreting a quantitative analysis, including regression results, reported in an economics journal article
  - showing what economic and statistical concepts and principles are used in economic analyses published in articles from daily newspapers and weekly news magazines

- Learn by doing, i.e., manipulate real data using Minitab (a statistical computing program) and explicate a number of economic controversies that are currently in the news, in a team setting.

(Chizmar, 1998)

Learning goals for development of autonomy and social responsibility

Habermas's third area of cognitive interest relates to that knowledge which results from individual experience. Such knowledge, which Habermas calls 'self-reflective', encompasses personal responses to works of art, literature and music, insights gained through reflection, meditation or challenging experiences, understandings which derive from experiences as a member of a particular ethnic or cultural group. It aligns with Marton's sixth and highest conception of learning – learning conceived as 'changing and developing as a person' (Marton *et al.*, 1993). Such knowledge is often devalued in academia, because it is regarded as too personal and individual to have any predictive power. But its role in pushing out the boundaries of academic knowledge has often been overlooked. The feeling that the dominant theory cannot explain one's own experience can be the starting point for new explorations. The literary critic bell hooks described just such a process:

> Years ago I was thankful to discover the phrase 'the authority of experience' in feminist writing because it gave me a name for what I brought to feminist classrooms that I thought was not present but believed was valuable. As an undergraduate in feminist classrooms where woman's experience was universalized, I knew from my experience as a black female that black women's reality was being excluded. I spoke from that knowledge. There was no body of theory to invoke that would substantiate this truth claim. No one really wanted to hear about the deconstruction of woman as a category of analysis then. Insisting on the value of my experience was crucial to gaining a hearing. Certainly the need to understand my experience motivated me as an undergraduate to write *Ain't I a woman: Black women and feminism*.

(hooks, 1994: 89)

In Habermas's view, the drive to develop self-reflective knowledge is linked to the human desire for freedom – the need to investigate our own experiences and to understand the social, political and cultural forces which have shaped our responses, so that ultimately we may make more considered choices about the ways in which we choose to be and act in the world. One of the tests of self-reflective knowledge is that it should produce a commitment to action. The resultant actions might range from founding a new political movement to being able to overcome one's tendency to procrastinate.

If as teachers we want our students to engage in this kind of learning within the subjects that we teach and to become better at self-reflective knowing, what kinds of learning objectives can we set for them? How is progress measured? What constitutes satisfactory performance? Does it make sense to ask such questions about this kind of learning?

In higher education, learning goals for self-reflective learning are most often specified in courses which prepare students for professions which involve a high degree of human interaction. The following statement from a unit on paediatric practice for occupational therapists attempts to show students the importance of this kind of learning in the professional context:

> Students are encouraged to identify their own values, attitudes and beliefs underlying their reactions (to clinical experiences), and to reflect further about where these came from, how valid these past engendering situations were to current therapeutic situations, and how those values, beliefs and attitudes might affect their work as a professional therapist and their inter-actions with clients, families, other staff and administrators.
>
> (Westhorp, 1994)

The students' progress toward this learning goal is assessed through a journal which documents their reactions to their clients and their clients' families and to the issues which arise in their own development as therapists.

It is far more unusual to find goals for self-reflective learning in subjects like mathematics. However, the learning objectives below were created by a lecturer who wanted his students, destined to be mathematics teachers, to examine the experience of *learning* mathematics. The aims and objectives of his unit on transformation geometry encompass objectives for all three of the categories of knowledge which we have been discussing:

Aims and objectives: transformation geometry
The discipline of mathematics is huge and there is much choice in the content that could be included in your degree programme. For this reason it should be made clear that the aim of this course is not just to teach you transformation geometry, as any one of a number of content areas could rightfully be in your programme. Rather, the aim of this course is to get you to think about mathematical processes and your own learning of these as you go about learning the content of transformation geometry.

With this aim in mind, the objectives for this course are listed below. This list is given as a set of increasingly cognitively complex 'performances' for the student:

1. • Be able to describe, and give examples of, the various transformations of the plane geometry covered in this course
   • Be able to *use* the vocabulary of transformation geometry correctly
   • Be able to *apply* the algorithms and methods of transformation geometry to problems that are similar to those discussed in class
2. • Be able to *solve* problems from plane transformation geometry that have not been discussed before
   • Be able to *reflect* on what they have learnt as a result of doing some activity or task

3. • Be *aware* of, and actively *use*, a mathematical approach in the processes of inquiry. That is, not only use strategic approaches to problem solving but also to *generate* and *explore* questions that arise to them as they are working through problems and ideas
   • Be able to *demonstrate* a coherent overview of plane transformation geometry
4. • Be able to *compare and contrast* the approach of transformation geometry with other approaches to geometry that they have seen
   • Be able to *relate* the development and/or the study of transformation geometry to the development/study of other areas of mathematics. For example, by looking for commonalities in things like the kinds of problems tackled, the way concepts have grown, the way proofs are done, and so on
   • Be able to *generate, modify* or *evaluate* their own views on what it means to learn mathematics as a result of their experiences in this course.

(Roberts, 1997)

In general then, goals for self-reflective learning will usually require students to articulate a personal position on some aspect of their course, be able to identify the views and experiences which shaped their current thinking and show that they understand the impact that their beliefs will have on their own practice. The evidence that an assessor might ask for to demonstrate progress in this kind of learning is implicit in the goal statement. It usually involves an examination of one's position, either over a period of time (as in a journal) or at a certain point, such as a reflective essay at the end of a unit. The journal or paper serves as both the learning activity and the evidence of progress.

As one example, the designers and teachers of a unit entitled 'Urban Society and Sociology' in a degree course for urban and regional planners have the goal that students come to 'appreciate the extent to which their own backgrounds (predominantly middle class, suburban and white) are likely to influence the way they approach their role and the decisions they make' (Nightingale *et al.*, 1996: 99). As part of the assessment for the unit and as evidence that they have become able to do this, students must write a paper in which they identify specific incidents from their own life which were significant in forming and confirming their values and sense of identity. They must be able to evaluate how their particular collection of characteristics, values and opinions is likely to be an advantage or a disadvantage in a planning career. These requirements then become the learning objectives for the subject as well as the requirements for assessment.

The teachers of this unit point out that the content of the subject addresses concepts of socialization, class, power, and relationships between the professions and the structure of society which could be found in many sociology courses, but the students must apply their understanding of these topics to themselves as potential agents of community influence and control. Because such understanding is so individual it cannot be assessed in any 'objective' way.

Students can only construct their own accounts of the current state of their understanding, how that understanding has developed and the factors which support or challenge their current beliefs. It is quite possible that students will not be able to adequately express all that they know, and so teachers may underestimate their achievements. On the other hand, the highly individual nature of the responses makes cheating or guessing virtually impossible, so overestimation of students' knowledge is not the danger that it is with other forms of assessment.

The importance of the different categories of knowledge in different disciplines

It is important to recognize that these three kinds of knowledge occur in all disciplines, although the emphasis given to each certainly changes from discipline to discipline. It is a common misconception that the sciences are confined to technical or conventional knowledge and the humanities are exclusively concerned with negotiating meaning. Much of mathematics involves technical and conventional knowledge but if, for instance, we require students to understand how a mathematical model represents a system or process, we are asking for a different kind of understanding. If we want mathematicians to be able to model complex situations, such as the workings of the national economy, then their awareness of their own beliefs and values may be critical, as they choose which elements or variables in the situation are significant enough to warrant inclusion in the model and which may be ignored.

Another illustration of how all three kinds of knowledge might be related within a discipline could be found in medicine, where trainee doctors might learn how to prescribe drugs safely and effectively; try to understand why some patients will abuse drugs; and consider their own personal areas of compulsive behaviour, the needs that they serve, why they are so difficult to change and why some addictions are socially accepted while others are not. It could be argued that doctors need to develop understanding in all of these areas if they are to be able to help patients with problems of addiction. Whether or not all three kinds of knowledge will be found in the curriculum will largely depend on the beliefs and ideologies of its designers and teachers.

Characteristics of effective learning goals and objectives

To sum up: useful learning objectives assist course designers in deciding what needs to be learned and assessed. Equally, they make clear to students the purpose of the unit and what they need to do in order to be successful. Where flexibility is possible, they provide the framework within which students and teachers can negotiate agreement on acceptable learning outcomes. Useful learning goals and objectives have the following characteristics:

- *Learning objectives need to represent real goals.* Too often learning objectives are formulated for relatively trivial outcomes, like being able to list the components of something or state the definition or the law. These are usually assessment tasks in the guise of objectives. They are not real goals of learning. We learn laws and principles and components so that we can investigate certain kinds of situations and predict outcomes. Memorizing elements, principles or rules is just one step on the way to a real goal of being able to interpret or predict or act more effectively in the world we inhabit. Trivial learning objectives will not motivate anyone – as Ramsden points out, they are more likely to encourage surface learning than real understanding (Ramsden, 1992). A significant learning objective tells students why they are taking this subject or module – what it is that they should be able to do differently or better as a result of this facet of their education.

- *Learning objectives must place academic skills or personal learning in the context of the particular subject matter in hand.* While technical or conventional knowledge is inevitably tied to particular subject matter, there is a tendency to express broad goals relating to other kinds of knowledge without indicating to students how they might achieve such goals in this particular unit of study. It will be necessary to clarify what characterizes critical thinking in accounting, or what kinds of communication skills engineers require.

- *Learning objectives should include* (either within the objective or in an associated set of assessment criteria) *a description of the kind of performances by which achievement will be judged.* Often the best way to be specific about how students must meet the learning objectives in a subject is by setting out the assessment tasks and the criteria by which these will be judged. The behaviourists were right about one thing – we can only make judgements about what students know on the basis of what they say or do. Of necessity, we assess behaviours or performances, often requiring a particular performance (such as writing as essay) not for its own sake but in order to get some evidence of the extent of the student's understanding. What is often not clear to students (and sometimes teachers also) is how or whether these behaviours – such as essay writing – relate to the goals of the subject. Either through the learning objectives or associated assessment criteria we can make clear to students whether they are being asked to undertake a particular task for its own sake (because it represents an intrinsically useful skill), or as a vehicle to provide evidence of the particular stage of understanding that they have reached. If we ask students to give a presentation, write a paper or produce a video, is it important that they learn about public speaking or video production or is it the content that matters?

- *Learning objectives should allow for either mastery or progress, depending on the nature of the learning.* As I have tried to make clear, in the area of technical and conventional knowledge we generally want students to achieve mastery. We want them to use the vocabulary of the discipline accurately, to carry out technical skills with care and precision. In knowledge concerned with generating understanding, negotiating meaning, becoming critical, re-creating ourselves, we are looking for progress. In these areas where 'infinite improvability' is the norm, what we are most likely to want from students is evidence that they are becoming more and more experienced in the *processes* which lead to greater depth of understanding and creativity.

- Lastly, *learning objectives should be memorable and limited in number*. Learning objectives for any unit of study need to be few enough and significant enough for teachers and students to keep them in mind. Only in this way can they guide planning and preparation for learning and teaching. And only if we can limit our learning objectives will there be the time in the curriculum for students to undertake the kinds of exploratory and expressive activities which deepen understanding and creativity.

8

Choosing Teaching Strategies

What is a teaching strategy?

A teaching strategy is not just about the activities of teachers, although that will be one component. It is actually a plan for someone else's learning, and it encompasses the presentations which the teacher might make, the exercises and activities designed for students, materials which will be supplied or suggested for students to work with, and ways in which evidence of their growing understanding and capability will be collected. A particular teaching strategy may not include the kind of activity that we commonly think of as teaching – a teacher formally addressing a group of students. The presentation of new information or new viewpoints may come via other media such as print, computer-based text and images, video or film. A teaching strategy, then, means all of the activities and resources that a teacher plans in order to enable students to learn.

In planning the teaching strategy a number of factors have to be taken into consideration. Obviously we need to focus primarily on what we want students to achieve, but we will also need to consider our students' own goals and whether their conception of achievement is likely to differ. What we know about how people learn will be an important factor in choosing learning activities, but the need to fit within an institutional, political and social context will also affect our choice.

Many studies have been carried out on the uses and effectiveness of individual teaching strategies, but they offer only limited guidance when it comes to choosing the strategy which we hope will achieve a specific outcome. In his work on students' choice of learning strategy, Biggs identified many factors other than their approach to learning which affected the achievement of learning outcomes. These factors include the student's prior knowledge, IQ, personality, background and motivation, as well as aspects of the educational context such as the nature of the subject, the course structure, the teaching strategy, the time available for the learning task and the nature of the assessment (Biggs, 1987).

Given that all of these factors will affect the eventual learning outcome to some degree, it is not possible to say with confidence that a certain strategy is the best choice for achieving a specific learning objective. Evaluative studies are usually careful to make the proviso that the strategy which worked for this group of students on this particular concept or skill, in this particular context, may not necessarily translate so effectively to other students, other topics, other contexts. Such studies can suggest strategies which would seem to have a better chance of success, but they cannot prescribe. Choosing a strategy for teaching a particular topic to a particular group of students is an art rather than a science. But telling new course designers that planning teaching strategies is an art which will be refined and developed through long experience is not especially helpful. If teaching is an activity too complex to be subject to a set of rules, what kinds of understandings or principles can guide our actions?

A very simple model of learning

Some years ago I was involved in designing workshops for part-time teachers in technical and vocational education. These teachers had little or no background in education, and the three-day workshops which we designed for them would probably be all the preparation for teaching that they would ever receive. Because most of them worked full time at other jobs they had little time for planning their teaching. To provide some kind of framework which would enable them to plan classes and choose learning activities in minimum time but still in a rational and strategic way, my colleagues and I developed a simple model of the learning process which could be used to guide the choice of activities (Hughes *et al.*, 1992).

This model proved very useful in working with this particular group of teachers and I think it can also be useful for many university teachers.

With this model (which I have modified slightly here), the experience of learning something, whether it is a concept, principle or skill, is set out in five stages through which each learner must progress. The stages are as follows:

1. Encounter or be introduced to the idea, concept, principle or skill.
2. Get to know more about it.
3. Try it out for oneself.
4. Get feedback.
5. Reflect, adjust and try again.

The later four stages can be repeated as many times as necessary until both learner and teacher feel confident that the student can take the new knowledge and use it to interpret, control or predict in different and 'real' situations.

Let's apply the model to an example of informal learning to see how it might work:

Coming to work on the bus, I read the daily paper. My eye is caught by a headline and a photograph. (I am introduced to the topic.) I read on. (I'm getting to know more about it.) I arrive at work and tell my colleagues

Encounter or be
introduced to the idea

Get to know more
about it

Try it out

Get feedback

Reflect and adjust

Figure 8.1   A simple model of the learning process

about what I just read. (I'm trying it out.) We discuss some of the issues involved, some of which are new to me. (I'm getting feedback, getting to know the topic better, trying it out again.) I relate the content of the article to a friend I see at lunchtime, confident of my grasp of its content, its ramifications and of my attitudes to it, and we discuss the issues. (I've refined and adjusted my earliest impressions and now I'm trying it out again and getting more feedback.)

Now let's explore these stages a little further.

The *introductory* stage may occur in the classroom, but in many cases students will have met the idea earlier in their lives. If you believe that it is likely that students have met the idea before, then in the classroom the introductory stage will consist of getting students to recall what they already know (or think they know) and checking for misconceptions. Sometimes the impact of a new concept is to bring tacit knowledge to light and to give students a different way to view previous experiences. Sometimes the best way to understand a new concept is by an analogy with something that students are familiar with. It is important to help students make these connections with what they already know, because to ignore what they have already learned is asking for trouble. Learning which derives from personal experience is very powerful. If that personal learning appears to contradict or undermine what they are hearing in the classroom, students are more likely to cling to their previous conceptions unless they are pushed to confront inconsistencies (Ramsden, 1988; Butler, 1996).

With this proviso about the need to take account of previous knowledge, there are many options available for introducing new knowledge, concepts or skills. You can simply tell students; you may be able to demonstrate; you might present an example, perhaps on video; or you might give them something to read in which the idea is introduced. Sometimes the best way for students to be introduced to the concept or the principle is to discover it for themselves (often called *discovery learning*). In this case the introduction might consist of a problem to think about, a case study to consider, an exercise to attempt, a game or simulation to experience.

The second stage (*getting to know more*) is an exploratory stage where learners acquire more information and begin to sort out for themselves the meaning of what they are hearing, seeing and feeling. Although the second stage often involves telling students more about the topic or getting them to read more about it, it should not be a passive experience for learners. They need to be able to ask questions to check their understanding and to be actively involved in exploring the internal detail of the topic and its links to their existing knowledge, skills and attitudes. This is essentially an investigative, cognitive processing step in which learners begin to make the content of the topic (be it knowledge, skill or attitude) meaningful and comprehensible. They begin to make it 'their own'.

If the introduction to the topic has been through some form of discovery learning, this second stage is particularly important. The initial experience with the problem, the case study or the game is often confusing and frustrating because learners do not yet have enough knowledge or experience to make significant progress. In the second stage of 'getting to know more' they begin to analyse their experience, identify what they have learned from the experience and, more importantly, what they still need to learn.

By the third stage (*trying out*), students begin to have some grasp of the topic and they can begin to try and use their new knowledge. This might involve attempting an exercise or trying a skill for themselves. Or it might mean answering a teacher's questions, finding new examples of a concept or giving their interpretation to other students in a tutorial group. One of the significant aspects of the 'trying it out' stage is that it frequently identifies for students the gaps in their knowledge. Before they receive any feedback from others, the experience of attempting the desired performance or trying to put the ideas into their own words will often make it painfully obvious which aspects are not yet under their control.

Feedback – the fourth stage – most commonly comes from the teacher or other students in the form of direct comment on one's performance. Such feedback varies considerably in its usefulness. The degree to which it facilitates further learning depends on whether mistakes and misunderstandings are clearly identified and whether any suggestions are provided as to how performance might improve. Less confronting (and often more helpful) feedback can often be obtained by comparing one's work with that of a skilled or expert performer. This might be as simple as checking one's maths exercise against the worked example in the textbook, looking at the solutions other students have found to a design problem, or reading examples of good student papers. This method of providing feedback is very common in some disciplines, where regular displays of student work may be accompanied by teachers or panels of experts explaining the criteria they use in judging and how these are applied. In other disciplines this method is almost never used, so that students may go through a whole degree programme without ever reading another student's paper or seeing how an expert might address their particular question.

Yet another form of feedback which students can be made aware of is that which is intrinsic to the situation. Sometimes this type of feedback is unavoidable, as when the student's computer program crashes because the bugs have not yet been eliminated. More often, students need to be prompted to look for and interpret feedback such as the reactions of patients, clients or colleagues, the responses of equipment or materials. Experts tend to rely heavily on intrinsic feedback in managing complex tasks, but this knowledge is often tacit and not communicated to students.

The stage of *reflecting on the experience* involves taking account of the feedback and deciding how one's performance needs to be adapted on the next occasion. Sometimes the effect of reflecting on the experience is to send students back to the stage of 'getting to know more'. They may realize that they are not ready for another attempt at trying out the knowledge that they have acquired thus far, and that they need to go back and do more research, reading or observation.

The reflection stage is usually a private one, although sometimes teachers may encourage students to reflect aloud on their experiences in pairs or small groups as a way of broadening their experience and helping them to clarify and focus their reflection and understanding. Other ways of making this stage more explicit are to ask students to keep journals throughout the unit of study or the work placement, or to ask students to write self-evaluations following a major piece of work. An argument can be made for including formal structured reflection activities when learning is complex – when students must integrate many different factors – and when critical, self-reflective knowledge is required, as when we want students to monitor and evaluate the quality of their own thinking and learning.

What happens when learners fail to complete all of the stages of the model? That is, when they don't get the opportunity to try out what they have learned, or they get no feedback, or they never reflect on how successful or unsuccessful they have been? We have probably all had many experiences of listening to a lecture which introduced us to a new topic and gave us some information about it, but did not go any further. Perhaps there was no time for questions, or we were too intimidated to ask, and there was no necessity to use the material in our work. The information which was provided in that lecture has almost certainly been lost to us, unless we have managed to engineer for ourselves occasions when we could process the information further, try it out in some way and get feedback on our level of understanding.

Think about some of the significant concepts, principles or skills that you have learned through formal education. Can you identify the five stages in your own experience of learning? Did the formal learning activities in your course provide opportunities for you to work through all of the stages or did you organize learning activities (such as a study group or informal discussions with friends) in order to learn effectively?

Faced with poor course design and poor teaching, some students can be very resourceful in organizing opportunities to try out their understanding and get feedback. Here a mature undergraduate student talks about her attempts to learn in a unit on 'Technological Change and Economic Development':

> There was no structure to the course and no structure to the lectures. I just had to go to the library, use the Internet, use the databases on the

CD-ROM. I felt very much as though I was constructing the course for myself, in my head. I would construct papers for myself, hand them in to the lecturer and wait to get feedback to know whether I had done it wrong or right. But we didn't really get any feedback, so I just plodded on. I would get very frustrated with this because I really wanted to understand. It upset me that I didn't understand what I was doing. I would get upset because there was no structure and we weren't getting any feedback. I went as far as tracking down and contacting one author [of one of the set texts] via the Internet so that I could get a better grasp of some information that he presented in the book that we were asked to comment on in a paper. I felt more satisfied, having corresponded with the author about that, that I was on the right track, I felt more like I knew what I was doing.

While we might admire this level of resourcefulness, we should not underestimate the frustration engendered, which is more likely to drive less mature and less determined students to give up the search for understanding.

The traditional methods used in university teaching are quite capable of supporting all of the stages of learning. Lectures and readings are used to introduce students to new material and provide them with significant amounts of information and a range of different views (*being introduced* and *getting to know more*). Laboratory work, tutorials, small-group work and assignments can give students the opportunity to try out their new knowledge, get feedback, reflect and try again.

However, frequently:

- The balance is wrong, with too much emphasis on the first two stages. It is common to have twice as much time scheduled for lectures as for practical or group work, and small-group sessions may be reduced further under budgetary pressure.
- There is little attempt in the first two stages to find out what students already know or to uncover their misconceptions.
- The activities don't occur in the best sequence. Lectures, tutorials and practical work may be out of sync so that the exercises and discussion topics are not related to the lecture material.
- Teachers lack the skills in planning and facilitating group work which would enable them to get students to participate: faced with a lack of student participation, small-group sessions are converted into mini-lectures.
- Opportunities for feedback and quality of feedback are particularly inadequate, owing to overcrowded classes and overloaded marking schedules.

Examples of the learning model applied to university programmes

There are, however, many examples of well-designed and well-executed programmes where the selection and sequence of learning activities supports all of the stages of learning. Below are four examples of different units of study, drawn from current practice.

Learning about classification schemes in psychology

The aim of this section of the course is to introduce students to classification schedules for mental illness. Through their experiences in class, students should understand how the schedules are used and be able to evaluate how adequate and useful they are.

Encounter / Get to know more
The lecturer introduces the topic by asking students what they know about classification schemes. The most commonly used schedule is introduced and explained with many examples. Further reading is provided in handouts.

Try it out
Within the tutorial group of around 20 people, students work in groups of three or four, trying to apply the classification schedule to the people depicted in brief case studies.

Get feedback
Feedback is provided by other members of the small group. In the plenary session which follows, each group presents its conclusions for consideration and discussion. Further feedback is provided by class members and by the teacher.

Try it out
Assigned to new groups of three or four, students compare their experiences of using the schedule and the difficulties they experienced.

Get feedback / Reflect, adjust
Again, feedback is provided by small group members and ultimately by the whole group as it comes together to finalize its conclusions about when and how the schedule might be used appropriately.

Try again
A second chance to try out some of the course material is provided through the written assignments.

Get feedback
Written assignments are initially evaluated by the tutor and two peers, with formative comments only.

Reflect, adjust and try again
Students reassess their own work, taking into account the feedback provided. A final version of the assignment is produced by each student and given a mark by the teacher.

Learning clinical skills in nursing

This final clinical placement in the nursing programme provides an opportunity for the student to specialize in an area of interest or to take advantage of unique learning opportunities which a placement might offer. Learning objectives for each student are therefore negotiated in individual learning contracts.

Encounter or be introduced
The nursing student meets with her academic supervisor and clinical supervisor to discuss the learning possibilities for the placement. The clinical supervisor highlights the particular opportunities for learning which the placement can offer. A number of learning objectives are agreed, together with assessment requirements.

Get to know more
During the placement the student discusses the area(s) of practice covered by the learning objectives with the clinical supervisor and other specialist staff. She observes expert practitioners and researches the literature on the topic.

Try it out
The student nurse works with patients and other staff under supervision, practising the skills agreed in the learning contract.

Get feedback
She receives feedback from patients, the clinical supervisor and other members of the clinical team. Some feedback is informal, but regular meetings are scheduled with the clinical supervisor, at which written feedback on progress against the learning objectives is provided.

Reflect, adjust and try again
The student keeps a journal of her experiences, including reflection on and analysis of her own performance. This journal is submitted to her academic supervisor at intervals for further feedback.

Self-paced learning of laboratory skills in physics

This unit requires students to master basic laboratory skills which they will need throughout their physics course, such as the use of common measuring equipment, and graphical presentation of results.

Be introduced
First-year students are given an introductory class for this strand of the course in which they are given an overview of the skills that they need to master.

Get to know more
Each student is provided with a manual providing more information and setting out exercises designed to develop the requisite skills.

Try it out
Students work through the exercises in the laboratory at their own pace until they feel that they have mastered the requisite skill.

Get feedback
Demonstrators are on call to provide assistance. When the student feels that he has mastered a particular skill, he can schedule a test with the demonstrator. Students are encouraged not to schedule a formal assessment until they have tested themselves against the checklists and criteria provided.

Reflect, adjust and try again
The demonstrator will indicate any areas where performance is inadequate. The student can schedule a re-test when ready. Once a satisfactory standard is reached, students proceed to learn the next skill.

Learning about paediatric nutrition through a problem-based course in medicine

This problem, designed for the first year of the medical course, is intended to introduce students to problems of growth retardation and malnutrition. Having worked through this problem, students should be able to identify growth retardation problems, know the nutritional requirements for normal growth and how the body extracts nutrients from the diet, and they should have given some consideration to the question of how adequate nutrition can be achieved for the disadvantaged.

Encounter
First small-group session: the student group views a video of 3-year-olds at play and identifies one child as small for its age. The group formulates the possible problem as apparent growth retardation, hypothesizes possible causes and identifies learning issues.

Get to know more
Individual study: the student group disperses to research identified learning issues from recommended texts, handouts and video material.

Try it out / Get feedback
Second small-group session: the students present and compare their findings, narrow down the hypotheses and settle on a diagnosis. Continuous feedback on reasoning is provided by group members and the tutor.

Encounter (a new aspect of the problem)
Second small-group session continues: the students identify a new problem: what is the appropriate treatment and management for this case? Learning issues are identified.

Get to know more
Students attend lectures and laboratory sessions on biochemistry and anatomy and review recommended text and video materials.

Try it out
Students meet without the tutor to prepare a patient management plan.

Get feedback / Reflect, adjust and try again
Third small-group session: the tutor provides feedback on the patient management plan. The whole case is reviewed, leading to identification of new problems and learning issues relating to community health education and malnutrition.

Differences in the nature of learning activities according to the stage of the learning model for which they are used

One of the implications of this model is that the same kind of activity can be used for different stages of learning, but will be used in quite different ways that will alter the character of the activity. Let's look at role play as an example.

A role play might be used in the first stage to introduce students to the topic for study. Let's say that the topic is to do with discrimination and inequality in society. Students may be introduced to the experience of discriminating or being discriminated against by taking part in a role play in which each student is given a different character and a scenario to act out. Once the role play is over, students will be encouraged to reflect on their experience and the feelings it engendered. The teacher may then help them to see this experience in a wider context and to theorize about it (students are now moving into the second stage – *getting to know more*). Later in their studies they will try out what they have learned in other assignments or exercises.

This kind of role play can be especially tricky to manage because of the emotions it may arouse, and the links that students may make to difficult personal experiences. On the other hand it can be a powerful form of learning, particularly for those students who have no real-life experience of the issues.

Role play might also be used in the second stage of learning, to help students extend their understanding of a topic to which they have already been introduced. Let's imagine that the teacher introduces students to a particular aspect of working with clients or patients by talking about it. Then, as part of the 'getting to know more' stage, she may demonstrate what she is talking about by role-playing with a student. The rest of the class watches. This use of role play has few of the difficulties associated with the first use. A volunteer can usually be found to take part in the demonstration, providing that there is no chance of their being humiliated by a poor performance. This possibility can be avoided if the teacher takes the role of the expert and the student has only to play the part of a member of the public or a similar role which requires no special knowledge or skill.

Of course role play can be really useful in the third stage where students begin to try out what they have learned. If we suppose that students are learning some kind of communication skill – interviewing, say – then the role play offers a way for students to practise before they have to work with real interviewees. In this case it will be desirable for all students to have the opportunity to practise and so the role plays will be set up in pairs. The numbers involved may make this more difficult to manage than the demonstration role play. However, because everyone is involved and thus there is no audience, the participants are not likely to find it particularly stressful. If it is clear to students that they are practising a skill which will be an important part of their professional repertoire, there is unlikely to be much resistance.

Lastly, role play might also be used to facilitate feedback by introducing a third person into the exercise described above. The third person takes the role of an observer and provides feedback to each of the actors. Roles usually rotate so that everyone experiences all roles. Feedback can also be provided, by the person playing the client/patient, on how the experience felt from that perspective.

While not all teaching/learning strategies are as versatile as role play, many can be used for more than one stage of the learning process. As we have seen with the role play example, the stage of the learning process for which an activity is used will make a significant difference to the way it is planned and managed. A problem-solving activity, used to introduce students to a topic or a concept, is a different proposition to a problem used to enable students to try out knowledge or skills which they have already begun to master. When an activity is set up as a form of experiential or discovery learning (i.e. it is used at the introductory stage), you can expect to have to manage students through a period of frustration as they try to make sense of their experience and identify what they need to learn in order to solve the problem. The 'getting to know more' stage which follows will probably take more time, as students try to make sense of their experience in terms of the theory which is now introduced. In comparison, activities which require students to apply what they have already learned provide a much more straightforward experience. The fact that the same activity can be used in different ways for different stages of learning is rarely directly acknowledged in the literature. It can often result in some confusion when teaching/learning strategies are being discussed. When choosing a learning activity it is therefore important to consider what stage of learning will be involved.

The educational literature contains much advice on selecting and using learning activities. Some, such as the '53 Interesting Ways' series (Gibbs *et al.*, 1984; Habeshaw *et al.*, 1987) seem to imply that choosing a learning activity for students is simply a matter of selecting something to your taste from the smorgasbord available. On the other hand, the instructional systems approach exemplified in Romiszowski's work (1981, 1984) suggests that if only all of the variables in the teaching situation can be analysed accurately, then the 'right' method can be found. In preparing for the classroom, lab or lecture hall, the teacher as course designer has to balance educational purpose with the flexibility necessary to meet continually changing circumstances. What I have tried to do with the simple model of learning that I have introduced here, is to provide a rule of thumb which will enable teachers to structure and sequence learning activities in a purposeful way. Work by Brookfield (1990), Laurillard (1993) and Biggs (1999) offers more detailed discussion of the choice and use of both activities and media than can be provided here.

Choosing materials and media

The choice of materials and delivery media becomes much easier when it is considered in the light of this learning model. Obviously a wide range of media is suitable for use in the introductory and exploratory stages. Print materials of all kinds are a staple of academic teaching. They offer considerable flexibility, portability and student control of pacing and timing. They are cheap and easily produced. Transferring print materials to computer for delivery via the Internet, as has recently become fashionable, offers few if any advantages in educational terms. Computer-based text is less easy to access and use than print. However, it may have administrative advantages in reducing printing and distribution costs for materials.

Television, video and film offer particular advantages. By presenting incidents from real life, they can provide opportunities for students to identify what aspects are significant and to formulate problems for themselves without the mediation of an author. In the example of problem-based learning we looked at earlier where medical students are learning to identify cases of childhood malnutrition, video is preferred as the presentation medium for trigger material because it fosters the observation skills of student doctors. Alternatively, video and film can present a powerful representation of a particular viewpoint – a chance for students to experience another person's position vicariously. Their capacity to show movement, to represent complex activities accurately and economically, makes them essential for many demonstrations for which access to the real experience is not available. Audio tape and other forms of sound recordings have the disadvantage that they offer no visual focus. Consequently many students find it difficult to concentrate on audio material for any length of time. They offer obvious advantages, of course, when students have vision problems and when there is a need to reproduce and analyse particular sounds.

The chief advantage of CD-ROMs and Web-based systems, which allow students to search and link large amounts of text and illustrative materials, is that they compress very large amounts of material in a very small space and allow students access to resources which they might not otherwise have. They can also provide the opportunity to track ideas in multiple configurations more easily than in any other media.

So far we have been talking about the kinds of materials that are useful in the first two stages – being introduced to the topic and getting to know more about it. It is more difficult to find media which allow students adequate opportunity to try out new ideas and skills, to get feedback and to reflect on their experiences. Computerized tutoring systems offer drill and practice with automated feedback, but cannot cope with complex learning or evaluate complex responses. Computerized simulations provide opportunities for students to try out different approaches and see the results, but have limited applications. Video conferencing and audio conferencing can reproduce classroom interchanges to some extent. But audio conferencing, although relatively cheap and easy to operate, eliminates the visual aspects of the communication and the possibility of using visual materials. Video conferencing, requiring cameras in each location, is expensive to set up and relatively difficult to operate, often requiring technical support on hand.

Increasingly e-mail discussion groups and Web-based bulletin board discussions are coming to replace audio and video conferencing when students have computer access. Their chief advantage is that access is not time-bound and students can easily present both formal written work and informal opinions for feedback from teacher and fellow students. However, computer-mediated discussions certainly lack the spontaneity of small-group work and students may be reluctant to expose risky opinions to the scrutiny that a bulletin board allows, unless the system permits anonymity.

As the British Open University has shown, resource-based learning as a substitute for traditional lectures has much to offer in the initial, exploratory stages of the learning process. But there are still so many limitations inherent in trying to encompass the interactive stages of learning through mediated systems that it makes more sense to retain the tutorial, the small class, the practical or laboratory session wherever possible. It is here, working closely with other students and their teacher, that students have their best opportunity to deepen their understanding and make the material their own.

Designing learning activities to encourage transfer

There are two aspects that we might consider under the heading of transfer:

- how we can encourage students to transfer their knowledge of concepts, ideas, principles and processes from one unit of study to the next, and
- how we can encourage the development of what are often optimistically called transferable skills. The transferable skills, also known as generic skills, are likely to include the kinds of abilities identified in programme goals and graduate profiles – abilities such as communication, critical thinking, problem solving, interpersonal skills and the ability to work collaboratively.

While transferability to other working or disciplinary contexts sounds highly desirable, many academics would settle for improving students' abilities to apply the so-called transferable skills to the range of contexts which they will encounter within their own discipline. The extent to which individuals can use the knowledge and skills which they have learned in situations different from those in which they were acquired has been the subject of much debate. The many studies that have been undertaken produce conflicting results: in some cases, students fail to apply knowledge and skills acquired in formal education to problems encountered outside the classroom; in others, impressive transfer takes place (see Salomon and Globerson, 1987, for a summary of much of the research in this area).

Salomon and Globerson have posited that the extent to which transfer takes place is largely attributable to the degree of *mindfulness* which students bring to their learning. Mindfulness is characterized by openness, by willingness to explore the cues and meanings associated with the task, by generating alternative strategies and gathering information on which to base decisions, by reflecting on outcomes, abstracting principles and generating new theories. Those principles and theories which students have derived themselves from their involvement in learning represent the kind of knowledge which is most likely to be successfully transferred to new contexts. Mindfulness on the part of learners can be significantly enhanced by the kinds of teaching and assessment strategies which are chosen. Probing and challenging on the part of teachers, requiring students to relate new material to knowledge which they already possess, asking students to teach others and to work in teams, are all strategies which appear to increase mindful learning and consequent transfer to new situations. The other factor which Salomon and Globerson have found to be particularly important in developing transferable learning is having many opportunities to practise new skills and knowledge. Practice consolidates the key elements, while mindful reflection allows students to analyse the adaptations which must be made for different contexts.

The same principles apply to the development and transfer of 'generic' skills as to other kinds of knowledge. If, for example, we wish students to master some key concepts and associated technical skills while at the same time developing their ability to work cooperatively, we need to consider how each of these (concepts, skills and collaborative working) will be introduced to students. We also need to consider how they will get to know more about each area, what opportunities they will have to try out their new learning and get feedback and how they can be encouraged to reflect on their own performance. The question of how we work collaboratively needs to become the subject of exploration, practice, feedback and reflection, just as much as the subject content. The research which has been done on transfer of learning points to the importance of giving students many opportunities to develop academic and 'generic' skills in a variety of contexts and to encourage their awareness of what it is they are doing.

Planning for all stages of the learning process

Obviously a number of the different stages of the learning process might be combined within the one class period and others assigned as out-of-class activities. But it is important that, as far as possible, provision be made for all of the stages. Highly motivated students will devise their own methods of trying out new learning and will seek out feedback for themselves. However, without the kind of structure which requires involvement, those students who find the particular topic difficult or uninteresting will be inclined to settle for surface learning.

It will always be possible to devise many teaching strategies for the same topic, and different strategies will appeal to different students. More or less structured activity may be required to enable students to master the material according to their level of ability and the complexity of the subject matter. That is, they may need to go through the cycle of the learning model – getting to know more, trying out, getting feedback, reflecting and adjusting – several times on the same topic. To plan adequate opportunities for students to interact in this way with the material often requires cutting back on the amount of material which can be 'covered', and academic teachers often find this a hard decision. It may be some comfort to consider that with any kind of complex learning, coverage without this degree of engagement with the material is unlikely to bring about understanding or the ability to transfer what one has learned to new situations.

9

Assessment

Making decisions about the assessment scheme

Although individual academics often have considerable freedom to decide what and how they will teach, when it comes to assessment it seems that everybody has a stake and makes demands on the assessment system.

Students want to know first of all what is expected of them. Their previous experience has usually led them to believe that expectations and standards can vary markedly with each new teacher and that it is necessary to work out what will be required here. While they may have noted the learning outcomes and objectives in the course description, past experience tells them that these will have little to do with what is assessed. Their first requirement of the assessment scheme is that it should be as clear as possible about what needs to be done and how it will be judged.

Then they need to know how they are getting on – whether they will pass the course, whether they are doing as well as they think they are. If they are not doing well they want to know what they would have to do in order to do better, what good performance looks like. And many want recognition of their achievements, something that they can show to future employers or graduate schools.

Teachers also need to know how they are getting on. They want to know whether their students are understanding the key concepts and mastering the skills, and whether they are ready for more advanced work. They also use assessment tasks to motivate students to study and keep up to date. They want to know that their assessment standards are comparable with colleagues' and that, if they maintain high standards, students will not desert them for easier marks elsewhere. And on occasions they want to use their students' assessment results to prove to others that they are effective teachers.

Institutions need to be able to show that their standards are high; that graduates are achieving the high standards set for them; and that they are fit for professional practice or graduate study. They want to distinguish the best performers by honours and scholarships. They prefer faculties and departments to use assessment schemes which enable easy comparison of individual and departmental performance.

Communities need to know what kinds of abilities they can expect of graduates and what grades and degrees signify. Some governments have gone as far as requiring institutions to introduce 'standards-based' or 'criterion-referenced' assessment in an effort to make assessment systems in higher education more transparent (Ministry of Education, 1991). Communities want to be assured that new professionals are competent to practise and that public institutions provide value for the funds they receive.

These many different expectations cannot be satisfied with one kind of assessment. In the past, assessment of students in higher education has often been thought of as a process for making a judgement about the innate ability of the student which had little connection with what had been taught or what the student hoped to achieve. So we have situations like the following, where a lecturer in medicine, reflecting on whether his faculty's assessment system reflected the core knowledge and skills for beginning practitioners, commented:

> In medicine we often assess the most esoteric and trivial knowledge, on the grounds that if they know the esoteric stuff they *probably* have the more basic and important knowledge. But by testing for really obscure information we can sort out a few top students and keep everyone else on their toes.

The problem with this kind of assessment is that although it serves the function of sorting out a few high-performing students, it does not tell us whether they or the rest of the group have mastered the most important knowledge and skills, and it provides little in the way of useful feedback to the teaching staff. It may not even do a good job of sorting out the best students, as it is quite possible that other bright students in the group have acquired a different collection of peripheral facts but haven't had the opportunity to demonstrate what they know.

To satisfy as far as possible the many expectations of assessment in higher education, one needs to use a range of different assessment techniques and (as always with curriculum issues) one needs a strong awareness of one's goals and purposes and those of other users of the system. It also requires an acceptance that it will not be possible to meet everyone's expectations completely. To do so would mean that students spent all of their time being assessed and had no time for unpressured learning and experimentation. Sometimes, in order to preserve everyone's time and sanity, one assessment task or technique has to serve conflicting purposes even though theoretically two different assessment tasks might do a better job.

Assessment decisions for the whole course

In designing or redesigning a course of study, which parameters of assessment do we need to agree on as a group, and which can be left to individual teachers or subject coordinators? Which aspects of assessment should be consistent throughout the whole course and which can be allowed to vary with individual units?

The qualities, skills and attributes to be developed and assessed

First of all it is essential for members of the design team to remind themselves of the goals and purpose of the course. If, in the initial stages of the design process, a graduate profile was prepared which indicated the kinds of knowledge skills and attributes that the course aimed to develop, now is the time to consider how these might be assessed in the context of each unit. If a core set of attributes has been identified, such as ability in critical thinking, problem solving and communicating, is it reasonable to assume that these will be developed and assessed through all of the units that make up the programme of study? If not in all units, then which ones?

Universities and faculties which have developed graduate profiles may ask that documentation for each programme of study shows the extent to which the desirable qualities of graduates will be developed and assessed in each unit. Table 9.1 is one example of the way that this has been attempted in an engineering degree (University of South Australia, 1998).

Table 9.1 An example of a year-of-study profile

	Engineering mathematics 1	Science for engineers	Mechanics and materials	Computer applications and graphics	Engineering mathematics 2	Electricity and electronics	Computer fundamentals	Communication and the profession
Body of knowledge	4	3	4	0.5	3	3	2.7	
Lifelong learning				0.5	0.2			
Effective problem solvers	0.5	0.6	0.5	1	1	1	1	1
Work alone and in teams		0.6		0.5	0.2	0.2	0.5	1
Ethical action								0.3
Communicate effectively		0.3		2	0.1	0.3	0.3	2
International perspective								0.2

Note: It is possible to 'map' the degree to which activities and assessment in each unit contribute to the ways that graduates achieve the necessary qualities through the course. This table shows (in credit points) the contribution of the first year to the development of qualities (University of South Australia, 1998).

The system of grading

Another significant assessment decision which needs to be taken at the course level concerns the grading system to be followed. Specifically, we need to look at how many levels of performance we should attempt to distinguish and whether the outcomes of all units should be graded in the same way.

Part of the decision about grading concerns whether grades and marks should be distributed according to the student's performance relative to the other students in her group (norm-referenced) or according to the standard that she has met (criterion-referenced). These two systems are not as far apart as their proponents might lead us to believe, the standards in a criterion-referenced system usually being derived from some idea of the norms for performance at a given level of the course. But they do have some important differences.

The marking system used in most universities and colleges requires that assessable work is given a numerical mark, that marks for all pieces of work are combined into a percentage and that a grade classification is then allocated using either a letter grade (A–F) or categories such as 'fail', 'pass', 'credit', 'distinction', 'high distinction'. Grades are often expected to fall into a pattern approaching a 'normal' distribution and may be adjusted to ensure that they do so. That is, the system in use is basically norm-referenced.

The advantages of a marking system like this, based on marks out of a hundred, is that it allows for fine distinctions to be made between students. Such distinctions are very useful when it comes to allocating scarce resources, such as university medals or postgraduate scholarships to prestigious universities. But in many cases it is hard to justify and defend, let alone replicate, such fine distinctions. Falchikov and Boud (1989) have pointed out the difficulties. When assessors are required to evaluate a piece of work or a performance by rating the work on a number of criteria using a hundred-point scale, they are being asked to make literally hundreds of distinctions at the same time. This level of discrimination is probably impossible to achieve with any degree of reliability. Certainly, some studies have shown that the greater the number of performance levels that the marking scheme attempts to distinguish, the less reliability there is likely to be among markers (Heywood, 1989: 65–8). In much university assessment the number or mark assigned to a piece of work has no numerical significance. Rather, it is a code for a qualitative judgement which might have more meaning for all concerned if it were expressed in words.

Criterion-referenced marking schemes usually attempt to distinguish fewer levels of performance, precisely because it is difficult to define standards for each of the different levels in words. One of the significant advantages of criterion-referenced schemes is that they force teachers to make their assessment standards explicit – difficult though this often is. Hidden assessment criteria have long been used as a powerful mechanism for keeping students in their place and have undermined much of the educational function of assessment. And while some students are spurred on by the knowledge that there are few places at the top, others find norm-referenced grading demotivating and unfair, as this student explained:

One lecturer . . . told us on the first day of classes that we would be marked in a certain way. He even told us how many people in the class would get an A, B, C, D, etc. He said that this was how it was done. Only a few people do really well and a few really poorly and the rest are in the middle. He gave the impression that the 'best' work would get an A (even if the standard was low) and the 'worst' would fail even if the standard of class work was really high. I don't think this is a fair and accurate way of assessing.

(Fourth-year student, quoted in Cartwright, 1997: 107)

Perhaps more important than precise (if somewhat artificial) ranking of students is achieving a clearer understanding among students, markers and the community about what different grade levels signify. Over the years many departments, faculties and institutions have attempted to explain what their grades mean, but these attempts have rarely gone beyond general descriptors of the 'poor', 'fair', 'good', 'excellent' variety.

One attempt to make clear what constitutes the quality of intellectual accomplishment at the different levels of performance signified by conventional letter grades is the grading scheme proposed by John Biggs based on his taxonomy of educational outcomes. The SOLO (Structure of the Observed Learning Outcome) taxonomy has been used frequently for classifying students' achievements in research studies but less often as an assessment tool in the classroom. Biggs's grading scheme, based on his taxonomy, provides the following explanation of intellectual performance needed to achieve each of five grade levels (Biggs, 1992).

The A grade performance requires students to show thorough understanding of the concepts that they have been taught but also to be able to use the concepts and ideas beyond the immediate applications they may have studied. It is characterized by a high level of abstract thinking which enables students to generalize to new contexts, make applications or draw conclusions that are apparently original. In Biggs's words, the A level 'involves a level of originality, elegance or generalization which is more what we would like rather than what we might reasonably expect'.

For a B grade students need to show that they have a clear understanding of major concepts and ability to see applications – that they can understand the question, put up a good argument, show judgement about what is important and what is less important.

C class performances show understanding of most the concepts dealt with, but little evidence of integration. Students have not been able to relate all aspects in a coherent whole, or think through all of the implications of specific applications. However, there is evidence of some understanding, coverage and effort.

Performances at the D level shows some understanding of one or a few basic aspects of the unit. There are some serious problems with the work but to fail it would be too drastic. Resubmission may be required.

The F (failing) grade is reserved for irrelevant, incomplete or plagiarized responses.

A scheme such as this makes sense to most academics, and Biggs has shown that it can be readily understood and accepted by students (Nightingale *et al.*, 1996: 92–4). By insisting on a high *quality* of performance at the upper grade levels it avoids the situation which can often occur whereby students are rewarded for the *quantity* of information they present, rather than their ability to synthesize and use it. For a scheme like this to be adopted as the guiding principle throughout a course of study requires, however, that there also be a commitment to devising the kinds of assessment tasks which allow students to perform at the highest levels. At present, in too many cases, the highest level required is that students present an understanding of the concepts dealt with, without any need or opportunity to go beyond that.

Mechanisms to ensure fairness

Another set of decisions that needs to be considered at the programme level concerns the mechanisms that will be put in place to ensure comparability of standards and to provide students with an avenue of appeal about assessment decisions. When more than one marker will be evaluating the same assessment tasks, what means will be used to establish agreement on standards before the assessment exercise begins? Would it be desirable to carry out a standard-setting exercise in which all of the markers assess the same sample of work and compare results, discuss and negotiate until they have agreed on standards at each level? Is it sufficient to provide assessors with marking guides which indicate the key points to look for?

Will any attempt be made after the event to bring marks presented by different assessors into similar distribution patterns? (i.e. will the marks be moderated?) What will happen if a student appeals against an assessment? Will the work be re-marked by the original marker? A second marker? What will happen if two markers disagree?

It is desirable for these issues to be agreed before the programme begins so that both markers and students have confidence in the integrity of the process.

Within this framework other decisions about assessment can usually be made at the level of the unit of study, allowing for considerable variety in the kinds of assessable tasks that a student will meet over the prescribed course of study.

Assessing different kinds of learning

In thinking about the kinds of knowledge, understanding, skills and personal attributes which could or should be assessed as part of a degree programme, it can be illuminating to look again at Habermas's construct of three different kinds of human interests which result in distinctly different kinds of knowledge or understanding:

- The interest in control or mastery of one's environment, leading to the development of technical, empirical and conventional knowledge
- The interest in developing shared understanding with others and in communicating and negotiating meaning, leading to interpretive or hermeneutic knowledge
- The interest in freedom – freedom from unthinking acceptance of social and political systems and individual limitations – leading to the development of self-reflective and critical understandings.

The characteristics of each of these different kinds of knowledge imply distinctly different kinds of assessment. The distinguishing feature of technical, empirical or conventional knowledge is that it is the object of general agreement and acceptance. Rules, formulae, vocabulary and procedures all represent codified and established knowledge. Tests of this kind of knowledge allow very little room for interpretation or individual response. There is a 'right answer'. Objective tests, such as multiple choice, true/false or sentence completion, are perfectly suited to assessing this kind of knowledge. The ability to carry out standard procedures and operations can be similarly assessed on a can/can't do basis, using observation and standard checklists of the steps in the process. Such assessment tasks are relatively easy to mark. There is little room for disagreement between different markers and so reliability is high. The weighting given to technical knowledge, and the extent to which such knowledge is believed to be worth assessing separately from more complex kinds of understandings, will depend on the nature of the discipline and on what is valued by the course designers and teachers.

Many courses use short tests and quizzes at regular intervals to test technical and conventional knowledge (and as a way of motivating students to study regularly). A nursing programme contains a fairly high proportion of technical, conventional and procedural knowledge. The following example describes how nursing skills are assessed in a clinical unit of a nursing degree:

Assessing technical/conventional knowledge in nursing

Students in their third year learn clinical nursing skills in laboratories which simulate the hospital setting. Students are introduced to the skills through inquiry-based learning packages so that skills are contextualized and students are always required to relate the associated knowledge and principles to the skills being practised or assessed. Nursing skills are assessed in this programme in two ways: a videoed skill assessment worth 10 per cent of the marks, and two objective structured clinical examinations (OSCEs), one undertaken in the middle of the year, worth 10 per cent, and the other at the end of the year, worth 15 per cent, of total marks. In addition the assessment programme includes two written examinations worth 25 per cent each and a group-learning contract worth 15 per cent.

The OSCE is a practical examination to assess competence. Unlike assessments of competence carried out in the workplace (such as the hospital ward), the OSCE uses simulation – including actor 'patients' – to ensure that all students are assessed on the same task in the same context. Assessments of students' clinical skills during hospital placements have been found to have poor reliability. The personal relationship between the student and the clinical supervisor may have more impact on the result than the student's actual clinical performance (Borbasi *et al.*, 1993). The variability among real clinical situations also makes fair comparisons difficult. In the OSCE students circulate through a number of stations or simulated nursing situations. Through the use of such structured simulations the OSCE attempts to overcome the difficulties and limitations which the workplace imposes on assessment.

Students circulate around a series of six stations, three of which require a written response and three of which involve assessors observing the performance of skills, using a previously prepared checklist. The performance stations require students to carry out tasks such as preparing intravenous medications. Those which require a written response usually test knowledge related to the skills required at the performance stations, such as the ability to interpret the cardiac rhythm displayed on an ECG monitor.

The skills, techniques and procedures assessed in this way have been analysed into their component steps or parts and prepared in the form of checklists. The checklists which will ultimately be used in assessing the students' performance are distributed to students as part of their course. They are encouraged to use the checklists during all their laboratory sessions and at independent practice sessions.

The Faculty of Nursing which developed this OSCE also introduced assessor training to improve reliability among assessors. A video was made of a student performing one of the skills. In training workshops, assessors scored the video performance using the checklist, discussed discrepancies in their scores and developed ground rules for overcoming problem areas.

At each OSCE, a seventh and optional station is set up where students can obtain general feedback on their performance. Results from the OSCEs are combined with the other assessment components to produce an overall grade for the course.

As a method of assessing clinical performance in areas such as history taking, examination and treatment, the OSCE provides a more reliable method of assessment than 'on the job' assessment. It has the potential for testing a wide range of nursing knowledge, but the skills that can be tested in one OSCE are naturally limited. For this reason an additional videotaped skill assessment was included in this unit. Staff hoped that it would also encourage students to practise skills regularly throughout the semester.

Four work areas were set up in the nursing labs, each equipped with a video camera on a stand, a monitor, teaching video tapes which demonstrated a particular skill, and a checklist of the correct procedure to be followed in performing the skill to a safe standard.

At the beginning of a four-week teaching block, students are introduced to the video self-assessment process and instructed in the use of the camera. Students then book three 20-minute video sessions at one of the times when a teacher facilitator will be present. They work in teams of two to four, depending on the nature of the skill being assessed and whether it involves a simulated patient and more than one nurse. At each practice session a partner will video the student performing the required skill. A viewing room is available following the taping session, where the student assesses his or her own tape using the checklist provided. The teacher facilitator is also available for feedback if the student requests it. When the teacher is happy with the performance, the student submits the best performance, together with a completed self-assessment checklist and responses to reflection questions. Students may book additional practice sessions, but they may only present for assessment tapes which have been made when a teacher facilitator is present.

The instructional tape provided to students is one which includes two versions of the skill being performed. One shows an expert (usually one of the teaching staff) performing the skill and the other version shows a competent but novice practitioner carrying out the same skill. (These examples are usually drawn from those of the previous year's students who performed well.) Students easily distinguish between the novice and expert performances, but find it encouraging to see the skill demonstrated by a peer. They also comment that they appreciate the fact that the staff are prepared to submit themselves to the same process (being videotaped performing a skill) that they require of students.

The videotaped skill performance is worth 10 per cent of the final mark for the subject. As students have already assessed their own performance a number of times and only submit work when they feel they have achieved adequate competence, the teacher's marking acts essentially as a quality control mechanism. Staff members teaching on the programme feel that students learn far more from assessing their own performance than they do from watching a demonstration. They also become much better at organizing their own learning. Most importantly, they get a real understanding of how much practice it takes to master a skill to the required standard.

The OSCE and the videoed skill assessment represent just two ways of assessing technical and conventional knowledge. The OSCE is labour intensive and therefore expensive to run. It requires considerable development time and the involvement of the whole teaching team. Its benefits lie in its high validity, good reliability and a high level of acceptance by students. The advantage of the videoed skills self-assessment lies in the strong, positive impact that it has on students' learning.

(Toohey and Magin, 1996)

Assessing communicative and interpretive understanding

The nature of communicative and interpretive understanding is such that it is difficult to be highly specific about what might constitute a 'right answer'. While there are elements of fact (names, dates, terminology) that we wish students to use correctly, these are incidental to the understanding that has been arrived at. Because it is impossible exactly to define in advance the correct response, those forms of assessment in which students are asked to identify the right choice from a predetermined set of responses are inappropriate. To have any real chance of understanding what the student has come to know we must ask him to construct his own response to the question or the problem. Among the criteria we apply in assessing his response will be:

- the range and quality of evidence he has called upon;
- the consideration he has given to other views and interpretations; and
- his ability to synthesize these into a coherent position.

In other words, while the student's construction of the ideas is important, so too is evidence of the processes he undertook to arrive at his current state of understanding.

The understanding that the student constructs through interaction with texts and colleagues and life experiences is always capable of further development and refinement. Indeed, so is the understanding of the teacher. Although the teacher may construct a model response to aid in marking, setting out the ideas and the arguments she would expect students to make, it is quite possible that her own understanding will change as she marks, in response to the interpretation and meanings made by students.

Assessment of interpretive and communicative understanding will always involve the student constructing his own evidence of understanding in forms like essays and reports, plans, projects and portfolios. Because this kind of understanding is always subject to further development, evaluation of the evidence will need to consider the student's present level of understanding and his demonstrated ability to use the processes which will enable him to continue to refine and deepen his understanding. Unlike technical and empirical knowledge, which can often be machine marked, this kind of assessment needs considered expert opinion.

Interpretive understanding is usually associated with the humanities, but I would like to look at one example of how this kind of knowledge is developed and assessed in mathematics.

The assessment scheme described here comes from a calculus course which runs over a full year (Roberts, 1996). There are four different forms of assessment: mastery tests, assignments, concept essays and a final, optional, exam. The mastery tests assess students' ability to 'do' calculus. They are made up of the same kinds of exercises as students work on in their small-group sessions. Three different versions of each mastery test are offered at weekly intervals. Students may chose to sit the test only once, or to sit it up to three times and present their best result. The mastery tests, of course, assess primarily technical and conventional knowledge.

Interpretive understanding is assessed in this unit through the assignments and the concept essays. The assignments (one per semester) require students to explore significant applications or investigations. For example, the first assignment requires students to do some preliminary mathematical modelling for demand function for a newly designed automobile. Students are asked to consider more than one possible model and to explore the assumptions that have been made so as to arrive at each; to compare the results from these models; to refine one model to make it more realistic and analyse the results from this model; and finally to suggest how the model might be developed further.

The concept essays provide another way for students to demonstrate their growing understanding of calculus. Students write six of these short papers (1–2 pages) over the year. Readings are suggested for most topics. Samples of some of the questions include:

> In about half a page or so each, give an explanation of the concept of a function as appropriate to:
>
> (i) a layperson
> (ii) a high school student
> (iii) a university mathematics student.

> Make sure you illustrate your explanations with examples and counter-examples where necessary. Also try to include a sentence or so explaining, at an appropriate level, why such definitions are indeed useful. Finish off by writing a paragraph or so explaining why we need a number of different definitions for the idea of a function. You might try to use the history of the development of the function concept in your explanation.

> In your own words, explain how the ideas of differentiation have been extended to apply to functions of two variables and to vector functions of one variable. Take about half a page to a page for each. Use diagrams to help your explanations. Try to explain why the extensions have been done the way you have explained and not some other way. For example, explain why partial derivatives are the central idea for functions of two variables as opposed to, say, finding the slope of the tangent plane.

> Summarize, in your own words, in about a page or so, the factors which existed in the seventeenth century which led to the main ideas of calculus being invented at that time.

The final concept essay for the year requires students to write about how (if at all) their view of calculus has changed as a result of doing this course. If students describe changes in their views, they are asked to try to identify the factors that influenced them.

Originally the assignments were together worth 24 per cent of the marks for the course and the six concept essays counted for 12 per cent. Malcolm Roberts, who devised these assessments, commented that were he running the course at present, he would increase the value of the concept essays because of the profit that students seemed to derive from them and the amount of work that they put into them.

One of the problems in contemporary higher education is that, owing to the desire for simplicity and certainty and perhaps for ease of assessment, much interpretive knowledge is taught and assessed as though it were empirical knowledge. This is particularly likely to occur when students are learning about theories which attempt to explain the workings of individuals, societies, economies and political systems. Ellen Langer and Jennifer Joss, of Harvard University, have carried out studies which examine the effects of presenting theoretical models to students in absolute or conditional terms. When the model was described in absolute terms, it was presented as though the information was certain and true for all contexts. When it was presented in a conditional way it was described as 'one possible model' and the researchers used terms like 'could be' and 'may be'. Langer and Joss showed that when students were taught and tested on theoretical material presented in absolute terms they were much less likely to be able to put the information to creative use. And students taught in this way are not even likely to notice when new cases are presented which do not fit the model at all (Langer, 1989: 127–9).

Assessing self-reflective and critical knowledge

The development of self-reflective and critical knowledge requires another form of assessment – this time on the part of the student. It requires students to step aside from their involvement in acquiring and applying new knowledge to ask questions like:

- What preconceptions or mindsets do I bring to this task?
- How did I acquire them?
- What other ways of framing this problem might there be?
- Whose interests are served by this particular way of framing the problem?
- What personal or contextual factors prevent me from acting as I would like to act? Or prevent others from pursuing their best interests? How might those factors be changed?

Even more than with interpretive knowledge, it can be difficult to define a specific outcome which the student must reach. The mechanisms for developing this kind of knowledge are likely to provide the evidence which will be used for assessment. Self-reflective and critical knowledge develops out of engagement with and reflection on real tasks. Discussion in which conceptions are challenged may be the best starting point, but other forms of reflection in writing, such as journals, autobiographies and evaluations of one's own performances, may provide assessment evidence for the student's progress in self-reflective and critical knowledge. Because it is so hard to define an acceptable result beforehand, assessment criteria for this kind of knowledge are most likely to concern process. We are looking for evidence that the student has engaged in the process of self examination.

Two examples follow of teachers in different fields attempting to develop and assess self-reflective knowledge. David Stewart teaches a course on

'Homelessness and Public Policy' (Stewart, 1997). This course focuses on understanding homelessness from a public policy framework – its incidence and prevalence, its consequences, and strategies for its prevention and amelioration. But Stewart also attempts to help his students understand the experience of homelessness. In this unit students engage in reading and critical reflection, but also undertake structured field experiences and volunteer at an agency that works with homeless people.

The unit has a number of assessment requirements, including a journal and a take-home exam which requires students to prepare input to a recent government policy initiative on homelessness. (The emphasis on learning from experience and translating learning back into social action is typical of a socially critical approach to course design.) An additional assessment task requires students to write a two-page paper on each of the five 'structured experiences' which form part of the unit. Here are three examples of the structured experiences which students must undertake.

Structured experience #2

For at least two hours of one day, render yourself homeless. Do not carry money, identification or food. Spend this time in a place where homeless people tend to congregate. Later write about your experiences and reflections. Note especially what you do (how you spend your time), what your chief concerns are, how you manage your creature comforts, how you view yourself and how others view you.

Structured experience #4

Go to a government or non-profit agency that offers income, employment, housing and/or food assistance to homeless and/or low-income people. Find out everything that is required for someone to enrol in that programme, perhaps by making an appointment with a caseworker. Reflect on how you felt as a potential social welfare beneficiary. How were you treated by staff members? Describe the process of obtaining benefits. Reflect on whether there are sacrifices in becoming a beneficiary of such a programme.

Structured experience #5

Do something to help a homeless person. Reflect on how you give help, the response, the consequences of this response, how you view yourself, how you view the person you are helping, and how the homeless person views you.

In their two-page papers, students are asked to describe their experiences, discuss their thoughts and feelings and analyse their experiences using their assigned readings and lecture notes. The structured experience papers are worth approximately 20 per cent of the marks for the unit.

Journals of work placements or course experiences, and reflective essays, are probably the most common vehicles for assessing self-knowledge and critical understanding. But a problem for many teachers is how such writing should be assessed. Fran Everingham teaches on a graduate programme in health sciences education which features reflective assessment tasks in many units. She has developed a set of criteria for evaluating reflective writing, based on Boud's work on the cycle of reflection (Boud *et al.*, 1985), which is used throughout the programme. Whatever form the reflective writing takes, students are assessed on their ability to:

- identify and describe significant incidents and the feelings that accompanied them;
- distinguish factors that affected their performance;
- analyse their performance in terms of their knowledge and skills and make connections with previous experiences or different contexts;
- balance personal interpretation with objective interpretation or feedback from others;
- identify strengths and weaknesses and select aspects for improvement.

(Everingham, quoted in Toohey, 1996: 85)

The choice of assessment method

The choice of assessment method will be influenced to a considerable extent by the kinds of learning that one wants to assess. The schema that we have used above suggests certain types of assessment methods as more appropriate than others for different kinds of learning. When choosing the set of assessment tasks that make up the assessment scheme for a unit of study a number of points need to be considered:

- The extent to which the assessment reflects the learning goals of the course (i.e. the *validity* of the assessment).
- The extent to which the results of the assessment can be trusted (i.e. the *reliability* of the assessment). The same work, assessed by different examiners or marked on different occasions, should produce very similar results. Work by students of comparable ability should achieve similar results.
- The extent to which the assessment supports and promotes real learning. The demands of assessment are a key factor in pushing students towards a surface approach to learning. Some assessment methods are more likely than others to encourage students to reduce what is to be learned to a series of unconnected facts which can be reproduced for assessment purposes (often referred to by students as 'cram and dump' assessment).
- The cost of the methods chosen. It would be naive to pretend that cost does not play a very significant role in the choice of assessment methods. Assessment tasks perceived as having greater validity may be more expensive to mount or more time-consuming to mark; mechanisms to increase reliability, such as double marking, standard setting exercises and assessor training, involve additional costs. Good assessment practice is not cheap, and needs to be constantly defended when the resource base is continually under threat.

Balancing all of these factors is not easy. Perhaps the most important thing to remember is that no one method will deliver them all. A range of methods, within units and over the whole programme of study, is most likely to produce a reasonable balance among validity, reliability, support for learning and cost.

A comparison of assessment methods

'*Objective' tests, including multiple-choice, true/false and short-answer,* are most useful for testing knowledge and understanding. Some variations, such as the patient-management problems found in medicine and the interpretations of legal cases used in law, require students to apply knowledge to 'real' situations. However, objective tests cannot assess the ability to construct an argument, defend one's judgement or display any original thinking. They allow broad coverage of the syllabus, often at the expense of depth. Objective tests (with the exception of short-answer tests) can be time-consuming and therefore expensive to design, if questions are to be clear and unambiguous and all of the responses plausible. Marking, however, is reliable, cheap, and can often be done by computer – probably the most significant advantage in the eyes of course designers. Speed of marking could be an advantage to students if it meant prompt feedback; more often feedback is withheld to save the expense of constantly designing new tests. As with all assessments carried out under examination conditions, there is little question that the work is that of the student.

Essay examinations and assessments are more appropriate for testing higher levels of thinking and more complex intellectual performances. Essay assignments require students to research and synthesize information, develop an argument and provide evidence for their judgements. Unless they are made explicit, students may not understand that an academic essay requires the presentation of an argument. Instead they may see it as an opportunity to describe all that they know about the topic without much evaluation or synthesis. The possibility of demonstrating higher-level intellectual skills will be sacrificed to some extent when essay questions are set under exam conditions. In exams there is likely to be more emphasis on remembering and organizing information and less on the quality of the argument. The compensating factor is that one can be confident of the authorship – which may not be the case with assignments and take-home exams.

Open-book exams may overcome some of these disadvantages – but they must be designed to test problem solving and the application and interpretation of knowledge, rather than students' ability to look up the right answer. They are more likely to promote a deeper and more thoughtful approach to studying for the exam.

Case study or problem-centred exams and assignments require a performance closer to professional practice than essay assignments, which have been criticized as bearing little relationship to 'real-world' tasks. In setting the case or the problem it can be difficult to find the level of complexity which is close enough to reality to be challenging, but is also manageable within the time frame.

Precisely because they are set to assess complex intellectual performances, long-answer questions are difficult and time-consuming to mark. This is particularly so if the student is to be given the kind of feedback that will help to improve the next performance. Marking is often unreliable and marking guides, which are intended to enhance reliability, often emphasize content at the expense of any weighting for synthesis of material, logical argument and clarity of expression.

Practical/professional tasks may include straightforward applications of knowledge and skills (such as often found in the Objective Structured Clinical Examinations/Assessments and many laboratory exercises) or more complex *projects* which involve identifying and defining a problem, or planning and carrying out a design solution or an intervention. While they have clear relevance in professional education they can also be used to good effect in more academic disciplines. History students can be asked to research and write about an aspect of local history; literature students can review novels and plays or edit a work for specific purposes.

Production of works of art and performances in music, theatre or dance also fall into this category. Depending on the scope of the project, these kinds of tasks may allow for the assessment of knowledge application, technical skills, interpersonal skills, problem-solving ability, ability to interpret an artistic work, creativity and the ability to follow procedures scrupulously and document results accurately.

The advantage of making such tasks part of the assessment is that the task is a significant vehicle for learning rather than an artificial hurdle, and the assessment closely resembles assessment in real professional or academic work (Romiszowski, 1981).

What is assessed will vary with the task. Many of these practical and professional tasks will result in some kind of assessable product: a work of art, a design solution, a patient-management plan or a lesson plan. Where there is no product and the task results in a 'real-time' performance it will need to be assessed by observation. The difficulties of assessing live performances are obvious. Preparation of markers' checklists and training of assessors may be necessary to ensure reliability, and such performances are frequently assessed by a panel of assessors. In addition to the performance or the product, many teachers will want to be assured of the process by which the product or performance was developed. To this end students are often required to keep journals of the project or work placement. Journals may form part of the final assessment, and have the advantage of increasing confidence about the authorship of the work.

The assessment of practical and professional tasks may be more time-consuming and expensive than assessment of paper-and-pencil tests, although this is not always the case. However, it often has considerable advantages for students in that the assessment process becomes far more open. Products and designs may be displayed, and students attend performances and project presentations. In contrast to paper assessments, the standard of work is available for all to see, and when students are themselves involved in giving feedback they come to have a better understanding of the assessment process.

Oral assessments usually take the form of seminar presentations, project presentations, oral exams or vivas, and sometimes the assessment of class participation. Oral assessments may be included because the development of skills in oral communication is a goal of the course, or as a means of levelling the playing field when a significant number of the students come from cultural backgrounds where oratory is more highly valued than skill in writing. For example, some New Zealand institutions have a policy of offering some oral assessment throughout their programmes in recognition of the strong oral tradition of Maori students.

Oral presentations and seminars, like written assignments, can provide a way of assessing students' ability to research and organize information and develop an argument. More interesting is likely to be the student's ability in making an oral presentation and leading a discussion – aspects in which students often receive little or no preparation. As one lecturer commented ruefully, after meeting much criticism from students who felt that they had not been adequately prepared for oral assessments:

> They were cross that we didn't do something on oral presentations before we did them . . . Oral presentations, like writing, are taken for granted as a skill you have – that everyone knows how to write and everyone knows how to speak.
>
> (Cartwright, 1997: 43)

As with all 'real-time' performances, the assessment of oral presentations and seminars tends to be highly subjective. For this reason, video and audio tapes are sometimes kept as a reference and more than one marker may be used to increase reliability. *Assessment of class participation*, usually justified on the grounds that it improves preparation, attendance and the quality of discussion, is even more problematic. Here the teacher must assess not one but many performances at the same time, and the criteria for successful performance are often unclear to all parties.

Oral exams and vivas are most likely to be useful as a follow-up to the assessment of a practical or professional task. Here they can be used to check the reasoning behind actions and judgements, and to see whether the student can reason from a particular context to other cases. Because oral exams tend to be less reliable than written forms of assessment, they should not be used for testing knowledge which could just as easily be tested in written form – unless there is some factor which makes writing difficult, such as student disability. Oral exams are often highly stressful for students. They should certainly be used if oral communication skills are necessary for performance in the discipline or profession, but students do need to be adequately prepared.

Reflective tasks include professional journals, diaries and logs, together with reflective essays and autobiographies. They are used to assess reflection on practice, growth in understanding, reasoning behind judgements and actions, and the development of professional attitudes. Although students often find journals unfamiliar and difficult, they do force most students to think more deeply about practical exercises and field placements, and may help to integrate theory and practice. Because it is difficult to specify performance standards for professional journals they are often assessed on a 'satisfactory/ unsatisfactory' basis.

Useful works which offer more detail on assessment methods include Gibbs *et al.* (1986), Brown and Knight (1994) and Nightingale *et al.* (1996).

The choice of assessors

Apart from academic assessors it is worth considering whether others should be brought into the assessment process. The most common choices are practitioners of the discipline or profession, and the students themselves.

Using practitioners as assessors

Although it is often thought desirable to involve practitioners more closely in the assessment of professional education, time and work commitments usually make this difficult. Two situations where they are commonly used are the assessment of work placements and the assessment of major projects.

Workplace supervisors are regularly involved in the assessment of students in cooperative education, clinical placements and other kinds of fieldwork because they have the most direct experience of the student's performance. Many workplace supervisors find this difficult, however, and report feeling a conflict between their roles as mentor and as assessor, which inhibits them from making realistic and accurate judgements about student performance. Many strategies have been used for improving the assessment of work placements, including negotiating learning objectives and assessment criteria through a learning contract, providing detailed criteria and training for workplace assessors and using the educational supervisor as a co-marker (Anderson *et al.*, 1996; Toohey *et al.* 1996).

Practitioners are also sometimes invited to form part of the assessment panel for major projects. The same need for guidance on assessment criteria and standards is evident, and briefing sessions, together with written and weighted assessment criteria, are often introduced to improve reliability. Being assessed by prominent professionals in their field may make the jury assessment even more stressful for students and extra consideration may need to be given to creating a positive and supportive climate for feedback.

Students as assessors

Convincing arguments have been made in the educational literature for the value of involving students in the assessment process in order to assist them in taking responsibility for their own learning – as they will need to do after graduation. The decision to introduce self- or peer assessment can be contentious, because it affects people's perceptions of standards. It is therefore best discussed and agreed during the design or review process.

Analyses of the many studies of student self-assessment that have been undertaken show that there is no general tendency for students to either overestimate or underestimate their own performance, although both have occurred in different studies. A tendency to over- or underestimate performance is more likely to result from the students' understanding, or lack of understanding, of the assessment criteria, or from the kind of rating instrument which is used, than from any general student characteristics (Boud and Falchikov, 1995).

On the other hand, able students and students who have considerable experience of the subject matter have been shown to make more accurate judgements of their own performance than inexperienced students and less able students. In general, the less able students are, the more likely they are optimistically to overestimate their own performance.

With peer assessment, the chief concern seems to be that students will not take the process seriously and will mark on the basis of personality and popularity. (Academics, of course, would not do this. Although one described his departmental practices in the following terms:

> When we find that we have a student whose mark is on the borderline between two honours grades we tend to ask ourselves: 'Is this person diligent, cheerful, willing to help out around the place?' If they are we generally push them up to the higher grade.)

Making self- and peer assessment more trustworthy

> I do not believe that peer assessment as it is currently practised is entirely the correct way to assess students. For example, students need to know *what* they are actually assessing and *why*.
>
> (Fourth-year student, quoted in Cartwright, 1997)

The student quoted above sums up the requirements for good self-assessment and peer assessment. Students need to be prepared for the seriousness of the process with careful explanations and examples of how self- and peer assessment is carried out in academic and professional work. The provision of explicit criteria is as important as it is in other forms of assessment. There is evidence that when students are involved in setting and negotiating the assessment criteria, their understanding and ability to apply the criteria accurately are further increased. However, complicated and lengthy rating instruments confuse inexperienced assessors.

In many cases it will be more useful to help students distinguish a limited range of performances (say, 'excellent', 'competent' and 'acceptable') than to ask them to award marks – which are, after all, irrelevant to professional self- and peer assessment.

Opportunities to develop and practise assessment skills whereby students have the opportunity to practise assessing one or two pieces of work, and then discuss differences which arise in applying the criteria, have been shown to improve reliability.

Finally, the use of a second marker (usually the teacher) to moderate individual self-assessment and the use of multiple markers in peer assessment can increase confidence in the results, particularly where they contribute to a final grade.

The research literature shows that the majority of students welcome the opportunity to become involved in assessment – both of their own work and that of their peers – provided that they have been given sufficient guidance to feel that they can do a good job.

Changing conceptions of assessment

The way in which assessment in higher education is conceived has changed quite significantly over the past two decades. Previously assessment was seen by many academics as a series of hurdles which would progressively eliminate weaker students. Success was more about identifying innate ability ('the first-class mind') than anything to do with the quality of teaching. But as conceptions of knowledge have broadened and educational research has focused on relationships between learning and teaching, ideas about assessment have also changed. At the American Association for Higher Education Assessment Forum, Marcia Mentkowski summed up the changes:

> Lately . . . I've . . . begun to identify some of the educational assumptions that are beginning to drive higher education assessment more broadly. I can see three intertwined but distinct aspects: First, expanding the outcomes of college to include not only what students *know* but also what they are able to *do* has led to development of alternative assessments, including performance and portfolio assessment. Second, expanding learning to include active collaboration with others, and more reflective and self-sustained learning, has led to assessment of projects produced by groups of students and to more attention to self assessment. Third, expanding educational goals to include personal growth has led to assessment of broad developmental patterns over time . . .
>
> (Mentkowski *et al.*, 1991: 13)

10

Implementing the New Course

With the new curriculum we are supposed to have cut the content of each of the core units by 25 per cent. Then how can it happen that the assessment looks exactly the same?

(Lecturer at an assessment review meeting 12 months after implementation of a major curriculum revision)

The biggest risk in reviewing and redesigning a curriculum is not that wrong choices will be made about content or teaching methods or the sequence of units; it is best to accept from the beginning that these aspects will need fine tuning in the initial stages and continuous improvement thereafter. The biggest risk is that after months of evaluating, planning and designing new approaches, the forces of inertia and the pressures of other demands will take over and very little will change.

Universities are not alone in this. Educational institutions of all kinds have proven highly resistant to change. The history of educational innovation is littered with failures. For example, Fullan and Stiegelbauer (1991) cite an investigation of federally sponsored educational programmes adopted in 293 sites in the United States, which found that local implementation failed in the vast majority of cases; typically the new programmes were abandoned after a relatively short time.

On the one hand, it is easy to dismiss changes that we don't want to get involved with as educational fads and wait for them to pass. But it is stretching credibility to assume that nothing has been discovered in the past 50 years about how to make teaching and learning more effective that couldn't profitably be used to reshape the curriculum. And regardless of whether or not we want to change, the social context in which we work continues to evolve, making yesterday's programmes less appropriate for today's students. As Michael Fullan has pointed out, it is necessary to exploit change before it victimizes us (Fullan and Stiegelbauer, 1991: 345).

What causes such resistance to curriculum change? And how can we overcome this resistance so that worthwhile changes have a chance to succeed?

The pressures for inertia

Some of the factors which inhibit and undermine change in higher education include the following:

- Staffing systems may insulate teaching staff from students and their concerns. In many cases the most influential senior staff teach only large lecture classes or individual postgraduate students. Small-group teaching is handed over to junior staff and teaching assistants. Thus students are more likely to approach junior staff with problems, but junior staff are the least able to initiate changes in the course design.
- Research funding is closely linked to individual or team efforts, but funding for teaching is not. Thus there is constant pressure to be active and successful in research but little corresponding pressure on teaching performance.
- The staff investment in the development of new courses, the introduction of educational technology or curriculum revision may not be recognized or rewarded in the promotion system.
- Professional bodies which accredit courses may be conservative, prescribing the hours to be spent on core units and the forms of assessment.
- Little evaluation may be carried out which might reveal student dissatisfaction or difficulty. Or, when student evaluation of teaching is used, any problems that are uncovered are regarded as the sole responsibility of the person teaching the unit. There is often no mechanism whereby the course teaching team as a whole evaluates issues such as whether units ought to be compulsory or elective, whether they ought to be redesigned to avoid content overlap or whether sequencing could be more effective.
- Norm-referenced assessment may hide the impact of changes such as large increases in class sizes. Recent studies have shown that increases in class sizes reduce the number of students who achieve at high level (Gibbs *et al.*, 1996). This effect may be lost sight of if results are routinely scaled to produce a constant grade pattern.

These are obviously powerful factors. Not all of them will apply in a particular institution, but many will, and the list gives us some idea of what the course design team is up against when contemplating significant change.

Along with these structural factors which militate against change is the personal reality. Even when individuals accept and initiate changes, teaching and assessing new material in different ways will be stressful. For some individuals it will call into question the knowledge and skills that they have developed over a working lifetime and undermine their concept of themselves as successful and competent teachers. Boyatzis, Cowen and Kolb, in their case study of radical change in an MBA curriculum, describe a shift from the traditional view of teacher-as-expert to a focus on student learning outcomes and the tailoring of programmes to fit individual needs. Many of the teaching staff found the resulting shift in identity, role and responsibilities difficult. One commented that the change required, 'giving up the limelight and centre stage in the classroom . . . changing how I think I am contributing to [the students'] development . . . and covering less material than should be covered in order to spend more time focusing on what material they are learning' (Boyatzis *et al.*, 1995: 210).

Creating pressure and support for change

How can we moderate those forces which maintain the status quo and create some impetus for improving what is offered to students? Studies of successful projects for change in education have shown that two key factors are necessary for success: *pressure* for change and *support* for people while they engage in the process. Pressure creates the need for change. It can come in a great variety of forms, such as the pressure created by falling enrolments, departmental budgets, poor evaluation data from students and the community, changes in the discipline or profession. Sometimes these pressures are obvious to everyone, but if the project leaders are attempting to look ahead and think strategically, they may be picking up factors in the wider environment which are not yet visible to many colleagues. Boyatzis and his colleagues report that initially many in their faculty saw no need for anything more than incremental curriculum change – after all, enrolments remained steady and quality of students high. It took a survey of organizational leaders to provide evidence that potential employers were unimpressed with traditional MBA programmes, together with wider evidence that the philosophy of management education inherent in the school's management degrees was rapidly becoming obsolete (Boyatzis *et al.*, 1995: 23).

Pressure creates the need for change, but support makes change possible. We frequently find ourselves in situations where we see a need for things to be done differently but either we don't know how or what to change or we don't have the time and resources to make the changes. Support for curriculum change usually means providing time and money for people to engage in development work, but also means supporting staff as they learn how to do things differently.

The planning stages

In earlier chapters we have discussed the importance of managing the planning process for curriculum change so that key factors are taken into account. It is worth reiterating these here.

- *Establish the need for change in everyone's mind.* Gut feeling (or professional judgement) may be sufficient impetus for change if all are agreed, but otherwise more objective data and a wider variety of opinion will be needed. This might include gathering evaluation data from current students, graduates, employers, professional bodies and academic leaders. Even more important than gathering the data is that the owners of the programme (those who work on it) should jointly analyse it and come to a shared understanding of its meaning and significance.

- *Choose the best project team and the process for planning.* The project will benefit if the key figures possess good analytical and interpersonal skills and open minds. But the project team should not have full responsibility for decision making. As far as possible, the project team gathers, analyses and reports data and proposes approaches, structures, unit outlines and sequences, but the whole teaching team makes the final decisions.
- *Seek high-level support and ownership early.* Those whose commitment needs to be obtained include departmental and faculty leaders and anyone else in the organization who has rights of approval over the programme or who might feel that they have the right to be consulted, such as other departments who provide some teaching. Influential professional bodies should also be included.
- *Negotiate resources and an adequate time frame.* It is important to distinguish between the resources needed in the design phase and the resources that will be required to run the course. Resources needed in the planning phase might include teaching release time for those heavily involved in the project, the cost of employing an educational design specialist, the cost of any staff development workshops or large-scale planning meetings, and design and production costs for materials. Project management processes, such as preparing a critical path for the project, can be particularly useful in determining a realistic time frame.
- *Manage conflict.* Where difficult decisions have to be made in large-group meetings, the use of an independent facilitator and structured processes can help to clarify points of contention, ensure all views are heard and ensure that conflict does not descend to personal attacks. Educational support units often contain individuals who combine expertise in education with good facilitation skills; their services may come free of charge. Some departments have found it worthwhile to employ their own educational specialist for the first year or two of the project. Such a person can fill a variety of roles: assisting with the design, facilitating meetings, and providing training and development closely targeted to the needs of staff and the specific course.

The kinds of structured processes which can be helpful in managing large meetings include procedures like the 'nominal group technique' (Delbecq *et al.*, 1975). Nominal group technique can help to bring a large group to agreement over questions such as which topics or units must be considered essential and which optional. Using this process, all of the options (or topics or units) are listed on a board or in some other form so that they are visible to all members of the meeting. Similar items are clarified and consolidated. Each person is then given a limited number of points (usually ten) and asked to distribute them among those items to which they give highest priority. All points can be given to one item, or they can be spread over as many as ten. The points allocated to each item are then totalled, and the results show the priorities of the meeting as a whole. Because the process is transparent, it usually produces general acceptance of the result.

For the individual working as one of the team driving a course design project, Peter Bloch's work in the management field provides useful advice on how to deal with opponents and adversaries on a one-to-one basis (Block, 1990). He suggests ways of approaching antagonists and soliciting support and recommends using opposition to test ideas and strategies and to clarify and refine one's own position.

Implementing the new course

Clarify what the change involves

The first step in implementation should involve clarifying as concretely as possible what the change will mean for all of the participants. If the change involves different kinds of goals and objectives it will be necessary to spend time exploring the ways in which the new knowledge, skills or attributes will be taught or developed, how their acquisition will be assessed and the criteria that will be used in assessment. If the change involves a component of workplace learning for students, it will be necessary to talk through the logistical difficulties that might ensue – how placements will be found, what will happen if sufficient placements cannot be organized, who will be responsible for liaison between the educational institution and participating organizations, what form that liaison is expected to take and how frequent contact is expected to be. In this way, many problems can be foreseen and avoided. In addition, those responsible are likely to have revisited the goals of the programme and the reasons for change and recommitted themselves to the new direction.

Support staff learning

Any significant curriculum change will probably require teachers to learn new teaching techniques. But it may also require them to adopt new ways of conceptualizing teaching. Recent research has shown that the way in which university teachers think about teaching and learning constrains the kinds of teaching strategies they are prepared to use (Trigwell *et al.*, 1994; Prosser and Trigwell, 1997). It can be quite fruitless to take a straightforward skills approach, demonstrating new methods and expecting teachers to use them, if their concept of teaching does not allow them to see the point. Education rather than training will often be required.

Timing is another issue in the provision of developmental support. It seems obvious that workshops or seminars should be organized before teaching begins, but it usually has to be accepted that this will not be enough. Some staff will not be motivated to seek assistance until they have had experience with the new curriculum, and others will want further help in solving problems or making modifications.

Help students adjust

Staff are not the only ones who may need help in managing the changes. Students may also feel uncomfortable, particularly if only one aspect or section of the course has changed. Where the entire course design is new or represents a complete departure from an earlier course, students will naturally be aware of this and may feel that they are guinea pigs constantly subject to experiment. It may be just as important to convince students of the need for change as it is with staff on the programme. When this occurs, and students are given opportunities to evaluate the new approaches and help to fine-tune the design, they often respond with enthusiasm.

Monitor progress

It is a delusion to believe that the design work is over once the approving authorities have signed off on the paper work and the course is about to begin. It is essential to monitor progress and look out for difficulties. Administrative structures and systems may create difficulties for the new curriculum and require modification. Problem solving groups for teaching staff can monitor the appropriateness and effectiveness of teaching and assessment strategies and the workloads of students and staff.

Implementing a new design for a core unit – a case study

Michael Briers is the coordinator for a core second-year unit in management accounting. The unit regularly attracts 700–800 students and requires a teaching team of between eight and ten staff. Briers has been responsible for initiating and managing a significant redesign of the unit over the last few years. His description of the process has been published elsewhere (Briers and Barber, 1995). In the interview below he talks about the reasons behind the changes in content and teaching:

> In the discipline area of management accounting there has been quite dramatic change in the types of management accounting technologies that organizations are using. We found that the standard material in textbooks was outdated very quickly. We had to develop a way of being able to handle new material as it was coming in, and we needed to develop a mechanism or framework for that to happen. With my own experience and involvement with professional education associations, particularly an experiential learning group, I also saw opportunities to tie in those changes with experiential learning. I started to experiment with different ways of doing things and talking with other people about what I was doing, and I came to see that if you set up the right processes, other staff would take on some of these ideas and move towards a more open and experimental type of teaching.

A lot of accounting people believe that accounting is very technical – which I guess it is – but one of the problems we identify is that students tend to see it as a shopping list of techniques. They were learning those techniques in isolation from any organizational setting so they didn't have any sense of how this worked in context. So the main aim of our content change has been to contextualize the techniques. The students coming into second year have very little organizational experience, but they need to develop their judgement about which tools and techniques to use in what kinds of situations.

The initial pressure for curriculum change here is caused by the need to keep up with rapid change in their discipline. However, an equally powerful influence is the course leader's interest in educational issues, allied with his feeling that the learning outcomes for students should be broader and more focused on the judgement needed to apply knowledge in complex organizations. As a result, both content and teaching approach have undergone substantial change.

The content of the unit now includes a much greater focus on organizational dynamics and the management of change. The broad thrust of the content changes has been to develop an overarching framework concerned with understanding what constitutes effective resource management, the nature of work processes, how such processes can be improved, what constitutes an improvement, how improvement opportunities can be prioritized and monitored, what problem-solving tools are available and what the change management process involves.

But to support the new direction in the content of the unit, changes have also been made in two other areas. One is the actual management of the course – the staff coordination process. The other is the teaching practices, which are now based on a more experiential model. Students are regularly asked to reflect on the nature of work processes in familiar organizations, such as the university bookshop or their own project teams. The aim is to identify opportunities for improvement. Teachers continually try to help students make connections between their own experiences and what organizations do. But the focus on student experience in the course has also given rise to a whole new repertoire of teaching practices in the small group sessions (the tutorials). As Briers describes it:

> We are still constrained within the traditional lecture-and-tutorial format because of the very large numbers on the course. We still believe that lectures have a role but we don't believe that you can learn a great deal from lectures. Effectively we have come to see a lecture as a support for the tutorial. We see that the tutorial is where the learning occurs, and the way we start to think about the lecture is to ask what sort of information we can convey in a lecture that will help them with this tutorial. We try and have some sort of conceptual diagram for each week and for the course overall. So we use the tutorial to point out the interrelations between each unit of work and the previous unit of work and the themes in the subject.

It's a two-hour tutorial. One tutorial might have a debate, another a role play, another a simulation game, a whole host of things. The idea is that at the end the students can associate a particular topic with something very concrete, something that they've done, an exercise that stands out. Tutorials are highly interactive, but they are also highly structured. It's not left to chance. It wasn't always this way but we've grown in confidence with it.

Managing the process

Apart from changes to the content and teaching approach, the other significant area of change has been in the management of the course and the introduction of a continuous improvement process. Because enrolments are so high – about 700–800 students – the unit requires a teaching team of between eight and ten staff members. As a way of continually improving the course design, and to ensure consistency among the different tutorial groups, the course is managed through a weekly meeting which follows the block of tutorials for that week. For that meeting each staff member prepares a semi-structured reflection sheet. It indicates the good things that happened in the tutorial, any aspect that did not go well, what needs to be improved and how this would be done. The focus is not only on the content of the material for that tutorial but also on how it was delivered – the mix of activities and the focus on one major theme. Briers describes the way in which these meetings operate as follows:

In the first half hour of the meeting we discuss the reflection sheet. We look at the previous week's tutorials and how they went and people offer their comments and suggestions on whether those activities should change the next time. At the end of the first half hour, the senior member of staff who is responsible each week for a particular week fills out an improvement sheet which basically summarizes what everybody said, and that goes into a file for next year.

In the second half of the meeting, the person who is responsible for the next tutorial outlines the approach to that tutorial. So we spend the second half of the meeting focusing more on the learning activities. Sometimes I might demonstrate a particular activity with the staff there. Occasionally we invite professionals from other areas – educational specialists. For example we had someone come in and talk to us about role playing when we were trying to develop our role playing exercises. Next year I've got in mind someone who is going to come and help us with some cross-cultural issues that we're trying to cover in the course.

Incidentally we make this process transparent to students. Students know that we have this weekly meeting and are told of any improvements or any changes that we make. They see us trying to improve – again, building on the course's change and improvement theme. We are trying to model the change and quality improvement process for the students as they learn about it as the content of the course.

These weekly meetings provide an excellent example of the kinds of staff development processes which really work to support staff as they explore new approaches to teaching and new teaching techniques. The focus is always on practical advice, learning from experience and calling on specialist help as required.

Overcoming resistance

Changes of this extent will not be welcomed by all staff. I asked Briers if he had met with much resistance.

> When we first introduced the changes, there was some resistance – I must say it wasn't wholesale resistance. The resistance came from the older members of staff who were happy going through a textbook chapter by chapter and were fairly comfortable with the chalk-and-talk model, which gave them much more control in the classroom.
>
> But we also had young people, and particularly some very bright young staff who really hadn't had much background in tertiary teaching. We found that they took on these changes and different styles of teaching with gusto, and mostly they would outscore the senior staff on student evaluations. I guess that made the senior staff, who were more reticent about the changes, start seeing that if they didn't do it they were going to be left out.
>
> I think that we made this work because we structured the meeting in a very collegial, open manner. We don't dictate, we try and allow for individual experimentation. We do have a structure, and part of the principles of change management is this notion of standardizing. Because we have lots of large courses and large numbers of staff we have to standardize to some extent, but we also have to allow scope for individual experimentation. In the meetings, we talk about the comfort zone, and how we all have different comfort zones. What we've found is that people now say, 'Look, I just don't feel comfortable doing that', and so we come up with alternatives. They might try something a bit different which suits their particular style and we encourage them to talk about how that went in the next meeting. Even though some more conservative staff members don't want to go as far as some of the younger staff, we find that they can still make a contribution by making modifications to what they do and doing what they feel more comfortable with.
>
> In those sorts of ways we try to have an open, consultative, cooperative process and encourage any contribution and acknowledge any difficulties people are having. It is not something you can achieve overnight, but after four or five years of doing this, people coming on to the course have an expectation that when they come to teach on this course they have a one-hour weekly meeting. Casual staff know that they get paid for this one-hour meeting and they don't want to miss it. The last few years we have

had 100 per cent attendance except for sickness, and the staff have started to see that this is a very important way of contributing to the course. We try to stick within the one-hour limit, we try and start exactly on the hour and finish on the hour. Initially people didn't like the idea because they thought it was just another meeting. It took some convincing that an hour at this meeting would save them two or three hours in preparation. Being able to talk through the ideas and making people comfortable with the material is far more effective than a written description.

But at the meeting they do get a document that outlines the desired learning outcomes, the class exercises and questions, and the suggested teaching approaches. So there is that structure – but there's a fine balance between standardizing and providing a structure that allows for individual differences, I guess.

The impact of the changes

In considering curriculum change it is always difficult to know whether it is better to start with small projects or to opt for major overhaul of the entire curriculum. Fullan suggests that the most powerful and long-lasting changes are likely to occur when small pilot projects first demonstrate that effective change is possible and those changes are then taken up and promoted by senior managers who provide structural support to enable change to happen on a wider scale (Fullan, 1994). In the management accounting course being described here, the department has not yet adopted this approach throughout its curriculum but a wider impact has been discernible. Briers comments on the impact of his work:

The most tangible impact of the changes is that the student ratings have been quite excellent: we've graphed them and there has been a steady improvement in all dimensions. Most striking is the students' engagement with the course. They are very willing to give feedback on all aspects. They think it's a very positive thing, knowing that the staff are trying to model the process that they're going through. In addition, staff have been able to translate some of the techniques and activities we do to other courses that they teach. I continually get feedback on how they go there.

Sometimes if you're going to make some changes you wonder where to start. Do you start on a grand scale or do you start on a small scale and build on your successes? We started on a small scale and it's worked really well for us. The staff who were teaching on the subject developed confidence. People now talk about how they push back their comfort zones and what they can do in classes. We have a very strong research emphasis in the school, but people are starting to see that they don't have to feel bad about spending so much time on teaching because they're getting so much reward from it and enjoying their teaching time.

Evaluation and the politics of survival

Evaluation will occur whether planned or not. Those who come in contact with the programme are likely to make some informal evaluation of it, particularly if it is in any way different from the norm. These informal evaluations are often based on limited experience or anecdotes passed on by others. Outsiders are likely to judge the programme against criteria which do not necessarily reflect the course designers' goals – looking at aspects like cost, performance on standardized tests of knowledge, and the 'efficiency' of delivery methods – when the programme may have been redesigned to improve interpersonal skills or self-directed learning abilities. It is human nature to make such judgements, but it is also human nature to mistrust the unfamiliar. Off-the-cuff judgements can be damaging to a new programme, particularly when they are made by those in positions of influence. It is therefore important, as part of the course design, to develop an evaluation programme which will provide evidence of the degree to which the programme meets its own goals and which also attempts to evaluate the programme from other perspectives.

To try to bring greater open-mindedness and different perspectives to curriculum evaluation, Michael Eraut has developed and used what he calls *divergent evaluation*. He proposes that the following questions be asked in developing an evaluation plan:

- How is the programme viewed from divergent value positions?
- By what criteria do people decide whether it is worthwhile?
- Are there any additional criteria it would be appropriate to introduce?
- What arguments could be used to justify or criticize the programme?
- What value judgements or empirical judgements would these involve?
- How well supported by evidence are the arguments?

(Eraut, 1984)

Evaluating a controversial medical degree

The medical course at the University of Newcastle in New South Wales was designed around problem-based learning with a particular focus on early clinical experience, population medicine and ongoing, self-directed learning. Students in the programme are selected through a comprehensive interview and testing process and represent a broader range of ages, backgrounds and academic achievement than is usual in most Australian medical schools. As the first problem-based medical degree in an Australian university it has been the subject of some controversy, and its programme and graduates have come under considerable scrutiny.

The Faculty of Medicine is also unusual in that it maintains its own Programme Evaluation Office. Since the inauguration of the degree in the late 1970s, extensive research has been carried out on those aspects which distinguish the Newcastle medical programme. In particular research has focused on three questions:

- What admission variables (such as age, gender, academic preparation) are associated with graduates' performance as interns?
- How do graduates from Newcastle perform and how do they compare with others?
- What are the factors that influence graduates to practise in rural areas? (The programme has a focus on community medicine.)

Research done in the school has been able to establish that neither age, gender, high-school marks, previous degrees nor admission scores could predict performance as an intern. Only previous study in both humanities and science prior to medical school, rather than science alone, was a predictor of higher-rated performance as an intern. These results have been used to vindicate the school's broader admissions policy.

On the second question, evaluations of Newcastle graduates by clinical supervisors have been analysed against those for all other medical graduates practising as hospital interns in the state. This analysis, carried out since the early 1990s, has shown that Newcastle graduates are more highly rated than their peers from traditional medical schools on their ability to interact with others, self-directed learning and reliability.

And finally, the research on those graduates who take up the hard-to-fill places in rural Australia has shown that they are more likely to come from a rural background themselves. This information has been used to ease the admissions criteria slightly in favour of students from rural backgrounds (Rolfe and Pearson, 1997).

Findings such as these provide assurance that the programme is meeting its goals and can be used to demonstrate its strengths. But the Newcastle faculty have also researched those areas which they believe may potentially be perceived as weaknesses in their programme. One of these is the question of how the basic sciences are learned in an integrated curriculum, based on clinical problems, when study groups may be led by clinicians rather than scientists and the students must identify and investigate basic science issues for themselves.

Analysis of taped tutorial sessions and students' written reports showed that most students could and did recognize and investigate the basic science issues underlying clinical problems to appropriate depth. However, a significant minority did not, leading the researchers to recommend that clear guidance must be given to students in problem-based learning groups to ensure that basic science issues are tackled at appropriate depth and feedback provided on results to correct any misapprehensions. On the question of whether students are likely to be disadvantaged in groups led by generalists, it was found that the personal style and tutoring skills of the group leader were more important than disciplinary background in helping students identify basic science issues (Rostas and Olson, 1997).

Evaluation studies of this type provide significant benefits to the programme by suggesting areas for improvement; they also help to counter criticism. It is not easy to get time and resources to carry out evaluation studies, but it is possible. University development grants and quality improvement funds are likely sources of funding, and professional associations have also provided funding. When well designed and executed, such studies can be published and form part of the department's research contribution. In any case the investment involved in designing and mounting a degree programme, and the increasing importance of well-designed programmes in attracting income to the institution, may encourage administrators to make resources available.

Ensuring the continuing quality of the course

In the past decade governments have instituted a variety of mechanisms aimed at making universities and colleges accountable for the quality of their teaching programmes. Examples include the external evaluations of teaching and learning provision in subject areas undertaken by the Quality Assessment Division of the Higher Education Funding Council for England (HEFCE, 1998); the Ministry of Education requirement in New Zealand that universities and polytechnics define learning objectives and assessment criteria (Harvey and Knight, 1996: 89); and the Australian government's offers of additional funding to those universities who could demonstrate that they had the best quality assurance procedures in place (NBEET: HEC, 1992).

All too frequently, such mechanisms result in people and institutions focusing on the form rather than the substance. (Do all units have documented aims and objectives? – tick. Has the content been updated in the past five years? – tick. Do we allocate firsts, seconds and thirds in the correct proportions? – tick.) At worst, these well-intentioned requirements do nothing except generate work which distracts academics from the possibility of improving their teaching.

When mechanisms like external reviews and accreditation procedures do improve the curriculum offered to students, it is because the process manages to engender the two key factors of pressure and support described earlier. For this to happen there must be a real possibility that the review process will fail to accredit the course, and the review process must generate opportunities for staff to learn new ways of doing things. Richard Henry, Professor of Paediatrics at the University of Newcastle, has described the impact of the development of a system of formal accreditation of medical schools by the Australian Medical Council. Initially, some medical faculties assumed that the process of accreditation would be virtually automatic, but complacency was shattered when three of the ten Australian schools and one New Zealand school received only limited accreditation rather than the maximum ten-year accreditation.

The accreditation process required each medical school to put together a portfolio documenting curriculum, facilities, admissions policies and research performance, and this was followed up by a week-long visit from a team of five to ten academics from other medical schools. Henry describes one of the unforeseen benefits of this process:

Another consequence of accreditation was that senior academic members of medical faculties were exposed to the curricula of other medical schools in a way that many had not previously experienced. The accreditation process fostered a collegiate approach. Some academics who had viewed with considerable scepticism, and sometimes hostility, any educational practices different from those conducted in their own institutions, came to appreciate that there were many examples of good teaching and learning elsewhere. At the same time there was a growing realization that there were deficiencies within their own curricula.

Perhaps all the changes that have occurred subsequently would have taken place without the AMC and its accreditation process. Three of the ten medical schools elected to overhaul their courses completely. Admission policies were changed (in three schools to graduate entry with criteria for interview that were no longer exclusively academic) and problem based learning, self-directed learning, population medicine and critical reasoning all became popular terms.

(Henry *et al.*, 1997: 1–2)

Evaluation by students is another mechanism that has been widely promoted as a means of assuring the quality of teaching. Unfortunately, evaluation on its own does nothing to improve poor teaching. Many academics who receive poor student evaluations do not improve over time – their evaluations remain consistently poor. A study of how academics use their student evaluation data demonstrates how this happens. Busuttil (1996) found that the academics at the university that he studied fell into three groups in respect of their use of student evaluation data. One group, largely comprising academics with some formal preparation for teaching, actively used the student evaluation process to improve their teaching. They designed and inserted their own questions into the standard evaluation instrument to find out about particular aspects of their teaching that they were currently experimenting with. A second group of academics, who predominantly taught small classes with whom they had a high level of interaction, saw the student evaluations simply as confirmation of what they already knew from their close contact with students. This group largely consisted of experienced academics whose teaching was well received by students. The third group, teaching both large and small classes, received poor evaluations but had little idea what might be done to improve them. Coming from departments where teaching had a very low profile and was not discussed, these teachers had no obvious sources of advice within their immediate environment. They tended to rationalize their poor reception by assuming that others had been evaluated equally badly, although this was clearly not the case. Lacking any obvious sources of help and tolerated by their departments, these academics stumbled on from year to year, disliking the large proportion of their time spent in teaching but seemingly unable to find the courage and the motivation to do anything about it. While the evaluation process required by the university brought some pressure to bear, their departments failed to provide the support which might have enabled them to change.

Key factors which support improvement

In my experience there are two factors more important than any others in maintaining the quality of a course. These are the existence of a collaborative culture, and a commitment to critical examination among the teaching staff.

Such a culture and commitment assumes that the educational programme of the department is a communal responsibility; that course design and delivery is a complex activity that will need to be fine-tuned over time; that teaching projects, like research projects, benefit from the scrutiny and suggestions of academic peers; and that design of teaching methodologies, like design of research methodologies, can often be improved by being talked through with colleagues.

The role of leaders

Departmental leaders can assist the development of such a culture by taking whatever opportunities arise to improve relationships among staff and relations with the discipline's community, and by creating occasions when different aspects of the department's teaching are up for examination, comment and discussion. Good course coordinators and heads of department create many such occasions, including informal seminars to present a colleague's teaching innovation, lunchtime discussions of teaching problems, collaborative review of teaching and support of teaching teams.

Importance of course review

Course review is an important part of the process. While individual units may be fine-tuned and updated yearly, this in itself creates a need to review the whole course at intervals if coherence is to be maintained. The length of the intervals may be mandated by the institution or an accrediting body or be left to the judgement of the department itself. Difficult though it is to find the time to look at the course as a whole, it is important to do so. I have encountered at least one course where, although the content of individual units was updated regularly and independently by the academics involved, the whole course of study had not been reviewed in over 15 years. The increase in the workload alone, owing to the fact that the 'owner' of each unit was continually adding new information and deleting very little, warranted a major review of the course.

Bringing in new members of the teaching team

Good induction for new staff members is also vital in ensuring that the course remains true to the original intentions. While new staff members are usually informed about the content for which they will be responsible, the aspects most likely to be neglected are the philosophy of the course, the teaching team's beliefs and values, and the core abilities which it is important for students to develop. These omissions commonly occur even when the course has recently been developed and much time and effort has gone into reaching agreement on goals and purposes. One academic who had been teaching on a course for three years, after joining it two years after it was inaugurated, undertook an investigation of the course development process as part of a postgraduate course in higher education. After interviewing members of the original design team she commented:

> I now feel that the concerns that I had at the outset are perhaps attribut-able to the approach to teaching and learning taken by individual lectur-ers in some units, rather than to the curriculum itself. In planning the curriculum the designers began with a focused vision – the education of professionals which encouraged the development of critical intellectual skills. Has this been achieved? I believe that to a large extent it is true to say that it has. The educational principles underlying the degree are consist-ent with this vision, as are the objectives. However, it may also be true to say that others who do not share this vision or beliefs may have comprom-ised these principles.

Knowing the intentions of the original course designers enabled her to see a logic in the choice and structure of units which had not been apparent before. It also enabled her to see that the original clear focus of the course was in danger of being lost because newer members of the teaching team had not been exposed to the educational principles on which the course was based.

Conclusion

Until recently, most programmes of study have been put together as collections of individual units. Individual academics have been given responsibility for each unit and left to develop the detail of content, teaching and assessment as they see fit. It is assumed that academics are teaching those topics which fit their particular research interests and thus will bring a high degree of enthusi-asm and expert knowledge to teaching. What is wrong with this model? Why is it necessary to change?

The first point to note is that the idea that academics teach only in those areas which are the subject of their research interests is clearly no longer true (if it ever was). Harvey and Knight report that in 1992 between 30 per cent and 60 per cent of academics in the UK taught for 21 hours or more per week during term time. These very high teaching loads mean that only a very few of those hours will actually reflect academic research interests. The majority of them will involve the academic as a generalist, teaching the fundamental knowledge of the discipline. This foundation teaching may be rotated among staff, but without a collaborative approach to course design, each staff member is left to reinvent the unit and bring his or her particular slant to the subject matter involved. Many academics do not feel particularly confident or comfortable in the area of course design. Most lack any training in this aspect of their work and have little exposure to different approaches and innovative examples. It is an aspect of academic work where many could benefit from the support provided by collaborative work, particularly if expert advice is also available.

But the possible benefits to academics through a more coherent and collaborative approach to course design are minor compared to the benefits for students. The traditional curriculum, in which each unit is an artefact of the individual academic, in which the educational purpose is neither stated nor discussed and assessment requirements are unclear, has a very negative impact on many students. It quickly becomes apparent to them that the most important lesson to learn concerns the lecturer. What topics does she think more important? What are his particular quirks, his likes and dislikes? What is it that she wants?

This focus on personalities is bound to distract students from the real work in hand. While some students accept it as the natural order, others resent their dependence and powerlessness. Certainly, it is hard to see how critical thought and independent judgement can be fostered through such unequal relationships.

Real learning in higher education needs to take place between consenting adults. Ideas about what is important, what knowledge and skills are essential to learn, what might constitute progress in learning or competence to practise or even excellence, need to be brought out into the open and discussed. As part of their education students need to understand what the educational process is about and how their contributions will be judged.

Clarity is one important goal of course design and integration is another. Integration is not something that teachers can do for students. It does require teachers to create opportunities whereby students are pushed to make connections between different domains of knowledge, whereby they must consider a problem from different viewpoints and must begin to construct the basis of their own future expertise. Creating opportunities for integration in the curriculum requires staff to plan together, to have some understanding of the requirements of other parts of the course, together with a sense of where the course as a whole should lead.

As a postgraduate student in the United States, I undertook a considerable amount of course work as part of my degree, in a department which subscribed to what might now be called a capabilities-based approach to course design. As a consequence, the learning goals and objectives of all units were clearly laid out and linked to the assessment tasks. Learning and assessment tasks usually required the application of knowledge to 'real' and complex problems.

Compared to the confusion and uncertainty I experienced in my very traditional undergraduate degree, I found this clarity of purpose and expectations absolutely liberating. It was particularly valuable to me as a student coming into another culture, which, although English speaking, was at times surprisingly alien. It enabled me to bring a clear focus to my work and I felt that when I succeeded it was by design rather than by accident. Although many of my professors were exceptional teachers, not all of them were. To a great extent, however, the clear structure and purpose, the coherent design of the course provided the support which enabled students to succeed.

For many students at present, higher education is a negative and frustrating experience. More than anything, it is about getting a qualification which will enable one to leave and do something else. As student numbers and class sizes grow, so does the potential for more students to experience inferior education. Increasing pressures on higher education make it even more necessary to think clearly about what we want to achieve educationally and what might be the most important experiences and outcomes for students. I would like to think that with more imaginative, more coherent, more collaborative and more transparent approaches to course design more students might find higher education a truly liberating and educational experience.

Acknowledgement

I would like to thank Geoff Scott, who has helped me to develop many of the ideas in this chapter about managing educational change.

References

Albanese, M. and Mitchell, S. (1993) Problem-based learning: a review of literature on its outcomes and implementation issues, *Academic Medicine*, 68(1): 52–81.

Allan, J. (1996) Learning outcomes in higher education, *Studies in Higher Education*, 21(1): 93–108.

Alverno College Faculty (1994) Course outcomes for EN210 Perspectives on literature: the storyteller's art, in *Student Assessment-as-Learning at Alverno College*. Milwaukee, WI: Alverno College Institute.

Anderson, G., Boud, D. and Sampson, J. (1996) *Learning Contracts: A Practical Guide*. London: Kogan Page.

Ash, S., Gonczi, A. and Hager, P. (1992) *Combining Research Methodologies to Develop Competency-based Standards for Dietitians: A Case Study for the Professions*. Canberra: Australian Government Publishing Service.

Auckland Institute of Technology (1995) *Bachelor of Business Degree: Definitive Document*. Auckland: AIT.

Barnett, R. (1994) *The Limits of Competence*. Buckingham: SRHE and Open University Press.

Belenky, M. F., Clinchy, B. M., Goldberger, N. R. and Tarule, J. M. (1986) *Women's Ways of Knowing: The Development of Self, Voice and Mind*. New York: Basic Books.

Benner, P. (1984) *From Novice to Expert: Excellence and Power in Clinical Nursing Practice*. Menlo Park, CA: Addison Wesley.

Biggs, J. B. (1979) Individual differences in study processes and the quality of learning outcomes, *Higher Education*, 8: 381–94.

Biggs, J. B. (1982) Student motivation and study strategies in university and college of advanced education populations, *Higher Education Research and Development*, 1: 33–55.

Biggs, J. B. (1987) *Student Approaches to Learning and Studying*. Hawthorn: Australian Council for Educational Research.

Biggs, J. B. (1989) Approaches to the enhancement of tertiary teaching, *Higher Education Research and Development*, 8(1): 7–25.

Biggs, J. B. (1992) A qualitative approach to grading students, *HERDSA News*, 14(3): 3–6.

Biggs, J. B. (1995) Student approaches to learning, constructivism, and student centred learning, in *Twentieth International Conference on Improving University Teaching*. University of Maryland: University College.

Biggs, J. B. (1996) Enhancing teaching through constructive alignment, *Higher Education*, 32: 347–64.

Biggs, J. B. (1999) *What the Student Does: Teaching for Quality Learning in Universities*. Buckingham: SRHE and Open University Press.

Biggs, J. B. and Collis, K. F. (1982) *Evaluating the Quality of Learning: The SOLO Taxonomy*. New York: Academic Press.

Bligh, D. (1975) *Teaching Students*. Exeter: Exeter University Teaching Services.

Block, P. (1990) *The Empowered Manager: Positive Political Skills at Work.* San Francisco: Jossey-Bass.

Bock, H. (1983) What are remedial problems? A tentative analysis, in C. Webb and H. Drury (eds) *The Communication Needs of Tertiary Level Students: Proceedings of the Australasian Tertiary Study Skills Conference.* University of Sydney: Language Study Centre.

Bocock, J. (1994) Curriculum change and professional identity: the role of the university lecturer, in J. Bocock and D. Watson (eds) *Managing the University Curriculum.* Buckingham: SRHE and Open University Press.

Borbasi, S., Shea, A., Mulquiney, J., Wilkinson, M. and Athanasou, J. (1993) *An Investigation of the Reliability and Validity of the Objective Structured Clinical Examination (OSCE) as an Instrument in Assessing the Clinical Competence of Undergraduate Nursing Students.* Sydney: University of Sydney, Faculty of Nursing.

Boud, D. (1995) *Enhancing Learning Through Self Assessment.* London: Kogan Page.

Boud, D. and Falchikov, N. (1995) What does research tell us about self assessment?, in D. Boud (ed.) *Enhancing Learning through Self Assessment.* London: Kogan Page.

Boud, D., Keogh, R. and Walker, D. (1985) *Reflection: Turning Experience into Learning.* London: Kogan Page.

Bowden, J. A. and Masters, G. N. (1993) *Implications for Higher Education of a Competency-based Approach to Education and Training.* Canberra: Australian Government Publishing Service.

Boyatzis, R. E. (1995) Gatekeepers of the enterprise: assessing faculty intent and the student outcome, in R. E. Boyatzis, S. S. Cowen and D. A. Kolb *Innovation in Professional Education.* San Francisco: Jossey-Bass.

Boyatzis, R. E., Cowen, S. S. and Kolb, D. A. (1995) *Innovation in Professional Education.* San Francisco: Jossey-Bass.

Briers, M. and Barber, T. (1995) Continuously improving teaching and learning, in L. Hewson and S. Toohey (eds) *The Changing University: Proceedings of the Biennial Education Conference, UNSW Education '95,* Sydney: University of New South Wales: Professional Development Centre.

Brookfield, S. D. (1990) *The Skillful Teacher.* San Francisco, Jossey-Bass.

Brown, S. and Knight, P. (1994) *Assessing Students in Higher Education.* London: Kogan Page.

Brookfield, S. D. (1990) *The Skillful Teacher.* San Francisco, Jossey-Bass.

Brumby, M. (1984) Misconceptions about the concept of natural selection by medical biology students, *Science Education,* 68(4): 493–503.

Busuttil, A. (1996) 'A study exploring the linkage between student evaluation of teaching and teaching development', unpublished MHEd thesis. University of New South Wales.

Butler, J. (1996) Professional development: practice as text, reflection as process, and self as locus, *Australian Journal of Education,* 40(3): 265–83.

Candy, P., Crebert, G. and O'Leary, J. (1994) *Developing Lifelong Learners through Undergraduate Education.* Canberra: Australian Government Publishing Service.

Cartwright, N. (1997) *Assessment and Feedback: A Handbook for Tertiary Teachers.* Ballarat: University of Ballarat.

Chizmar, J. (1998) *Course contract for ECO 131: Economic Reasoning Using Statistics.* At http:// 138.87.168.39/Jack_Chizmar/ECO131/syllabus131_981.html (on 2 January 1999). Department of Economics, Illinois State University.

Clampitt, S. (1998) *Introduction to Linguistics ENGL3073: Course Syllabus.* Inter American University of Puerto Rico at http://ponce.inter.edu/proyecto/in/huma/ENGL3073/main3073.html (on 26 April 1998).

Cohen, R., Flowers, R., McDonald, R. and Schaafsma, H. (1993) *Learning from Experience Counts: Recognition of Prior Learning in Australian Universities,* Commissioned Report for the Australian Vice Chancellors' Committee, Working Party on Credit Transfer and Recognition of Prior Learning. Sydney: University of Technology, Sydney.

Cohen, S. A. (1987) Instructional alignment: searching for a magic bullet, *Educational Researcher,* 16(8): 16–20.

Crombie, A. (1985) The nature and type of search conferences, *International Journal of Lifelong Education,* 4(1): 3–33.

Dahlgren, L. O. (1984) Outcomes of learning, in F. Marton, D. Hounsell and N. Entwhistle (eds) *The Experience of Learning*. Edinburgh: Scottish Academic Press.

Delbecq, A. L., Van de Ven, A. H. and Gustafson, D. H. (1975) *Group Techniques for Program Planning: A Guide to Nominal Group and Delphi Processes*. Glenview, IL: Scott Foresman and Company.

Diamond, R. M. (1989) *Designing and Improving Courses and Curricula in Higher Education*. San Francisco: Jossey-Bass.

Eisner, E. W. (1994) *The Educational Imagination: On the Design and Evaluation of School Programs*, 3rd edn. New York: Macmillan.

Elton, L. (1994) Enterprise in higher education: an agent for change?, in P. T. Knight (ed.) *University Wide Change, Staff and Curriculum Development: SEDA paper 83*. Birmingham: Staff and Educational Development Association (SEDA).

Entwhistle, N. J. (1981) *Styles of Learning and Teaching*. New York: John Wiley and Sons.

Entwhistle, N. and Ramsden, P. (1983) *Understanding Student Learning*. London: Croom Helm.

Eraut, M. (1984) Handling values issues, in C. Adelman (ed.) *The Politics and Ethics of Evaluation*. London: Croom Helm.

Falchikov, N. and Boud, D. (1989) Student self-assessment in higher education: a meta analysis, *Review of Educational Research*, 59(4): 395–430.

Feletti, G. and Wallis, B. (1985) Issues in course design, in D. Boud (ed.) *Problem-Based Learning in Education for the Professions*. Kensington, NSW: Higher Education Research and Development Society of Australasia.

Freire, P. (1970) *Pedagogy of the Oppressed*. New York: Seabury Press.

Fullan, M. G. (1994) Coordinating top-down and bottom-up strategies for educational reform, in *Systemic Reform: Perspectives on Personalizing Education* at http://www.ed.gov/ pubs/ EdReformStudies/SysReforms/fullan1.html (on 12 April 1998). US Department of Education: Office of Educational Research and Improvement.

Fullan, M. G. and Stiegelbauer, S. (1991) *The New Meaning of Educational Change*. London: Cassell.

Gagne, R. M. (1977) *The Conditions of Learning*, 3rd edn. New York: Holt, Rinehart and Winston.

Gardner, H. (1993) *Frames of Mind: The Theory of Multiple Intelligences*, 2nd edn. London: Fontana.

Gardner, H. (1994) *Creating Minds*. New York: Basic Books.

Gibbs, G. (1992) Improving the quality of student learning through course design, in R. Barnett (ed.) *Learning to Effect*. Buckingham: SRHE and Open University Press.

Gibbs, G., Habeshaw, S. and Habeshaw, T. (1984) *53 Interesting Things to do in Your Lectures*. Bristol: Technical and Educational Services.

Gibbs, G., Habeshaw, S. and Habeshaw, T. (1986) *53 Interesting Ways to Assess Your Students*. Bristol: Technical and Educational Services.

Gibbs, G., Lucas, L. and Simonite, V. (1996) Class size and student performance: 1984–94, *Studies in Higher Education*, 21(3): 261–73.

Gonczi, A., Hager, P. and Oliver, L. (1990) *Establishing Competency-based Standards in the Professions*. Canberra: Australian Government Publishing Service.

Habermas, J. (1972) *Knowledge and Human Interests*. London: Heinemann.

Habeshaw, S., Gibbs, G. and Habeshaw, T. (1987) *53 Interesting Things to do in Your Seminars and Tutorials*. Bristol: Technical and Educational Services.

Hart, M. U. (1992) *Working and Educating for Life: Feminist and International Perspectives on Adult Education*. London: Routledge.

Harvey, L. and Knight, P. T. (1996) *Transforming Higher Education*. Buckingham: SRHE and Open University Press.

Henry, R., Byrne, K. and Engel, C. (eds) (1997) *Imperatives in Medical Education: The Newcastle Approach*. Newcastle: Faculty of Medicine and Health Sciences, University of Newcastle.

Hewson, L. and Hughes, C. (in press) An online postgraduate subject in information technology for university teachers, *Innovations in Education and Training International*.

Heywood, J. (1989) *Assessment in Higher Education*, 2nd edn. Chichester: John Wiley and Sons.

Higher Education Funding Council for England [HEFCE] (1998) Assessing the Quality of Education: HEFCE Quality Assessment Report. at http://www.niss.ac. uk/education/hefce/qar/assess.html (on 27 April 1998).

Higher Education Quality Council [HEQC]: Quality Enhancement Group (1997) What are graduates? Clarifying the attributes of 'graduateness', *DeLiberations* at http://www.lgu.ac.uk/deliberations/graduates/starter.html (on 14 August 1998).

Hillman, M. and Hargreaves, J. (1994) *A Question of Balance: A Report on a Research Project into Socio-Legal Practice*. Sydney: Law Foundation of NSW and School of Social Work, UNSW.

hooks, b. (1994) *Teaching to Transgress: Education as the Practice of Freedom*. New York: Routledge.

Hughes, C. and Hewson, L. (1998) Online interactions: developing a neglected aspect of the virtual classroom, *Educational Technology*, 38(4): 48–55.

Hughes, C., Toohey, S. and Hatherly, S. (1992) Developing learning centred trainers and tutors, *Studies in Continuing Education*, 14(1): 14–27.

Hurley, J. and Dare, A. (1985) A problem-based program in management education, in D. Boud (ed.) *Problem-Based Learning in Education for the Professions*. Kensington, NSW: Higher Education Research and Development Society of Australasia.

Kemmis, S., Cole, P. and Suggett, D. (1983) *Towards the Socially Critical School: Orientations to Curriculum and Transition*. Melbourne: Victorian Institute of Secondary Education.

Kemp, J. E. (1977) *Instructional Design*, 2nd edn. Belmont, CA: Fearon Pitman.

Knowles, M. S. and associates (1984) *Andragogy in Action*. San Francisco: Jossey-Bass.

Langer, E. J. (1989) *Mindfulness*. Reading, MA: Addison Wesley.

Larson, L. E. (1993) The two classroom cultures: challenge to instructors, *The Teaching Professor*, December, 3–4.

Laurillard, D. (1993) *Rethinking University Teaching: A Framework for the Effective Use of Educational Technology*. London: Routledge.

Limerick, D. L. and Cunnington, B. (1993) *Managing the New Organisation*. Chatswood, NSW: Business and Professional Publishing.

Loacker, G., Cromwell, L., Fey, J. and Rutherford, D. (1984) *Analysis and Communication at Alverno: An Approach to Critical Thinking*. Milwaukee, WI: Alverno Productions.

Lovat, T. J. and Smith, D. L. (1995) *Curriculum: Action on Reflection Revisited*, 3rd edn. Wentworth Falls, NSW: Social Science Press.

Mager, R. (1975) *Preparing Instructional Objectives*, 2nd edn. Belmont, CA: Fearon-Pitman Publishers.

Marton, F. and Säljö, R. (1976) On qualitative differences in learning: I. Outcome and process, *British Journal of Educational Psychology*, 46: 4–11.

Marton, F., Beaty, E., Dall'Alba, G. (1993) Conceptions of learning, *International Journal of Educational Research*, 19: 277–300.

Mentkowski, M., Astin, A. W., Ewell, P. T. and Moran, E. T. (1991) *Catching Theory up with Practice: Conceptual Frameworks for Assessment*. Washington, DC: American Association for Higher Education.

Miller, C. M. L. and Parlett, M. (1974) *Up to the Mark: A Study of the Examination Game*. London: Society for Research into Higher Education.

Ministry of Education, New Zealand (1991) *Financial Reporting for Tertiary Institutions*. Wellington: New Zealand Government.

Mostyn, G. and Luketina, D. (1995) Major curriculum reform for environmental engineers, in L. Hewson and S. Toohey (eds) *The Changing University: Proceedings of the Biennial Education Conference, UNSW Education '95*. Sydney: University of New South Wales, Professional Development Centre.

National Board of Employment Education and Training: Higher Education Council [NBEET: HEC] (1992) *Higher Education: Achieving Quality*. Canberra: Australian Government Publishing Service.

Nicholls, A. and Nicholls, S. H. (1978) *Developing A Curriculum: A Practical Guide*, 2nd edn. London: Allen and Unwin.

Nightingale, P. and O'Neil, M. (1994) *Achieving Quality Learning in Higher Education*. London: Kogan Page.

Nightingale, P., Te Wiata, I., Toohey, S., Ryan, G., Hughes, C. and Magin, D. (1996) *Assessing Learning in Universities*. Sydney: UNSW Press.

Perkins, D. (1995) *Outsmarting IQ: The Emerging Science of Learnable Intelligence*. New York: Free Press.

Perry, W. G. (1970) *Forms of Intellectual and Ethical Development in the College Years.* New York: Holt, Rinehart and Winston.

Perry, W. G. (1988) Different worlds in the same classroom, in P. Ramsden (ed.) *Improving Learning: New Perspectives.* London: Kogan Page.

Posner, G. J. (1995) *Analyzing the Curriculum,* 2nd edn. New York: McGraw Hill.

Prosser, M. and Trigwell, K. (1991) Student evaluations of teaching and courses: student learning approaches and outcomes as criteria of validity, *Contemporary Educational Psychology,* 16: 269–301.

Prosser, M. and Trigwell, K. (1997) Relations between perceptions of the teaching environment and approaches to teaching, *British Journal of Educational Psychology,* 67: 25–35.

Race, P. (1989) *The Open Learning Handbook.* London: Kogan Page.

Ramsden, P. (1983) Institutional variations in British students' approaches to learning and experiences of teaching, *Higher Education,* 12: 691–705.

Ramsden, P. (ed.) (1988) *Improving Learning: New Perspectives.* London: Kogan Page.

Ramsden, P. (1992) *Learning to Teach in Higher Education.* London: Routledge.

Roberts, M. (1996) *Student Guide for MAQM235: Calculus Strand.* University of Newcastle.

Roberts, M. (1997) *Student Guide for Transformation Geometry.* University of Newcastle.

Rolfe, I. and Pearson, S. A. (1997) Programme evaluation: some principles and practicalities, in R. Henry, K. Byrne and C. Engel (eds) *Imperatives in Medical Education: The Newcastle Approach.* Newcastle: Faculty of Medicine and Health Sciences, University of Newcastle.

Romiszowski, A. J. (1981) *Designing Instructional Systems.* London: Kogan Page.

Romiszowski, A. J. (1984) *Producing Instructional Systems.* London: Kogan Page.

Rostas, J. and Olson, L. (1997) Making it work, in R. Henry, K. Byrne and C. Engel (eds) *Imperatives in Medical Education: The Newcastle Approach.* Newcastle, Australia: Faculty of Medicine and Health Sciences, University of Newcastle.

Roth, K. and Anderson, C. (1988) Promoting conceptual change learning from science textbooks, in P. Ramsden (ed.) *Improving Learning: New Perspectives.* London: Kogan Page.

Rowntree, D. (1981) *Developing Courses for Students.* London: McGraw Hill.

Ryan, G., Toohey, S. and Hughes, C. (1996) The purpose, value and structure of the practicum in higher education: a literature review, *Higher Education,* 31: 355–77.

Säljö, R. (1979) *Learning in the Learner's Perspective. I. Some Commonsense Conceptions,* Reports from the Institute of Education, No. 76. University of Goteborg.

Salomon, G. and Globerson, T. (1987) Skill may not be enough: the role of mindfulness in learning and transfer, *International Journal of Educational Research,* 11: 623–37.

Schön, D. (1990) *Educating the Reflective Practitioner.* San Francisco: Jossey-Bass.

School of Medicine: Emory University (1998) *Human Anatomy: Course Syllabus* at http://www.emory.edu/ANATOMY/AnatomyManual/Object.html (on 26 April 1998).

Schwab, J. (1964) Structure of the disciplines: meanings and significances, in G. W. Ford and L. Pugno (eds) *The Structure of Knowledge and the Curriculum.* Chicago: Rand McNally.

Scott, G. (1991) How clever are we in the way we train our workers? *Training and Development in Australia,* 18(2): 7–12.

Scott, G. (1999) *Change Matters: Making a Difference in Education and Training.* Sydney: Allen and Unwin.

Simosko, S. (1991) *APL – A Practical Guide for Professionals.* London: Kogan Page.

Southern Illinois University: School of Medicine (1998) Problem Based Learning Initiative, at http://edaff.siumed.edu/PBLI/Index.htm (on 12 August 1998)

Spencer, L. (1984) *Soft Skill Competencies: Their Identification, Measurement and Development for Professional, Managerial and Human Service Jobs.* Edinburgh: Scottish Council for Research in Education.

Stenhouse, L. (1975) *An Introduction to Curriculum Research and Development.* Oxford: Heinemann.

Stephenson, J. and Weil, S. (1992) *Quality in Learning: A Capability Approach in Higher Education.* London: Kogan Page.

Sternberg, R. (1996) *Successful Intelligence: How Practical and Creative Intelligence Determines Success in Life.* New York: Simon and Schuster.

Stewart, D. T. (1997) *Syllabus for HED/URBS 582: Homelessness and Public Policy.* San Francisco State University at http://thecity.sfsu.edu/~stewartd/hed_urbs.htm (on 15 April 1998).

Taba, H. (1962) *Curriculum Development: Theory and Practice*. New York: Harcourt, Brace and World.

Tompkins, J. (1996) *A Life in School: What the Teacher Learned*. Reading, MA: Addison-Wesley.

Toohey, S. (1996) Managing and developing oneself, in P. Nightingale, I. Te Wiata, S. Toohey, G. Ryan, C. Hughes and D. Magin (1996) *Assessing Learning in Universities*. Sydney: UNSW Press.

Toohey, S. and Magin, D. (1996) Performing procedures and demonstrating techniques, in P. Nightingale, I. Te Wiata, S. Toohey, G. Ryan, C. Hughes and D. Magin (1996) *Assessing Learning in Universities*. Sydney: UNSW Press.

Toohey, S., Ryan, G., McLean, J. and Hughes, C. (1995) Assessing competency-based education and training: a literature review, *Australian and New Zealand Journal of Vocational Education Research*, 3(2): 86–117.

Toohey, S., Ryan, G. and Hughes, C. (1996) Assessing the practicum, *Assessment and Evaluation in Higher Education*, 21(3): 215–27.

Trigwell, K. and Prosser, M. (1991) Relating approaches to study and quality of learning outcomes at the course level, *British Journal of Educational Psychology*, 61: 265–75.

Trigwell, K., Prosser, M. and Taylor, P. (1994) Qualitative differences in approaches to teaching first year university science, *Higher Education*, 27: 75–84.

Tyler, R. W. (1949) *Basic Principles of Curriculum and Instruction*. Chicago: University of Chicago Press.

University of South Australia (1998) *Developing the Qualities of a University of South Australia Graduate: Guide to Writing Courses and Subject Documents*. Adelaide: University of South Australia.

Van Rossum, E. J. and Schenk, S. M. (1984) The relationship between learning conception, study strategy and learning outcome, *British Journal of Educational Psychology*, 54: 73–83.

Van Rossum, E. J., Deijkers, R. and Hamer, R. (1985) Students' learning conceptions and their interpretations of significant educational concepts, *Higher Education*, 14: 617–41.

Wallis, B. (1985) Novelty as a motivator: the need for variety in problem-based formats, in D. Boud (ed.) *Problem-Based Learning in Education for the Professions*. Kensington, NSW: Higher Education Research and Development Society of Australasia.

Watkins, D. (1983) Depth of processing and the quality of learning outcomes, *Instructional Science*, 12: 49–58.

Westhorp, P. (1994) The experience and outcomes of action research and reflective teaching in occupational therapy, in B. Smith (ed.) *The Experience of Reflective University Teachers Addressing Quality in Teaching and Learning: The CUTL Action Research Project*. Adelaide: University of South Australia.

Wheeler, D. K. (1967) *Curriculum Process*. London: University of London Press.

Woods, D. (1985) Problem-based learning and problem solving, in D. Boud (ed.) *Problem-Based Learning in Education for the Professions*. Kensington, NSW: Higher Education Research and Development Society of Australasia.

Index

accreditation
  of medical schools, 199–200
  of prior learning, 115
action learning, 9, 62
Albanese, M., 104
Allan, J., 140, 141
alternative entry routes, 115–16
Alverno College, 74, 94–6
Alverno College Faculty, 145
Anderson, C., 120
Anderson, G., 61, 184
approaches to curriculum, 48–69
approaches to learning, 9–18
Approaches to Study Inventory (ASI), 11
Ash, S., 84
assessment
  and approach to learning, 14–15, 180
  cognitive view, 57
  community expectations, 168
  decisions at course level, 168–72
  of different kinds of learning, 172–80
  discipline-based view, 50
  and educational values, 47
  ensuring fairness, 172
  experiential view, 61
  institutional requirements, 167–8
  of interpretive understanding, 144
  methods, 180–4
  of performance, 182
  and resource pressures, 19
  self and peer, 61, 65, 101, 175, 178,
    184–6
  of self-reflective knowledge, 148–9
  socially critical view, 65
  student view, 167
  systems view, 54
  teacher view, 167
  see also feedback on learning

assessors
  students as, 184–6
  workplace supervisors as, 184
Auckland Institute of Technology, Bachelor
  of Business programme, 75–9,
  106–7
audio conferencing, *see* teleconferencing
audio-visual materials, 163
audio-visual technologies in assessment,
  174–5, 183
Australian Graduate School of Management,
  54
Australian National University, 51

Barber, T., 192
Barnett, R., 99
Belenky, M. F., 72, 131
Benner, P., 86
Biggs, J. B., 9, 11, 13, 16, 17, 100, 141, 152,
  171–2
Bligh, D., 119
Block, P., 191
block teaching, 121
Bock, H., 132
Borbasi, S., 174
Boud, D., 61, 170, 180, 185
Bowden, J. A., 7
Boyatzis, R. E., 40, 72, 188–9
Briers, M., 192–6
Brookfield, S. D., 162
Brown, S., 184
Brumby, M., 120
Butler, J., 154
Bygrave, J., 75–9, 106

Candy, P., 75, 91, 112
capability-based programmes, 9, 67
  case study, 75–9

see also Higher Education for Capability
    project
Cartwright, N., 183, 185
case study assessment, 181–2
CD-ROMs, 163
Center for Critical Thinking, University of
    Sonoma, California, 59
change
    clarifying the nature of, 42
    creating pressure and support for, 189–92
    establishing need for, 41
    factors causing resistance to, 188–9
    getting commitment to, 37–8
    implementing, 39
    learning to, 31–2
    managing, 39–43
    overcoming resistance to, case study,
        195–6
    and staff development, 41–2
    success factors in, 40–3, 189
Chizmar, J., 146
Clampitt, S., 143
class participation, assessment of, 183
classrooms, *see* teaching spaces
climate for learning, 15–16, 17, 60
Clinchy, B. M., 72
clinical placements
    assessment of, 174
    example of structure, 158–9
    for skill development, 125–6
    see also workplace learning
cognitive abilities and course structure,
    105–10
cognitive apprenticeship, 59
cognitive approach to course design, 48,
    55–9, 68
cognitive structures, 105–10
Cohen, R., 115
Cohen, S. A., 141
Colleges of Advanced Education, 7, 12
Collis, K. F., 11
competence standards, 81–2, 83
    and problem-based learning, 111
competency-based approach to course design,
    67–8
    see also systems approach
competency-based structures, 93–100
computer-assisted learning, 163
computer-mediated groups, 122–4, 164
concept mapping, 80
concepts and course structure, 105–10
conceptual change, 59
    and flexible delivery, 118, 120–4
conflict
    in beliefs and values, 68–9
    managing, 190, 191

content
    choosing, 28, 45, 79–90
    cognitive view, 57
    discipline-based view, 50
    experiential view, 61
    setting priorities for, 88
    socially critical view, 65
    systems view, 53
cooperative education, example from
    business, 77
course content, *see* content
course design
    and approaches to learning, 13–20
    case study of implementation, 192–6
    conflict in approach to, 68–9
    determining course framework, 26–33
    implementation of, 39, 191–6
    and motivation to learn, 17
    personnel, 28–35
    philosophical approaches to, 48–69
    problems in, 4–5
    starting points for, 21–5
course design teams
    case study, business, 77
    case study, engineering, 35–7
    choosing, 28–34, 190
    and research, 86
course documentation, *see* documentation
course level, 114–15
course structure
    based on cognitive development, 105–10
    decisions about, 27
    based on logic of subject, 92–3
    hybrid, 110–12
    performance or competency-based,
        93–100
    and professional education, 127–8
    project-, inquiry- or problem-based,
        100–12
Cowen, S. S., 40, 188
critical incident, 74, 85–6
    case study, 87–8
critical theory, 63–4
critical thinking
    and course structure, 107–10
    and flexible delivery, 121
    and group work, 121
Crombie, A., 81
Cunnington, B., 6
curriculum documentation, *see*
    documentation
curriculum organization, *see* course structure

DACUM (developing a curriculum), 84, 86
Dahlgren, L. O., 18, 120
Dare, A., 102

de Bono, E., 59
Delbecq, A. L., 85, 190
Delphi technique, 84–5
departmental climate, see climate for learning
Diamond, R. M., 89
discipline-based approach to course design,
    48, 49–51, 67
discovery learning, 154–5, 162
    see also inquiry learning
dispositions, development of, and flexible
    delivery, 118
distance education, 118
    and cognitive development, 58
    see also flexible delivery; resource-based
    learning
documentation, 79, 169

economic context of education, 7–8, 19–20
    and flexible delivery, 129
Education for Capability, see Higher
    Education for Capability project
educational developers, see educational
    specialists
educational specialists
    and problem-based learning, 105
    and resource-based learning, 128
    role in design process, 31, 33, 34
Eisner, E. W., 44, 45, 47, 48, 136–8, 164
Elton, L., 7
e-mail, for group interaction, 114, 119–20,
    122–4, 164
Emory University, School of Medicine, 143
empirical, technical and conventional
    knowledge
    and assessment, 173–5
    and objectives, 142–3
Enterprise in Higher Education Initiative,
    140
enterprise skills, 7
entry requirements, 114–16
Entwhistle, N. J., 9, 11
Eraut, M., 197
essay examinations and assessments, 181
evaluation, 88–9, 197–200
Everingham, F., 179–80
experiential approach to course design, 48,
    59–63, 68
experiential learning, 102, 162, 192
    see also experiential approach to course
    design
expressive activities, 138

Falchikov, N., 170, 185
feedback on learning, 153–4, 155–6
Feletti, G., 105
flexible delivery, 118–27

flexible entry and exit, 11[
flexible learning, 114
Foucault, M., 68
Freire, P., 66
Fullan, M., 39, 40, 42, 187
functional analysis, 83–4

Gagné, R., 93
Gardner, H., 2
generic skills, see transferable skills
Gibbs, G., 13, 162, 184, 188
Globerson, T., 141, 164
goals, see learning goals
Goldberger, N. R., 72
Gonczi, A., 83, 84
grading, 170–2
    norm-referenced, 170–1
    criterion-referenced, 170–1
graduate profile, 78, 169
    see also qualities of graduates
Gramsci, A., 68
group work
    computer-mediated groups, 122–4
    and conceptual change, 121
    and critical thinking, 121
    and flexible delivery, 121–4
    via teleconference or video conference, 122

Habermas, J., 68, 141, 144, 146, 172
Habeshaw, S., 162
Hargreaves, J., 87
Hart, M., 45
Harvey, L., 7, 72, 199, 202
Henry, R., 199–200
Hewson, L., 122
Heywood, J., 14, 96, 170
Higher Education Council, 71, 199
Higher Education for Capability project, 67,
    76, 140
Higher Education Funding Council for
    England (HEFCE), 199
Higher Education Quality Council (HEQC),
    70, 71
Hillman, M., 87
hooks, b., 146
Hughes, C., 122, 153
Hurley, J., 102
hybrid structures, 110–12

inquiry learning, 100–5
instructional designers, see educational
    specialists
integrated curriculum, 1, 77, 78, 106–7, 198
integration, 203
    of theory and practice in problem-based
    learning, 104

...lectual abilities and course structure, 105–10
interdisciplinary course, example from business, 75–6, 87
Internet, *see* e-mail; World Wide Web
interpersonal skills, 98
interpretive understanding
and assessment, 172–3, 175–8
and learning goals, 144–6
interviews, 82–3
case study in social work–law degree, 87

Joss, J., 178

Kant, I., 55
Kemmis, S., 48
Kemp, J. E., 51
Knight, P., 7, 72, 184, 199, 202
knowledge
cognitive view, 56
different kinds in problem-based learning, 101–2
different kinds of knowledge and the disciplines, 149
discipline-based view, 49–50
empirical, technical and conventional knowledge and objectives, 142–3
experiential view, 60
and human interests, 141–2
interpretive understanding and learning goals, 144–6
performance-based view, 52
self-reflective knowledge and learning goals, 146–9
socially critical view, 64
knowledge, technical, *see* empirical, technical and conventional knowledge
knowledge base
and problem-based learning, 102
structure of and learning, 18
Knowles, M. S., 59, 60, 61
Kolb, D. A., 188

Langer, E., 2, 178
Larson, L. E., 17
Laurillard, D., 162
leadership
and continuing improvement, 201
and curriculum change, 40–1
role of department head, 36–7, 40
learning
assessing different kinds, 172–80
cognitive view, 56
conceptions of, 130–1
different kinds and flexible delivery, 118–27

discipline-based view, 50
experiential view, 60
model, 153–62
resource-based, 118–27
self-directed, 81, 101, 111
skills, 46
socially critical view, 64–5
systems view, 52–3
transfer, 164–5
see also approaches to learning
learning contract, 60, 61, 62, 63
example in nursing, 158–9
learning goals
and assessment, 168–9
characteristics of effectiveness, 149–51
importance of, 132–3
and interpretive understanding, 144–6
for programmes of study, 70–9
and self-reflective knowledge, 146–9
socially critical view, 65
learning hierarchy, 94
learning objectives, *see* objectives
learning outcomes, *see* objectives; outcomes
level of course, undergraduate or postgraduate, 114–15
lifelong learning and problem-based learning, 104
Limerick, D. L., 6
Loacker, G., 74
Lovat, T. J., 141
Luketina, D., 35

Mager, R., 134–6
Magin, D., 175
Marcuse, H., 68
Marton, F., 9, 130, 131, 146
master performer analysis, 73–4
Masters, G. N., 7
Mentkowski, M., 186
mindfulness
in course design, 2
in learning, 164–5
Miller, C. M. L., 131
Ministry of Education, New Zealand, 168, 199
Mitchell, S., 104
modular courses, 1, 116, 127–8
Mostyn, G., 35, 37, 38, 39
motivation to learn, 17

National Board of Employment, Education and Training (NBEET), 71, 199
nested course, 116–18
Nicholls, A., 51
Nightingale, P., 148, 172, 184
nominal group technique, 190

objective tests, 181
objectives
  alternatives to behavioural model,
    137–141
  characteristics of effectiveness, 149–51
  cognitive view, 56–7
  content, 140, 141
  development of the concept, 133–7
  for empirical, technical and conventional
    knowledge, 142–3
  experiential view, 61
  and interpretive understanding, 144–6
  life skill, 139–40, 141
  methodological, 140, 141
  and self-reflective knowledge, 146–9
  and systems approach, 52, 53
observation of practitioners, 82–3
  case study, 87
Olson, L., 198
open book exams, 181
open learning, *see* flexible learning
  see also distance education
oral assessments, 183
organization, *see* course structure
outcomes, 140
  expressive, 137–8
  SOLO taxonomy, 11–12

Parlett, M., 131
Pearson, S. A., 198
performance assessment, 182
performance-based approach, *see* systems
    approach to course design
performance-based structures, 93–100
Perkins, D., 2
Perry, W. G., 72, 131, 133
personal relevance approach, *see* experiential
    approach to course design
personal transferable skills, *see* transferable
    skills
politics, organizational, 41, 42–3
polytechnics, 7, 13
Posner, G. J., 48, 55, 56, 57
prerequisite knowledge and skills, 93–4, 98
print materials
  choosing, 163
  and flexible delivery, 119–20
problem-based learning, 9, 62, 67, 75, 100–5,
    160–1
  case study in evaluation, 197–9
problem-centred assessments, 181–2
problem solving, 137–8
professional associations, 27
  as accrediting bodies, 82, 83, 188
  role in design process, 31
programme goals, 70–9

programme maps, 128
project assessment, 182
project-based courses, 100–5
Prosser, M., 12, 191

qualities of graduates, 70–2
quality assurance
  initiatives, 7
  and systems-based approach, 52
quality improvement
  continuing, 199–202

Race, P., 119
Ramsden, P., 9, 13, 59, 100, 150, 154
reflection, 153–4, 156
  and assessment, 178–80, 183–4
research techniques for course development,
    82–6
  case study, social work–law degree, 86–8
resource-based learning, 118–27, 164
  staff requirements, 128–9
resource pressures, *see* economic context and
    course design
Roberts, M., 147–8, 176–7
role play, 161–2
Rolfe, I., 198
Romiszowski, A. J., 52, 124, 162, 182
Rostas, J., 198
Roth, K., 120
Rowntree, D., 80, 90, 139–40, 141
Ryan, G., 125, 126

Säljö, R., 9, 130, 131–3
Salomon, G., 141, 164
Sampson, J., 61
Schenk, S. M., 12, 130
Schön, D., 59, 76
Schwab, J., 105–6
Scott, G., 30, 42, 84, 204
search conference, 80–1
self-directed learning, 81, 101, 111
self-instructional materials, 119–20, 125
self-reflective knowledge
  and assessment, 172–3, 178–80
  and learning goals, 146–9
Simosko, S., 115
skills
  development of, 46, 118, 124–5
  and flexible delivery, 124–6
Smith, D. L., 141
socially critical approach to course design, 48,
    63–6, 68
SOLO taxonomy, 11–12
  as grading scheme, 171–2
Southern Illinois University, School of
    Medicine, 100

Spencer, L., 74, 86, 98
Stenhouse, L., 136–9, 141
Stephenson, J., 67, 76
    see also Higher Education for Capability
Sternberg, R., 2
Stewart, D., 178–9
Stiegelbauer, S., 39, 40, 42, 187
student body, changes in, 6–7
student choice and approach to learning, 15, 128
student evaluation of teachers and courses, 88–9, 200
students
    and assessment, 167
    as assessors, 184–6
    entry requirements, 27
    involvement in course design, 31, 35–6, 38, 39, 59–63, 89–90 (*see also* self-directed learning)
    from minority groups, 96
    from non-traditional backgrounds, 98, 129
    support needs, 27
Study Behaviour Questionnaire (SBQ), 11
Study Process Questionnaire (SPQ), 11
surveys, 82–3, 89
systems approach to course design, 48, 51–5, 67–8

Taba, H., 51
Tarule, J. M., 72
teaching
    in blocks, 121
    conceptions of, 191
    student-focused, 133
teaching spaces
    and beliefs about education, 45–6
teleconferencing, 122, 163–4
textbooks, 119
thinking skills, 59
    see also cognitive abilities; intellectual abilities
Thorndike, E. L., 55
time allocation in the curriculum, 46, 67
Tompkins, J., 132
Toohey, S., 82, 98, 175, 180, 184

traditional approach, *see* discipline-based approach to course design
technical knowledge, *see* empirical, technical and conventional knowledge
transferable skills, 7, 71–2, 139, 140–1, 164–5
Trigwell, K., 12, 191
tutors, for open and distance learning, 122
Tyler, R., 51, 133–4, 141

University of New South Wales, Faculty of Law, 66
University of Newcastle, NSW, medical programme, 197–9
    evaluation, 197–9
    goals, 75
University of Sonoma, California, 58
University of South Australia, 169
University of Technology, Sydney, Faculty of Education, 63
University of Western Sydney, Macarthur, Faculty of Health, 80

Van Rossum, E. J., 12, 130, 131, 132
video conferencing, 122, 163–4
video materials, *see* audio-visual materials

Wallis, B., 103, 105
Watkins, D., 12
Weil, S., 67
Westhorp, P., 147
Wheeler, D. K., 51
Woods, D., 101, 102, 103, 138
workload and approach to learning, 13–14
workplace learning
    implementation of, 191
    for skill development, 125–6
    see also clinical placements
workshops
    planning and teaching, 121
    for skill development, 125
World Wide Web
    delivery mechanism, 119, 163
    and group work, 122–4, 164
    source of curriculum documents, 79